CREATIVE HOME ECONOMICS INSTRUCTION

Second Edition

Other McGraw-Hill titles from

The Home Ec Professionals

CHILD GROWTH AND DEVELOPMENT Hurlock
CONCEPTS IN CLOTHING Graef, Strom
FOCUS ON FOOD Peck, Moragne, Sickler, Washington
GUIDE TO MODERN CLOTHING Sturm, Grieser, Lyle, Roberts
GUIDE TO MODERN MEALS Shank, Fitch, Chapman, Ohl, Duyff, Hasler
HOW YOU PLAN AND PREPARE MEALS Carson, Ramee, Cobe
PARENTING AND TEACHING YOUNG CHILDREN Hildebrand
PERSONAL PERSPECTIVES Paolucci
SURVIVAL: A GUIDE TO LIVING ON YOUR OWN Kelly, Chamberlain
TEEN GUIDE TO HOMEMAKING Brinkley, Chamberlain, Champion
THE HOME: ITS FURNISHINGS AND EQUIPMENT Morton, Guthrie, Inman, Geuther
YOUR MARRIAGE AND FAMILY LIVING Landis

ABOUT THE AUTHORS

Valerie M. Chamberlain holds the rank of professor, and Joan M. Kelly, the rank of associate professor in the Department of Home Economics Education at Texas Tech University. They are involved in teacher education at the graduate and undergraduate levels and are also engaged in research studies in the field. Their other professional activities include in-service workshops and the development of games and articles for home economics publications. Dr. Kelly and Dr. Chamberlain are co-authors of McGraw-Hill's senior high school home economics text, *Survival: A Guide to Living on Your Own.*

Dr. Chamberlain, in addition to her university teaching, has taught high school home economics in Vermont and Florida. She is the co-author of McGraw-Hill's *Teen Guide to Homemaking.*

Before joining the faculty at Texas Tech, Dr. Kelly taught high school home economics in Maryland, New Jersey, and Florida.

CREATIVE HOME ECONOMICS INSTRUCTION

Second Edition

Valerie M. Chamberlain, Ph.D.
Professor
College of Home Economics
Texas Tech University
Joan M. Kelly, Ed.D.
Associate Professor
College of Home Economics
Texas Tech University

WEBSTER DIVISION
McGRAW-HILL BOOK COMPANY

New York St. Louis San Francisco Auckland
Bogotá Düsseldorf Johannesburg London
Madrid Mexico Montreal New Delhi
Panama Paris São Paulo Singapore Sydney
Tokyo Toronto

Editor: Martha O'Neill
Managing Editor: Alma Graham
Coordinating Editor: Mary Ann Jones
Design Supervisor: Margaret Amirassefi
Production Manager: Karen Romano

Cover Design: David Schiffer

This book was set in 9-point Times New Roman
by World Composition Services.

Library of Congress Cataloging in Publication Data

Chamberlain, Valerie M
Creative home economics instruction.

Includes index.
1. Home economics—Study and teaching. I. Kelly, Joan, joint author. II. O'Neill, Martha. III. Title.
TX165.C43 1981 640'.7'1 80-11698
ISBN 0-07-010424-7

CONTENTS

ACKNOWLEDGEMENTS

Camille G. Bell, Ed.D.; Chairperson, Department of Home Economics Education, Texas Tech University, for her original research related to teaching skills.

Mary M. Boswell, M.S.; Associate Professor, Department of Home Economics Education, Texas Tech University.

Barbara Brandenburg Young, M.S.; Dallas Independent School District, Dallas, Texas, for test questions on table setting.

Merrilyn N. Cummings, Ph.D.; Associate Professor, Department of Home Economics Education, Texas Tech University.

Linda Glosson, Ph.D.; Director of Home Economics Instructional Materials Center, Texas Tech University, for consultation on behavioral objectives.

Sandra Honeycutt, M.S.; Matthews Junior High School, Lubbock, Texas, for test questions on commercial egg beaters.

LaRue C. Manford, Ph.D.; Southwestern Texas State University, for test questions on clothing construction techniques.

Phyllis Poindexter, M.S.; Newton High School, Newton, Texas, for test questions on muffins.

Albie Rasmussen, M.S.; Kansas State University, Manhattan, Kansas, for the skit "High Pressure Salesman" (adapted and retitled "Camera Shy").

Virginia Tompkins, M.S.; Associate Professor, Department of Home Economics Education, Texas Tech University, for the Unit Plan and Lesson Plan.

Dun-Donnelley Publishing Corporation for "Four of a Kind" by Valerie M. Chamberlain and Joan Kelly. Reproduced by special permission from the January, 1974 issue of *What's New in Home Economics*. Copyright 1974, Dun-Donnelley Publishing Corporation.

PREFACE

The title *Creative Home Economics Instruction* conveys in a very real sense the contents of this book. The material presented is based on educational theory and research as well as on the experiences of the authors and other professionals, many of whom are former students of the authors.

The approach is a pragmatic one; the ideas, methods, and media are practical and can be implemented immediately by the teacher. The suggested learning experiences can be adapted easily to meet the needs, interests, and abilities of all students in home economics programs.

The contents of this book are devoted to areas that concern beginning teachers and to suggestions that will stimulate experienced professionals and provide new ideas for them. We want to share these ideas with you—the reader, the initiator, the professional.

CONCEPTS AND GENERALIZATIONS

1

Educators are faced with an enormous responsibility in deciding what to teach and how to teach it. It is not enough to teach facts that may be forgotten, outdated, or irrelevant by the time the secondary student is out of school. For these reasons, emphasis in recent years has been placed on analyzing the structure of various fields of knowledge by identifying and classifying concepts or key ideas relating to them. Organizing ideas helps to make knowledge more useful and meaningful to students than does memorizing material.

One of the primary goals of home economics educators is to help students analyze relationships that exist among concepts in the various home economics subject-matter areas. When students are helped to see these relationships, they are better able to formulate their own generalizations that tie together the various home economics content areas.

CHARACTERISTICS OF CONCEPTS

A concept is a key idea, topic, or main thought. It is what an individual thinks about a particular subject or topic. Because background experiences are different, each student will attach different meanings to a particular idea or concept. In planning the curriculum, a teacher needs to recognize that concepts vary from one individual to another and that these ideas are constantly changing because of additional experiences that may be gained inside or outside the classroom. Concepts usually develop slowly because they build cumulatively through a variety of experiences.

Concepts may be simple or complex. For example, when the question "What do you think of when I say 'food'?" is asked of five-year-old children, the response may be: "hot dogs, ice cream, cookies, lunch, eat." Foods that are particularly liked and simple concepts for which the children have a frame of reference will be identified. If secondary students are asked to do the same thing, the response may also include well-liked foods such as pizza and hamburgers. However, because older students' concepts of food are broader and more complex, they may identify nutrition, health, calories, diet, fun, party, and the like. On the other hand, if a dietitian were to talk about food, specific nutrients, dietary allowances, and quality control might be discussed. The individuals described think of food differently because their cumulative experiences relating to it are vastly different.

A primary step in curriculum planning is to analyze the needs of society in general and the needs of students in a particular class, course, or program in order to identify the concepts to be included. Other factors that are considered in selecting concepts are the family, socioeconomic, cultural, and academic backgrounds of the students as well as their interests, ability and motivation levels, values, and goals.

Concepts change and grow not only for an individual, but also within a society. At one time, the American family was usually thought of as a husband, a wife, and children. Today, families are recognized in many other contexts: one-parent families, couples without children, families without marriage, or people living in groups. For many, the concept of marriage has also changed. Concepts, then, deal with abstract meanings. They evolve through successive experiences that individuals encounter in a variety of situations.

When using the conceptual approach to teaching, skillful teachers will take advantage of opportunities to clarify and reinforce relevant and recurring concepts. For example, safety is a concept pertinent to home economics and might be included in such areas of study as child development, housing, food preparation, consumer education, clothing, and family living. Management, decision making, human relationships, art, and design are other examples of concepts that recur in a wide variety of home economics curricula. These illustrations point out that concepts are *not* taught, but rather concepts are clarified in a variety of contexts through successive experiences.

DEVELOPING A CONCEPTUAL FRAMEWORK OR CONCEPTUAL STRUCTURE

Concepts can be classified, grouped, or categorized into hierarchies. A conceptual framework, sometimes called a conceptual structure, is like a topical outline in that it is used to organize ideas into a logical system.

A conceptual framework may be developed for an entire curriculum, for a specific course, for a unit of study, or for one lesson. The major, main, or key concepts are identified first. Then the minor concepts or subconcepts are cited. These are organized in a sequence corresponding to the order in which they will be included in the curriculum. The conceptual framework should provide enough detail for any person familiar with the subject matter to know what is expected to be covered. It does not, however, indicate *how* the material will be covered. Concepts should be clearly and concisely stated. Nouns are the primary part of speech used in writing concepts; verbs and articles are not needed.

The conceptual framework that follows could be used in teaching art as it relates to housing or clothing. The major concepts are the *elements of art* and the *principles of design*. The elements are covered first because a basic understanding of them is necessary before the principles can be applied. Line is the first element to be studied because it is the easiest to comprehend and an understanding of it is necessary before form and shape can be explained. It would be difficult to cover the effects of color or harmonies without having studied hue, value, and intensity first. There is a logical reason for the order, or sequence, of each of the concepts and subconcepts included.

CONCEPTUAL FRAMEWORK OR STRUCTURE

A. Elements of art

1. Line
   a. Vertical
   b. Horizontal
   c. Diagonal
   d. Curved
2. Form and shape
3. Color
   a. Physical qualities
      1. Hue
      2. Value
      3. Intensity
   b. Psychological and emotional effects
      1. Associations
      2. Temperature and force
   c. Schemes or harmonies
      1. Monochromatic
      2. Complementary
      3. Analogous
      4. Triad
      5. Accented neutral
4. Texture
   a. Visual
   b. Tactile

B. Principles of design

1. Balance
   a. Formal
   b. Informal
2. Proportion and scale
3. Rhythm
   a. Repetition
   b. Gradation
   c. Radiation
   d. Opposition
   e. Transition
4. Emphasis
   a. Dominance
   b. Subordination
5. Unity or harmony

The length of time that it would take to cover this conceptual framework could vary from several days to several weeks, depending on the background experiences interests, and needs of the students. For some groups it would be feasible to cover each subconcept in depth and, perhaps, to add others, while for other students whose lower-level needs are more immediate, it might be meaningless to do more than touch on the main points.

SCOPE AND SEQUENCE OR CONCEPTUAL BLOCK PLAN

Scope refers to *what* concepts, or subject-matter topics, are to be covered, and sequence refers to *when* they will be covered. A daily scope-and-sequence chart may be the same as a conceptual block plan showing the days when certain topics are expected to be included in the curriculum. The term *scope and sequence*, however, may also be used to refer to the basic subject matter planned for various grade levels and/or for different courses.

A block plan may be simple or complex, including only major concepts or including broad and upper-level objectives, learning experiences, key generalizations, resources, and any other basic material a teacher may want to identify when making long-range unit plans. A teacher's plan book is often used for making a scope-and-sequence chart or block plan. Lesson plans are more detailed and may

DAILY SCOPE-AND-SEQUENCE CHART OR CONCEPTUAL BLOCK PLAN

MONDAY

A. Elements of art
1. Line
   a. Vertical
   b. Horizontal
   c. Diagonal
   d. Curved
2. Form and shape

TUESDAY

3. Color
   a. Physical qualities
      1. Hue
      2. Value
      3. Intensity
   b. Psychological and emotional effects
      1. Associations
      2. Temperature and force

WEDNESDAY

3. Color (*cont'd*)
   c. Schemes or harmonies
      1. Monochromatic
      2. Complementary
      3. Analogous
      4. Triad
      5. Accented neutral
4. Texture
   a. Visual
   b. Tactile

THURSDAY

B. Principles of design
1. Balance
   a. Formal
   b. Informal
2. Proportion and scale

FRIDAY

3. Rhythm
   a. Repetition
   b. Gradation
   c. Radiation
   d. Opposition
   e. Transition
4. Emphasis
   a. Dominance
   b. Subordination
5. Unity or harmony

include additional information such as specific and lower-level behavioral objectives, content notes needed by the teacher when presenting the material, key questions to be discussed in class, student activities, and assignments. See Chapter 4, pages 42–49, for an example showing how a lesson plan can be developed from a unit block plan.

The outline on page 12 shows one way in which the art concepts identified previously in the conceptual framework can be used to develop a daily scope-and-sequence chart or conceptual block plan.

Long-range scope-and-sequence plans show, at a glance, the development of concepts throughout an entire curriculum. The following example demonstrates one way in which concepts relating to consumer education could evolve.

SCOPE–AND–SEQUENCE PLAN

A. Consumer education I

1. Values
   a. How acquired
      1. Family
      2. Friends
      3. Community
      4. School
      5. Religious group
      6. Mass media
   b. Identification
   c. Changes
   d. Effects on consumer decisions
2. Goals
   a. Short-term
   b. Long-term
   c. Changes
   d. Effects on consumer decisions
3. Needs and wants
4. Managing resources
   a. Money
   b. Time
   c. Energy

B. Consumer education II

1. Sources of consumer information
2. Buying guidelines
   a. Clothing
   b. Food
3. Labels
   a. Care
   b. Use
   c. Nutrition
   d. Unit price
   e. Open and pull dates
4. Warranties and guarantees
5. Types of marketplaces
6. Checking accounts
7. Credit
   a. Open-end
      1. Charge accounts
      2. Credit cards
   b. Closed-end loans
      1. Installment
      2. Passbook
8. Advertising
9. Fraudulent practices
   a. Referral schemes
   b. Fake gift certificates
   c. Bait and switch

C. Consumer education III

1. Economic systems
2. Types of income
3. Buying
   a. Appliances
   b. Furnishings
   c. Housing
   d. Transportation
   e. Insurance
4. Renting
   a. Housing
   b. Equipment
5. Spending plans
6. Savings and lending institutions
   a. Commercial banks
   b. Savings and loan associations
   c. Credit unions
   d. U.S. government
7. Taxes
8. Consumer agencies
   a. Government
   b. Private
9. Legislation
10. Careers

A scope-and-sequence plan does *not* show how the subject matter will be covered. In other words, it does *not* suggest the learning experiences, activities, media, or materials that can be used to help students clarify the concepts that have been identified for inclusion at various levels.

CHARACTERISTICS OF GENERALIZATIONS

A generalization is a statement that expresses a complete thought and underlying truth and also has an element of universality. This means that a generalization can be applied in a number of situations and is equally valid anywhere in the world. Generalizations are the basic ideas, principles, and understandings that describe or explain facts and specific phenomena. They unify various aspects of a subject by showing the relationships among concepts.

There are three levels of generalizations. The first may be a simple statement of fact, definition, description, analogy, identification, or classification. A second-level generalization shows relationships among ideas or makes comparisons. It may include more ideas than a first-level generalization and involves greater depth and scope of subject matter. A third-level generalization explains, justifies, interprets, or predicts. It may be more remote in time and space than a first- or second-level generalization. Examples of generalizations at the three levels follow:

Level 1: Milk is a food.

Level 2: Your health is related to the food you eat.

Level 3: Your size is partially determined by the kind and quantity of food you consume.

The first example is a simple statement expressing a universal truth. The second shows that there is a relationship between health and food intake. The third example makes a subtle prediction by pointing out that the food people consume affects their growth and physical maturation.

The level of generalization that students can be expected to formulate depends upon their previous personal and educational experiences, their innate intelligence, and the learning activities in which they engage. Some students may seldom go beyond the first level, while others find little difficulty in formulating third-level generalizations. On the other hand, students may reach only the first level in some subject-matter areas and the third level in others, depending upon their own background experiences and familiarity with the subject matter. When planning lessons, however, it is generally advisable for teachers to try to help students form generalizations above the first level because at this first level generalizations often become shallow statements of fact such as "Milk is nutritious." Such facts, unrelated by higher-level generalizations, may be forgotten or become irrelevant in students' lives outside the classroom.

FORMULATING GENERALIZATIONS

Usually, twenty to twenty-two words is the maximum number that can be used to formulate a generalization without making it too complex to have real meaning. A generalization expresses only one idea; therefore, it is inappropriate to use a colon or semicolons in writing one. Value judgments are also inappropriate. Consequently, words and phrases like these are *not* used: it is *vital* that; it is *important* to remember; one *must*; a person *should*; and, this *ought* to be done so that . . .

The following phrases may be helpful in writing generalizations because they minimize the likelihood of making value judgments and facilitate making statements that show relationships:

is affected by	is an integral part of	may be enhanced by
is dependent on	is a product of	may be identified by
is limited by	is influenced by	may be necessary for
is promoted by	is subject to	may be modified by
is related to	may be associated with	constitutes a pattern for
is the result of	may be developed by	contributes to

Students should not be given generalizations but should be led to formulate their own. When students are given generalizations, they are denied the challenge and opportunity to think for themselves, using the higher-level thought processes. Teachers can guide students into developing appropriate generalizations more effectively when they have written generalizations in advance because this planning necessitates that teachers clarify where they intend to lead their students. It is the teacher's responsibility to plan learning experiences and activities that help students arrive at generalizations that are meaningful to them and that are stated in their own words. Most students will not state generalizations as their teachers would, but through the skillful use of appropriate and probing questions, teachers can encourage students to clarify and refine the generalizations they do make. Initially, students may be helped to generalize by being asked to answer questions such as the following:

- What have you learned from the lesson today?
- How can our discussion be summarized in a few sentences?
- What are the main ideas we have been talking about and how are they related?
- How does today's discussion relate to what we studied yesterday?
- How can these ideas be applied to new or different situations?

Answering questions like these not only helps students summarize the material that has been covered, but also aids instructors in evaluating the effectiveness of their teaching. Since most of the disconnected facts that are "learned" by individuals are forgotten in a short time, students must be helped to formulate generalizations that can be used as guidelines in the future as well as the present. When students are able to develop generalizations showing the interrelationships among concepts, they are better prepared to transfer learning from one situation to another.

Formulating generalizations when planning curricula is analogous to using a map when planning a car trip. There may be more than one way to get to your destination, but by planning the route in advance, much time and confusion may be eliminated. Planning, though, does not preclude the possibility of making a side trip along the way, stopping somewhere while en route, using another means of transportation at the last minute, or being detained because something has happened over which you have no control. Similarly, it is easier to accomplish your goals if you have planned how you will attain them, but you need to be flexible in your teaching to accommodate individual students' needs and learning styles, to take enough time to clarify points, to change your approach if it is ineffective, and to accept disruptions that are unavoidable.

After the concepts to be included in the curriculum have been identified and developed into a framework of hierarchies, and generalizations have been formulated that link the major concepts and show the interrelatedness among them, the next step in curriculum development is to plan the behavioral objectives the students are expected to achieve. Learning experiences are planned next, to enable students to meet these established objectives. The means for evaluating student achievement of the objectives is usually an ongoing and continuous process throughout the unit of study that may culminate at the end of the term in a final exam or project.

BEHAVIORAL OBJECTIVES 2

In the past, educators formulated their goals in broad, general terms with lots of loopholes. For example, all home economics teachers wanted their students to "gain a greater appreciation of homemaking." However, "appreciation" is a difficult factor to measure objectively. Furthermore, if students are to be graded on their "greater appreciation of homemaking," surely many are astute enough to bluff and to give at least lip service to their "appreciation." How, then, can teachers appraise and assess the students' sincerity? What and how much constitutes a "greater appreciation"? The preceding does not mean that all home economics teachers should not work constantly and diligently to help students develop positive attitudes toward their subject matter and toward the roles of men and women as family members, as managers of their resources, and as homemakers. Instead, the illustration is used to show the inherent weakness in nebulous and vaguely stated objectives.

Recent trends in education emphasize objectives that specify the ultimate behavior expected of students. The terms *behavioral, performance,* and *instructional objectives* are often used synonymously. Behavior can be measured objectively because there is concrete evidence of achievement. In other words, the objectives describe or define what the learners have to do to demonstrate their attainment of the objectives. Since the anticipated results of instruction are clear, there is measurable evidence of the outcome of the educational process. Behavioral objectives are applicable to learners of all ages and backgrounds in a wide variety of situations: classroom students, on-the-job trainees, 4-H members, athletes, student pilots, management trainees, or anyone else for whom there is an expected level of performance.

DOMAINS OF LEARNING

Objectives are divided into three categories of learning called the cognitive, affective, and psychomotor domains. The cognitive domain is concerned with rational learning—knowing and thinking. Knowledge, use of the mind, and intellectual abilities are emphasized. The affective domain deals with emotional learning—caring and feeling. Attitudes, appreciations, interests, values, and adjustments are considered. The psychomotor domain relates to physical learning—doing and manipulating. Speed, accuracy, and dexterity are concerns in developing physical skills in this domain.

No subject-matter area of home economics pertains exclusively to one domain. Each area involves all three domains to some degree, although the study of nutrition and textiles is most closely associated with cognitive learning, family relationships and human development with the affective domain, and food preparation and clothing construction with psychomotor development. Remembering, understanding, relating, analyzing, synthesizing, and assessing nutritional knowledge are not enough. Students also need to develop an interest in, appreciation for, and positive attitude toward using their knowledge. In addition, students have to be able to prepare food so that it is nutritious. Certainly, one of the major purposes of teaching clothing construction is to help students develop skills. However, students also have to develop a desire to perform these skills carefully and accurately. Few garments can be made without a basic knowledge of grainlines, pattern symbols, and alteration techniques. All three domains must be considered when planning strategies for teaching each home economics subject-matter area, although for each content area one domain may be emphasized more than others.

Each domain is divided into a hierarchy of levels—from the simplest to the most complex. Most students have to achieve objectives at lower levels before they can accomplish those at higher levels. To attain objectives at each of the specified levels, students generally have had to master the skills of the preceding levels in consecutive order. It is unusual for students to skip levels by intuitively grasping the subject matter. Therefore, behavioral objectives relating to one concept are planned and written to conform to the hierarchies of the domains, and rarely is more than one level omitted in the sequence. Plans may call for student achievement below the highest possible level; in fact, objectives formulated for some content areas may specify achievement that reaches only the first, second, or third step in the hierarchy.

This is not meant to imply that younger students or those of lower ability cannot use higher thinking processes. Students in the primary grades analyze, synthesize, and evaluate in relation to simple concepts. Low-ability students may need to be encouraged to use higher thought processes. Teachers select less complicated content for them to study than that presented to other students. The levels of learning are applicable to all students regardless of age, innate intelligence, or environmental background.

Not measurable - appreciate, ascribe, become familiar believe, develop a feeling, discuss, enjoy, enthuse, grasp, aware, know, learn, realize, recall, recognize, see the need understand, value

Cognitive Domain

In all three domains of learning, concrete, objective, and measurable evidence is needed for proof of the students' achievement. In the cognitive domain, teachers can gather this evidence by having students identify facts, give examples, apply principles, analyze situations, plan solutions to problems, and evaluate results. There are six levels of learning in the cognitive domain.*

Knowledge: recalling, remembering, and recognizing

This level emphasizes facts, information, and specifics. It serves as the foundation, or base, upon which the others are built. It involves remembering material in a form very close to that in which it was originally encountered. It depends on memorizing or identifying facts. It may be thought of as the student's "file" of information that can be recalled or brought to mind later. Examples of activity at this level include reiterating the names of color harmonies that have been studied, stating rules for furniture arrangement that have been given previously, and matching cooking terms with their definitions.

Objectives at the knowledge level include the ability to:

cite	label	recite
define	list	reproduce
identify	name	state

Comprehension: understanding and explaining

This level is concerned with grasping the meaning and intent of material. It deals with content and involves the ability to understand what is being communicated. A reading-comprehension test, in which students read a section and then explain what it means, is an example.

Objectives at the comprehension level include the ability to:

convert	give examples	paraphrase
describe	illustrate	summarize
explain	interpret	tell in one's own words

Application: using ideas

Application involves using what is remembered and comprehended. It applies learning to life in new or concrete situations. It includes the ability to use knowledge and learned material in meaningful ways. It may involve applying principles and rules, choosing appropriate procedures, or selecting solutions to problems that are similar to those presented previously. The role of application in the cognitive domain is not to be confused with that of developing manipulative and purely physical skills in the psychomotor domain.

* Benjamin S. Bloom, et al., *Taxonomy of Educational Objectives, Handbook I: Cognitive Domain*, David McKay Company, Inc., New York, 1956.

Objectives at the application level include the ability to:

apply
compute
construct
demonstrate
estimate
prepare
relate
show
solve
use

Analysis: reasoning

Analyzing involves breaking material into its constituent parts and determining the relationship of these parts to each other and to the whole. It may include identifying components, analyzing relationships among them, and looking at the principles involved in organization. It is taking one step, portion, or piece at a time to clarify the overall idea. Analyzing includes separating relevant material from trivia, distinguishing facts from hypotheses, and differentiating between objective data and value judgments. An example may include analyzing a floor plan for features such as possible furniture arrangements and groupings, traffic flow, placement of rooms to minimize noise and assure maximum privacy, and building costs.

Objectives at the analysis level include the ability to:

analyze
associate
determine
differentiate
discriminate
distinguish
outline
point out

Synthesis: creating

Synthesis is the ability to put parts and elements together into new forms. Ideas are organized into new patterns, and materials are put together in a structure that was not there before. Creativity and originality are emphasized. For example, in planning a unit of study for kindergarten-age children, it is necessary to consider everything that has been learned about child development, the subject matter to be taught, methods of teaching, media and materials, and ways of getting young children interested and motivated. Similarly, in designing a new toy it is necessary to synthesize knowledge concerning developmental levels of children, materials that might be used in making toys, and marketing techniques and procedures in order to create a toy that has never been produced before.

Objectives at the synthesis level include the ability to:

combine
compile
compose
create
design
develop
devise
integrate
modify
organize
plan
propose
rearrange
reorganize
revise
rewrite
write

Evaluation: making a judgment

Evaluation is concerned with learners' abilities to judge the value of ideas, methods, materials, procedures, and solutions by developing or using appropriate criteria. The criteria are the yardsticks used in making a judgment. Examples include comparing and contrasting theories of child rearing, assessing the facilities and services offered in a home for senior citizens, and weighing the advantages and disadvantages, in given situations, of buying clothes versus making them.

It should be noted that there is some disagreement among educators about whether evaluation actually involves the most complex level of cognitive thinking. Some put it just below synthesis, making the latter the highest step in the cognitive domain. In either case, teachers should strive to include in their teaching strategies learning experiences that necessitate some student synthesizing and evaluating.

Objectives at the evaluation level include the ability to:

appraise	conclude	judge
assess	contrast	weigh
compare	evaluate	

Unfortunately, too often only the knowledge level in the cognitive domain is emphasized and evaluated. Students are taught facts and specifics and are then asked to repeat them in various ways. What purpose does this information serve if students do not understand it and cannot use it? Facts, per se, will be forgotten within a short time. Therefore, it is the obligation of every teacher to work toward higher levels of thinking and to build on the knowledge students attain.

Knowing certain facts is essential, but it is not enough. To illustrate, students need to acquire a basic knowledge and understanding of facts relating to nutrition before they can apply them in planning nutritious meals.

Cautions for writing cognitive objectives

It is recognized that a behavioral verb suggested here to specify a certain level of learning can be used in a different context to indicate another learning level. If an objective states, "Compile a list of . . . ," this activity may be at the synthesis level or the knowledge level, depending upon the way in which the rest of the behavioral objective is worded and how the subject matter is presented in class. "State in your own words . . ." denotes the comprehension level because it involves explaining, which students can do only if they understand the material. However, "state" is more frequently used at the knowledge level in the sense of reiterating information or naming factors, such as "State the principal rule of storage." "Identify the solution . . ." implies solving an application problem, even though the word "identify" is generally associated with the knowledge level. These examples illustrate that the behavioral words indicated for each level in the cognitive domain should serve as guidelines only. An objective can be at a level different from that which the lead verb immediately suggests.

Sample objectives in the cognitive domain

The following behavioral objectives relating to types of housing provide examples at the sequential levels in the cognitive domain.

KNOWLEDGE: *List* types of housing available in the local area.

COMPREHENSION: *Explain* the characteristics, advantages, and disadvantages of various types of housing available in the local area.

APPLICATION: *Compute* the cost of living in various types of housing in the local area.

ANALYSIS: *Analyze* given situations to determine types of housing desirable for meeting the needs and life styles of various individuals, families, and groups.

SYNTHESIS: *Plan* various types of housing to meet the needs of different people and kinds of families.

EVALUATION: *Evaluate* housing available in the local area for the various types of individuals, families, and groups that predominate in the community.

Obviously, students have to identify the different types of housing, such as mobile homes, duplexes, town houses, apartments, and condominiums, before they can describe the homes' characteristics or summarize their advantages and disadvantages. Likewise, students must understand the provisions of living in various types of housing before they can estimate costs and savings related to maintenance, utilities, insurance, and income tax deductions. Similarly, these factors need to be applied when determining types of housing that best meet certain peoples' needs. Each succeeding level is dependent upon satisfactory achievement of the lower level. Occasionally a level can be bypassed, but this should be done with caution. In the preceding example, students could evaluate available housing without having designed any. Plans for teaching do not necessarily have to include behavioral objectives that proceed to the highest level. In this instance, it is conceivable that in a comprehensive survey course, it would be feasible to include only the first two levels of objectives related to types of housing. In a course in which housing is studied in depth, all six levels would probably be included, with several objectives at some of the levels, particularly the lower ones.

Affective Domain

It is much easier to formulate objectives and evaluate accomplishments in the cognitive and psychomotor domains than in the affective domain. A student's interest, attitude, or appreciation can only be measured through observable action. This action, or evidence of learning, needs to be clearly specified, as it is in this behavioral objective: "Show interest in child development by voluntarily participating in a community-service project planned for children, by relating baby-sitting experiences, or by doing extra readings in this area."

Five levels of the affective domain deal with emotional learning.* These range from being aware of a particular phenomenon to developing a total philosophy.

Receiving: attending and becoming aware

At this level, learners merely become aware of a situation, idea, or process. They notice and are willing to receive certain stimuli. Awareness is developed through the sensory organs. This level includes perceiving factors with discrimination and developing sensitivity, tolerance, and alertness. Teachers are concerned with getting, holding, and directing students' attention so that students will be willing to try certain behaviors.

Some behavioral tasks associated with receiving are to:

accept	be aware	perceive
acknowledge	show awareness	tolerate
be alert	notice	
show alertness	pay attention	

Responding: doing something about the phenomenon

In addition to perceiving a particular situation, idea, or process in responding, the learners do something with or about it. Students may make the first overt responses in order to comply, but later make them willingly and with satisfaction. Responding involves developing a low level of commitment. At this level, students follow through with directions, select their own problems, and respond voluntarily when given alternatives. They are actively involved in the learning process.

Some words and phrases used to indicate responding are:

accept responsibility	care for	follow
agree to	communicate	obey
answer freely	comply	participate willingly
assist	conform	read voluntarily
be interested	consent	respond
show interest	contribute	visit
be willing	cooperate	volunteer

Valuing: developing attitudes

Valuing means that learners accept the worth of an object, idea, belief, or behavior and also show a preference for it. They are consistent in responses

*David R. Krathwohl, Benjamin S. Bloom, and Berthram B. Masia, *Taxonomy of Behavioral Objectives, Handbook II: Affective Domain*, David McKay Company, Inc., New York, 1964.

concerning a particular issue and express opinions about it with conviction. In fact, they may give opinions publicly, whether they meet with approval or not. There is individual commitment to an underlying value that guides behavior. In other words, the person begins to prize and cherish the position chosen in relation to certain ideas and issues. In addition, at this level, behavior is consistent and stable enough to make students' values identifiable to others.

Because valuing relates to developing attitudes, some of the following words can be used to formulate objectives at this level:

adopt	desire	seek
assume responsibility	exhibit loyalty	show concern
behave according to	express	show continuing desire to
choose	initiate	use resources to
commit	prefer	

Organization: arranging values systematically

This level includes organizing values, determining interrelationships among them, and establishing a hierarchy of the dominant ones. Learners adapt their behavior to the value system they have selected. They also analyze evidence and form judgments about social responsibilities. Students may relate personal ethical standards to those expressed in biographies and fiction.

Since organization is arranging values in priority order, according to a system, some words that can be used to establish behavioral objectives at this level are:

adapt	classify	group
adjust	conceptualize	rank
arrange	disclose	reveal

Characterization: internalizing a set of values

At the highest level of achievement in the affective domain, beliefs, ideas, and attitudes are integrated into a total philosophy of life, or world view. Characterization may be expressed as devotion to a cause. Values are internalized to such a degree that there are persistent and consistent responses in similar situations.

It is extremely difficult to measure achievement objectively at this level. However, some behaviors that may be associated with characterization follow:

act upon	exemplify	maintain
advocate	exhibit	serve
defend	expose	support
display	influence	show consistent devotion to
devote	justify behavior	

Cautions for writing affective objectives

If measures of attainment and evidences of achievement have not been preestablished and clearly specified, evaluation of objectives in the affective domain may become highly subjective. Evidence of achievement in the affective domain is sometimes measured by cognitive behavior. Some examples follow:

- Show interest in children's clothing by *pointing out* self-help features.
- Express concern about the depletion of energy resources by *writing* an article or *preparing* an oral report about how to get better gas mileage when driving a car.
- Exhibit loyalty to the school chapter of Future Homemakers of America (FHA) by *organizing* a social for new members, by *writing* a code of ethics for officers, or by *proposing* a new installation service.

These affective objectives show that there may be alternative ways designated for measuring affective achievement. When attendance at a certain event is compulsory, when an assignment is required, or participation in an activity is mandatory, there is no behavioral evidence of affective achievement, change, or growth.

Affective objectives at the *receiving* and *responding* levels very often are indistinguishable from learning experiences. Learning experiences are the actual tasks and activities that enable students to achieve planned objectives. It is difficult to differentiate between the following as behavioral objectives or learning experiences:

- to *pay attention* to a demonstration
- to *care for* the plants in the department
- to *contribute* to a class discussion

Objectives at the knowledge and comprehension levels in the cognitive domain are often more appropriate than objectives at the receiving and responding levels in the affective domain. This is true because the intent of objectives at the receiving and responding levels is usually cognitive in nature. For example, in actuality, students pay attention to a filmstrip in order to cite, identify, or list certain facts or to repeat some cognitive information. When voluntarily answering questions, students are often giving examples, explaining, or summarizing in their own words. Therefore, cognitive objectives at the knowledge and comprehension levels might precede objectives at the valuing level more appropriately than would affective objectives at the receiving and responding levels.

Sample objectives in the affective domain

There are two primary reasons for the difficulty in measuring achievement in the affective domain: the variables are intangible and evidences of attainment need to be predetermined. These evidences may be specified by using phrases such as these:

by volunteering to	as proved through	by listing
as shown by	by deciding to	by giving examples
when participating in	by going to	when doing

The following examples of objectives relating to the guidance of children are appropriate for students enrolled in an occupational course in child-care services and illustrate the hierarchies in the affective domain:

RECEIVING: *Show* awareness of positive verbal-guidance techniques by noting examples shown in an appropriate film or videotape.

RESPONDING: *Follow* the guidelines established for positive verbal guidance when working with children under supervision in the school child-care laboratory.

VALUING: *Choose* positive rather than negative verbal-guidance techniques when working independently with children in a child-care center.

ORGANIZATION: *Adapt* behavior, in a wide variety of situations, to reveal values congruent with positive and established principles of child development.

CHARACTERIZATION: *Exemplify* a philosophy of child development that consistently reflects devotion to causes contributing to the welfare and improvement of community conditions affecting all children.

These examples illustrate the increased complexity of objectives as higher levels are achieved. At the lower levels the teacher does more structuring than at the higher levels, where students become more self-directive.

Psychomotor Domain

Psychomotor learning is concerned with developing physical skills. Proficiency is sought in performing motor tasks. Speed, accuracy, manual dexterity, and economy of effort are important. One author, a home economist, has identified five levels in this domain.*

*Elizabeth J. Simpson, "Classification of Educational Objectives, Psychomotor Domain," *Illinois Teacher*, Winter 1966–1967.

Perception: recognizing and detecting sensory cues

At this level, learners become aware, through the five senses, of objects, qualities, and procedures. In other words, sensory stimulation provides the basis for becoming aware of the action to be performed. Students observe so that they can recognize appropriate behavior and will be able to act accordingly. For example, the teacher may demonstrate kneading bread dough so that students can see and understand how it is done.

Some words that describe behaviors at this level are:

detect
feel
hear
listen
observe
perceive
recognize
see
sense
smell
taste
view
watch

Set: becoming ready to act

Set is a mental, physical, or emotional readiness for a particular kind of action or experience and the willingness to respond to it. Being physically set involves assuming a body stance appropriate for doing a particular task. In learning how to pick up a heavy object, for example, students bend their knees and keep their backs straight to achieve the correct body posture to perform the act.

Some words that describe behavior at this level are:

achieve a posture
assume a body stance
establish a body position
place hands, arms, feet
position the body
sit
stand
station

Guided response: imitating and practicing

This involves practicing the action under supervision through imitation or trial and error. Learners repeat one phase of a complex skill by doing it as it was demonstrated. In child development, the learner may repeat a finger-play exercise as illustrated. In food preparation, the student may practice making accurate measurements.

Some words that describe behavior at this level are:

copy
duplicate
imitate
manipulate with guidance
operate under supervision
practice
repeat
try

Mechanism: increasing efficiency

At this level, a learned response becomes habitual and is performed with some degree of skill and confidence. There is improved efficiency in performing the act. A student in a wage-earning program in home services may make a bed quickly, smoothly, and with a minimum expenditure of time and energy, using the "once-around" method. Behavioral tasks include the ability to:

complete with confidence
conduct
demonstrate
execute
improve efficiency
increase speed
make
pace
produce
show dexterity

Complex overt response: performing automatically

Learners perform more complicated acts automatically, without hesitation, efficiently, and with a high degree of skill and self-sufficiency. They proceed with assurance, ease, and muscular control. Students may prepare and serve several meals, managing their resources effectively and using a variety of food-preparation techniques skillfully. Some terms that describe behavior at this level are:

act habitually
advance with assurance
control
direct
excel
guide
maintain efficiency
manage
master
organize
perfect
perform automatically
proceed

Cautions for writing psychomotor objectives

Sometimes the application level in the cognitive domain is confused with psychomotor learning. Making a chart to show the characteristics of natural and synthetic fibers and their primary uses is a cognitive activity because it involves remembering, understanding, and applying information. The *only* physical skill involved is in drawing straight lines for the chart.

Psychomotor objectives at the *perception* level are often indistinguishable from learning experiences. For example, classroom learning experiences may consist of activities such as *feeling* the textures of different fabrics, *tasting* milk and cheese in a variety of forms, and *viewing* a film showing prenatal development. This situation is similar to the one that exists in attempting to write objectives at the receiving and responding levels in the affective domain. Low-level cognitive objectives appropriately precede *set* in the psychomotor domain so that *perception*-level objectives are not needed.

Sample objectives in the psychomotor domain

The following examples pertaining to clothing construction serve to illustrate progression through the levels of learning in the psychomotor domain.

PERCEPTION: *Detect* errors in the threading of a sewing machine after having watched a demonstration showing the correct procedure.

SET: *Assume* a body position at the sewing machine that minimizes fatigue.

GUIDED RESPONSE: *Practice* inserting a lapped zipper, using the step-by-step directions provided on the zipper folder.

MECHANISM: *Demonstrate* how to insert a lapped zipper quickly and efficiently without needing either written instructions or the teacher's help.

COMPLEX OVERT RESPONSE: *Proceed* skillfully through the steps in making a garment with a minimum amount of guidance and help from other people.

The words and phrases suggested for establishing behavioral objectives in all the domains are intended to serve only as guidelines. The context in which a verb is used can change the meanings and intents so that in actuality another level is indicated. For example, at the mechanism level, students could make a convenience-food product with skill, efficiency, and confidence, whereas at the complex overt-response level they might use a complicated recipe to make a quality food product, using appropriate procedures and efficient management techniques with assurance.

The context in which a behavioral term is used may indicate a domain that is different from that with which it is usually associated. To illustrate this, students could use rules in the cognitive sense of applying them, or they could use their resources to initiate policies in which they believe strongly and to which they are committed, or they could use acquired physical skills to perform a specified task.

GUIDELINES FOR WRITING BEHAVIORAL OBJECTIVES

Although some teachers encourage their students to write objectives beginning with "The student should be able to . . . ," the authors of this book believe that such wording is contradictory to the basic premise of using the behavioral approach. How do teachers know if students are able to, unless they actually do? Consequently, it is more logical to begin objectives this way:

The students will:

Name ______________________________

Describe ______________________________

Apply ______________________________

By using this format there is no need to precede every objective with "The students (or club members, or participants) will. . . ." Instead, each objective can be worded concisely, beginning immediately with a behavioral verb that indicates exactly what the students are expected to do.

Behavioral objectives are written to include only one verb and only one idea or variable. It is better to write separate statements for each objective than to include too much in one. If an objective is stated "Identify and analyze . . . ," students may be able to do the first part but not the second. Consequently, use only one verb in stating each objective and *never* use behavioral terms indicating different levels in formulating one objective.

An example of a *very poorly* written objective is: "Develop menus for nine consecutive days for children attending a camp for diabetics and for their non-diabetic counselors who need to lose at least ten pounds." There are two ideas expressed here, so there should be two objectives. One objective should pertain to diabetic diets and the other to weight-reduction diets. In addition, behavioral objectives are written without qualifying numbers. In this case, the number of days and the number of pounds should be omitted. Instead, this type of specificity may be included in the learning experiences that are planned to enable students to meet particular objectives. Improved behavioral objectives might be stated: "Plan appropriate menus for diabetic children" *and* "Develop a dietary plan for losing weight." Menu planning for diabetics should not be limited to camp situations, and there is no reason to restrict dietary planning for losing weight to camp counselors. Behavioral objectives are written in broader and more general terms.

When planning a unit or course of study, higher-level objectives are used. In the cognitive domain, these are usually at the analysis level or higher; however, occasionally a unit objective at the application level is used. These higher-level objectives may be called broad, overall, or terminal objectives. Objectives for lessons or small units of subject matter are called specific, daily, or enabling objectives. Their levels lead sequentially to the level of the broad, overall objective. For example, the broad unit objective, which relates to the major concept, may be at the synthesis level. Daily objectives or those relating to the subconcepts may be at the knowledge, comprehension, application, and analysis levels. Occasionally the concluding daily objective is at the same level as the broad objective. This is most likely to happen the last day of a unit. A specific objective, however, does not exceed the level of the broad objective. If it did, the broad objective would be inappropriate. Daily objectives planned for the beginning of a unit may stop several levels below the level of the broad objective. In the example of the menu-planning unit, the broad objective is at the synthesis level. The seven specific objectives for the first day of the unit might be developed so that there are three at the knowledge level, two at the comprehension level, and two at the application level.

Verbs to avoid when writing behavioral objectives

Objectives beginning with "to discuss" are extremely difficult to measure objectively unless teachers have previously established the exact criteria by which the discussion will be evaluated. Even when this has been done, students often bring up valid points teachers have not anticipated. When this happens and students do not include factors expected in the answers, teachers are faced with the problem of measuring responses fairly.

The following terms are sometimes used erroneously in formulating behavioral objectives. *These are not measurable behaviors unless they are qualified.*

appreciate	enjoy	recall
appreciate fully	enthuse	recognize
ascribe to	grasp the significance of	recognize the importance of
become familiar with	have an awareness of	see the need for
believe in	have faith in	understand
believe truly	know	value
develop a feeling for	learn	
discuss	realize	

Sharing Objectives with Students

There are advantages in stating behavioral objectives for students. Objectives provide guidance for studying. When it is time to review for a test or to prepare an assignment, students know what is expected of them. Some teachers write the objectives for the day on the board or give students duplicated copies of both broad, overall and specific, daily objectives. In some classes, students help plan the objectives. These may not be expressed in exact, pedagogic terms, but the students are participating in the teaching-learning process. Their contributions should be very worthwhile since they often have accurate and strong feelings about what they need to learn and know.

Evaluation is facilitated when behavioral objectives have been formulated carefully in advance because they predict the type of evaluation that is appropriate and the level at which achievement should be measured. Behavioral objectives also serve as the bases for selecting and planning meaningful learning experiences. Learning experiences are the tasks students perform and the activities in which they participate to enable them to achieve planned objectives.

COMPETENCY-BASED EDUCATION

The competency-based approach to education emerged in the late 1960s because of the growing emphasis in many sectors of society on *accountability*. Dissatisfaction with the educational system increased as it became evident that many students were leaving school while lacking the basic skills needed to function effectively in society. Since expenditures for education consume such a large proportion of the public tax dollar, concern also increased for the quality of teacher-education programs and the professional abilities of college graduates planning to teach. *Accountability* as it relates to teachers, then, encompasses relevancy, adequacy, effectiveness, and efficiency.

For students, competency-based education can be thought of as criterion-referenced education in which the desired outcomes relating to knowledge, attitudes, and behavior are stated as behavioral objectives. Students understand that certain specified competencies, or measurable and observable behaviors, are expected of them and that they must demonstrate attainment of the required competencies in order to pass. (This system takes the use of behavioral objectives beyond their usual application. That is, they are ordinarily a measure of *how well* a student has mastered the material, not *whether* the student has mastered it.)

The implementation of the competency-based approach to education has been primarily at the level of higher education. However, the impact of the movement has affected education at the precollege level because of the changes in teacher-education programs and the emphasis in teacher-training on achievement of specified objectives. Teachers who have been required to demonstrate their attainment of certain competencies may be inclined to approach their own teaching by stating student objectives in behavioral terms and evaluating student achievement in relation to attainment of these objectives. The similarities between the use of behavioral objectives and competency-based education are illustrated by examining the characteristics of competency-based education.

1. Competencies to be demonstrated, or objectives, are stated in behavioral terms and sequenced according to the needs and abilities of the students.
2. Student achievement is measured by determining if pre-established levels of competence, or performance, have been met.
3. Students are informed of the levels of competence, or objectives they are expected to achieve, as well as how they will be evaluated. The criteria for evaluation are also shared.
4. The instructional program provides a variety of learning experiences that use different teaching methods and media to enable students to reach the specified competency levels, or to achieve the stated objectives.
5. Since attainment of specified competencies, or achievement of objectives, is the purpose of the educational program, time is not a factor. Some students may need little time to reach specified competency levels, while other students need much more time.
6. Student assessment of competency performance, or achievement of objectives, is the primary source of evidence used in the evaluation process. A large amount of responsibility, therefore, must be assumed by the student for meeting these pre-established levels of performance. Accountability is thus shared responsibility of the student and teacher.

Terminal Performance Objectives

A terminal performance objective (TPO) represents a broad general area of a competency that serves as a major criterion for evaluating performance related to that component. A TPO is similar to a higher-level, broad, overall behavioral objective that relates to a major concept.

Enabling Objectives

A TPO can be divided into a series of enabling objectives. An enabling objective (EO) represents a specific criterion for measuring performance related to one component of a broad component of a broad competency. An EO is similar to a lower-level or specific behavioral objective. Attainment of enabling objectives contributes to the achievement of a TPO as attainment of specific, lower-level behavioral objectives contributes to the achievement of a broad, higher-level objective.

Competency-based education can be thought of as criterion-referenced education in which the desired outcomes relating to knowledge, attitudes, and behavior are stated like behavioral objectives. Students understand that certain specified competencies, or measurable and observable behaviors, are expected of them and that they must demonstrate attainment of the required competencies.

DESIGNING LEARNING EXPERI-ENCES 3

After the concepts to be covered have been identified, after the generalizations that students will be guided to make have been determined, and after the behavioral objectives have been formulated, the next step in planning is to select and develop learning experiences. These are the activities in which students participate at school, at home, and in the community to help them clarify concepts, arrive at generalizations, and achieve established objectives. Developing learning experiences involves designing the experience itself, choosing the appropriate teaching method, and deciding what media are to be used. Learning activities may be primarily physical, as in using various types of commercial cleaning equipment; social, as in having an open house in the department; emotional, as in portraying roles in a sociodrama; or mental, as in working a crossword puzzle or computing interest charges. Learning activities need to be planned that will help students meet objectives in all three domains: cognitive, affective, and psychomotor.

Various methods of teaching are the vehicles used for implementing learning experiences. Skits, role plays, sociodramas, discussions, debates, and field trips are a few of the teaching methods available for planning educational activities. The method selected indicates *how* the subject content will be presented. Educational media are the tangible visual and auditory products used to convey messages. Transparencies, flip charts, and flannel boards are visual media. Records and audio cassette tapes utilize sound. Many educational media such as films, video tapes, and film strips with synchronized records utilize both the sense of seeing and that of hearing. Other media, especially in home economics, use the senses of touch, taste, and smell.

CONSIDERATIONS IN DESIGNING LEARNING EXPERIENCES

Learning experiences may be carried out by individuals, by a few students working together, or by an entire class. They may be part of the classroom work, a home-experience program, or activities of a Future Homemakers of America (FHA) or a Home Economics Related Occupations (HERO) group. Many variables affect the learning experiences, teaching methods, and media used. However, the most important are the concepts to be covered and the objectives that have been established. Other variables to consider when developing learning experiences are discussed below.

Variety

In designing a learning experience for a given situation, you must first ask, "What is the best way to help my students clarify these concepts and reach these objectives?" It is important to select a variety of teaching methods and media, both from one day to the next and within the same class period. Nothing can be less motivating for students than doing the same old thing every day. Ideally, you will seek to have approximately three different types of learning experiences within each class period. Naturally, this does not apply to laboratory lessons. Nor will you change pace just because it is in the plans to do so. If students are highly stimulated by a particular learning experience, you may capitalize on the teachable moment and continue while interest is keen. There would be little purpose in beginning another activity when the students are still highly engrossed in what they are doing. However, it does not pay, in educational value, to continue or repeat activities simply because students enjoy them.

The Students

The length of the students' attention span will affect the number of different learning experiences planned. Their preferences for certain types of activities need to be considered. The makeup, or personality, of the class also influences the selection of learning experiences. If students are especially active, experiences that involve considerable physical participation may be appropriate. The ways in which students learn best must be determined. Whether they seem to get more from reading, from visual stimuli, from discussion, or from individual and group study projects is a very important consideration.

It is essential that all students become involved in the teaching-learning process. For some students, participation may be passive, whereas for others it may be active. Some students might be engaged in pencil-and-paper types of activities while others are doing something physical. The vehicle for participation can reflect individual preferences; the important thing is that each student be involved in some way appropriate for the individual.

Number of Senses Involved

Generally, there is a greater retention of subject matter when students use several senses in carrying out a learning activity. Whenever feasible, the students should not only hear about the topic under consideration but also see pertinent materials relating to it. Seeing may include reading or viewing appropriate visuals. Home economics teachers have a distinct advantage because it is possible to include the senses of touch, taste, and smell in many of the areas of subject matter studied. For example, in studying various types of fabrics, students can handle samples to determine the tactile effects of fiber content, weave, and various finishes. Tasting and smelling various types of cheese or forms of milk, such as skim, evaporated, and condensed, will leave a more lasting impression than only hearing or reading about their characteristics and qualities.

For the school population as a whole, retention of subject matter is about the same when students are told about or read about the material. However, if both senses—hearing and seeing—are involved, retention after a time lapse of several days is about three-and-one-half times greater. Consequently, you should make every effort to involve as many senses as possible in a learning experience without becoming repetitious, boring, or insulting to the students.

Time of Day and Year

Classes that meet early in the morning, just after lunch, or at the end of the school day often react to the same learning experiences very differently. The time of year must also be considered. In early fall or late spring the weather may be too warm to make some activities feasible. Furthermore, there are learning experiences that would not be well accepted at the beginning of the school year because the students and teacher are not yet sufficiently acquainted or at ease with one another. For example, students may be reluctant to discuss male-female relationships before rapport has been established within the class. Near the end of the school term, students may be restless. Special efforts often have to be taken to plan activities that are especially stimulating and interesting then.

Physical Facilities

The physical facilities, including the amount and availability of space and equipment, affect the learning activities that can be planned and carried out. For example, it is difficult to have a party for children or a fashion show in a small or crowded classroom. Sometimes rooms can be borrowed or exchanged for special events, but this possibility is less likely in a crowded school. If it is impossible to darken a room, films will lose their effectiveness, and if the necessary *hardware* is unavailable, many types of audiovisual media cannot be used. Whether a school is in a rural or urban area will influence the number and types of field trips that can be arranged, and guest speakers who can be expected to come.

Administrators' Attitudes

The attitude and philosophy of the school's administrators has a bearing on the methods of teaching you select. If your school is very traditional or slow to accept new ideas, this will influence the learning experiences you use. On the other hand, if you teach in a school where most of the teachers have creative and interesting teaching strategies, it will be easier for you to be innovative, too.

The Teacher

Naturally, you will favor some methods of teaching and types of learning experiences more than others because you feel comfortable and secure using them. When something has worked well in the past, it is only logical and practical to try it again. However, there is no reason to use only those activities that have proved successful. Students may suggest other ideas that are just as good and some that may be better than ones you have been using. Every teaching method or learning experience that is at all feasible should be given a chance so that you can see if it will work well for you. If you do not think it has been successful after trying it several times, there are always alternatives from which to choose. Unless you try a method, you have no way of knowing how successfully you can use it.

BASING LEARNING EXPERIENCES ON BEHAVIORAL OBJECTIVES

Sometimes all of the students in a class complete the same learning experiences and sometimes the students are offered choices. Some students may be able to achieve an objective after participating in only one activity, whereas other students may need to complete several learning experiences before they can achieve the same objective.

A learning experience must come up to the level of learning indicated by the corresponding behavioral objective but should not exceed that level. Although a learning experience often begins with components at a lower level of learning than that of the objective, ultimately it should reach and match the objective level to enable students to attain the objective. The following example illustrates an objective at the comprehension level and an accompanying learning experience that begins at the knowledge level and proceeds to the comprehension level:

BEHAVIORAL OBJECTIVE	LEARNING EXPERIENCE
Summarize the characteristics of different wall finishes. (Comprehension)	Read the chapter in the text on wall finishes. List advantages and disadvantages of various wall finishes discussed in the text. Examine samples of wall finishes. Describe to the rest of the class the characteristics of one sample wall finish. Take turns until all the characteristics of each sample have been explained.

Although an objective at the knowledge level, such as "List various types of wall finishes," might have been used here, it is not necessary. If it were included, the learning experience would be restated in two parts. Every stated objective has at least one separate and parallel learning experience planned to enable students to achieve it.

The following examples illustrate how learning experiences can be planned to help students attain behavioral objectives from the lowest to the highest level in the cognitive domain. Although every cognitive level is used here for illustrative purposes, a level is sometimes omitted if it appears that students can continue up the hierarchy without it. The *valuing* objective is included at a point corresponding to its parallel position in the affective domain. The concepts to be clarified are the types of maturity: chronological, physical, mental, emotional, social, and philosophical.

BEHAVIORAL OBJECTIVES	LEARNING EXPERIENCES
List the different types of maturity. (Knowledge)	Read about types of maturity in a selected textbook. Match the names of the types of maturity written on a chalkboard, poster, flip chart, or transparency with each definition, as it is given.
Give examples to illustrate the various types of maturity. (Comprehension)	Divide into groups of three to five students. Role-play situations depicting as a class the ways in which mature and immature behavior are illustrated by the characters in the dramatizations and/or draw cartoons illustrating various types of maturity and/or describe persons (anonymously) who are mature in some respects and immature in others.
Demonstrate the possible effects of mature and immature behavior. (Application)	Make up and present miniskits showing mature and immature behavior. Show how the situations could be handled differently to obtain more positive reactions from others.

Show a continuing desire to learn more about maturity by completing an extra-credit project. (Valuing)	Give a short oral report relating a situation from literature in which immature behavior had detrimental effects. Tell about an instance in which a literary character showed greater maturity than expected from a person that age. Discuss the effect this had on others or read a biography or autobiography about a person having many mature characteristics. Prepare a short written or oral report showing how this person expressed his or her maturity.
Analyze given situations to determine types and levels of maturity. (Analysis)	Read case studies. Point out various types and levels of maturity depicted by the people in the stories and/or watch a television soap opera or part of a movie in which the characters demonstrate various types and levels of maturity. Project the future consequences of the mature and immature behaviors shown by completing the story.
Propose ways to cope with immature behavior. (Synthesis)	Formulate answers to the letters in personal-advice newspaper columns that reveal immature behavior. Develop a set of guidelines for those who work with preschool-age children to use in directing the children's immature behavior into more mature actions.
Evaluate one's own level of maturity. (Evaluation)	Judge one's own maturity, using a scorecard, checklist, rating scale, or questionnaire that has been provided. Evaluate progress, after making a plan for self-improvement.

Learning experiences describe what learners have to do and how they are to do it. Like objectives, when written, they begin with behavioral verbs. Usually they are written so that the verb indicates what the students, rather than the teacher, will be doing. Either approach is acceptable, but consistency is important to avoid confusion about who is to do what.

Learning experiences that are planned for an entire unit of study may be described in general terms, whereas learning experiences that are part of a daily lesson plan are usually given in some detail. You will want to plan your learning experiences to include a variety of teaching methods and media that involve as many senses as possible. The interests, likes, and abilities of the students need to be considered as well as the time of day and year, the equipment and materials available, and the general philosophy of the school system in which you teach.

PLANNING 4

A plan for teaching is like a map or tour guide. It shows your destination and allows for adaptability and creativity in reaching your ultimate goal. If you are driving to a distant place for the first time, you have need to plan your trip in considerable detail and map out your route carefully in advance. If you have traveled to this location many times before, you may only have to refresh your memory about the route. In either case, you are free to detour, spend more time at an intermediate point than planned, or take an alternative road for part of the way. Likewise, when teaching you need to be open to student suggestions for changes in plans, sensitive to how they are reacting, alert to innovative ways of covering subject matter, and flexible enough to take advantage of your own second thoughts.

PLANNING UNITS

A unit is planned for the number of days or weeks you anticipate spending on one major concept within the curriculum. A unit plan is broad in scope and lacks the details that are an inherent part of a daily lesson plan. Lesson plans evolve from the unit plan which includes the following basics:

- *Conceptual framework or structure* that provides a topical outline of the subject matter to be covered.
- *Broad, overall, or terminal objectives* at the higher levels of learning. It may take several days to reach one broad objective, although occasionally attainment of more than one higher-level objective is anticipated in a single class period. See pages 17–33 for an in-depth discussion of broad objectives appropriate for use in planning units.

SAMPLE UNIT PLAN

<table>
<tr><th>Week 1. Monday</th><th>Tuesday</th><th>Wednesday</th></tr>
<tr><td colspan="2">I. SIGNIFICANCE OF FOOD ---------------→</td><td>II. MEAL PLANNING ----</td></tr>
<tr><td>A. Food habits
B. Cultural patterns
C. Social values
D. Psychological satisfactions</td><td>E. Fads and fallacies</td><td rowspan="2">A. Nutritional needs

TO: Plan meals considering nutritional needs, available resources, values, lifestyles and daily food patterns. (C-S) —</td></tr>
<tr><td colspan="2">TO: Analyze factors that affect the significance food has for individuals and families (C-An)</td></tr>
<tr><td>LE: Read and discuss case studies and own situations to determine factors influencing significance of food.</td><td>LE: Share examples of food fads and fallacies and discuss how they relate to the significance one attaches to food.</td><td>TO: Evaluate meals for nutritional content, utilization of resources, and requirements of lifestyles. (C-E) ---
LE: Judge given menus and special diets for inclusion of the basic food groups.</td></tr>
<tr><td>Week 2 -----------→</td><td colspan="2">III. FACTORS AFFECTING FOOD PURCHASES --------→</td></tr>
<tr><td>-------------→</td><td colspan="2">A. Income
B. Family composition and lifestyles -----------→
C. Technology
D. Trends in processing and commercial marketing</td></tr>
<tr><td>-------------→</td><td colspan="2">TO: Determine factors that affect food purchases. (C-An)</td></tr>
<tr><td>-------------→

LE: Exchange menus written on Friday. Work in small groups to evaluate menus for nutrition, use of resources, and appropriateness to lifestyles.</td><td>LE: Listen to guest speaker from university discuss relationship between food purchases and various other factors.

LE: Work in small groups to plan and present some of the following:
(Con't. Wed.)</td><td>1. Handout or news article of suggestions of ways in which proportion of income spent for food can be lowered.
2. Role plays showing how family composition and lifestyles affect food purchases.
3. Visuals on technology affecting food purchases.
4. Skits showing trends in food processing and commercial marketing.</td></tr>
</table>

Thursday	Friday	Resources
B. Resources 1. Money 5. Abilities 2. Time 6. Available 3. Energy foods 4. Equipment	C. Lifestyle D. Values E. Daily food patterns	*Focus on Food* Ch. 27, p. 348 Ch. 12, p. 136
		Films: "Mix & Match for Good Meals" "Food for Life"
LE: View pictures showing situations in which meals are being served that reflect use of resources. Point out ways in which resources seem to have been used to advantage. Suggest changes.	LE: Use RDA charts to plan meals that are nutritionally adequate for special groups such as vegetarians, athletes, and non-breakfast eaters.	Tupperware Ed. series
IV. PLANNING FOOD PURCHASES		
A. Food grades B. Food states and forms	C. Using ads and specials D. Trading stamps and premiums E. Shopping list	*Focus on Food* Unit IV, p. 277 *Consumer Decision Making* Ch. 20, p. 385
TO: Compare food grades, states, and forms in making food purchasing decisions. (C-E)	TO: Develop guidelines that utilize effective management of food purchasing skills. (C-S)	*This American Consumer* Ch. 9, p. 139
LE: Take field trip to supermarket. Listen to guide explain grades, forms, and states of food. Use worksheet to compare various grades, states, and forms observed.	LE: Present skit about going grocery shopping and analyze factors the characters do and do not consider in planning food purchases.	*Teen Guide to Homemaking* Ch. 19, p. 383

- *Major learning experiences or student activities and evaluation.* Only the most important activities, involving the higher levels of learning, are included in a teaching unit. Learning experiences used for evaluation purposes and other major plans for evaluating student achievement are usually included also.
- *Resources* such as teacher reference materials and media. Occasionally student resources are suggested.

In addition, unit plans may include a description of the school and community situation such as the kind and degree of support for the home economics program and availability of material and intangible resources. General observations about the interests, needs, and ability levels of student groups in each class are helpful. (As you write notes about students, however, keep in mind the possible legal implications of your assessments.) Plans for teaching the unit are derived from the data pertaining to the students, school, and community. If a justification is provided, it tells why the chosen concepts are appropriate for inclusion in the unit. If generalizations are included in a unit plan, they should be second- and third-level and should link the major concepts. First-level generalizations are inappropriate for unit plans because they are too narrow in scope.

Unit plans in block form are easy to use because they provide a daily overview of the teacher's broad and general plans for the coming weeks. By planning in advance, media can be requested or developed ahead of time, arrangements can be made for field trips and resource people, and pertinent references can be gathered and studied.

Note that in the sample unit plan on pages 42 and 43, more than one day is devoted to each of the four major concepts. This is often true, but sometimes only one day is planned for a concept. In the sample, the terminal objectives (TO) are at the analysis, synthesis, and evaluation levels; sometimes more than one objective is planned for a day. Only major learning experiences (LE) have been suggested. These enable students to meet the objectives and correspond to them in levels of learning. Labeling objectives in both unit and lesson plans with the following symbols, to indicate domains and levels of learning, facilitates the planning of learning experiences at appropriate levels:

COGNITIVE (C)	AFFECTIVE (A)	PSYCHOMOTOR (P)
Knowledge (C-K)	Receiving (A-Rec)	Perception (P-P)
Comprehension (C-C)	Responding (A-Res)	Set (P-Set)
Application (C-Ap)	Valuing (A-V)	Guided response (P-GR)
Analysis (C-An)	Organization (A-O)	Mechanism (P-M)
Synthesis (C-S)	Characterization (A-C)	Complex overt response (P-COR)
Evaluation (C-E)		

LESSON PLANS

The extent to which you plan daily lessons varies greatly depending upon your teaching experience, knowledge of the subject matter to be covered, and the types of lessons being planned. For the experienced teacher, this planning may be done primarily in the mind, with only a few key ideas written on paper. The beginning teacher usually has to plan more extensively in order to feel secure and confident when teaching. The student teacher is generally expected to plan lessons in detail. It is recognized that full-time, in-service teachers may not have the time or the need to plan as extensively as they once did. However, lesson plans should contain enough information to permit a substitute teacher with a background in home economics subject matter to use any given plan when a minimal amount of time is available to prepare for class.

Although you may not choose to write a justification for every lesson, you should ask yourself these questions: Why teach this lesson? How pertinent is this topic to contemporary life for these students? Some subject matter that has been a traditional part of the typical home economics curriculum for many years can be questioned today as to its relevance to changing family life styles. Justifying your lesson plan, at least mentally, will help you to keep your material interesting and fresh while retaining content of proven value. On the other hand, an idea need not be discarded just because it is traditional.

The unit plan provides the broad base from which lesson plans evolve. The sample lesson plan that follows is based on the second Friday of the sample unit plan.

SAMPLE LESSON PLAN

Course and Unit: Consumer Education (Consumer Buying-Food)
Class Period and Time: First, 8:35 a.m.–9:30 a.m.
Day and Date: Friday, September 13, 19XX

Major concept(s) from unit block plan:

Planning food purchases

- Using ads and specials
- Trading stamps and premiums
- Shopping lists

Broad objective(s) from unit block plan

Develop guidelines that utilize the effective management of food purchasing skills (C-S).

Introduction/establishing set

Ask students to unscramble the eight words written on a poster, all of which relate to shopping. Each word represents a factor to consider for a step to take before making food purchases. The letter found between the two vertical lines in each word is in its correct position and forms the word SHOPPING. (8–10 minutes)

D A	S	
H	H	L T A E
S E R	O	T S
M A T S	P	S
I	P	A L S S E C
T	I	L S
G N N	N	I L P A
	G	S R D A E

(Note: To save time, students could work in pairs on a single word. If this takes too much time, give students hints, so that establishing set does not take too long.)

Lesson body

SPECIFIC OBJECTIVES	CONTENT NOTES	LEARNING EXPERIENCES
1. List sources of ads consumers use to make food purchasing decisions. (C-K)	1. *Source of ads* –Newspapers –Magazines –Radio –T.V. –Flyers and circulars –Window display posters	*1. Name sources of ads that influence consumer decisions relating to food purchasing. (2–3 minutes)
2. List ways to identify specials. (C-K)	2.,3. *Ways to identify specials in newspaper ads* –Bold print –Large type –Different colors –Coupons	2. View ads on posters showing ways specials are emphasized. (2–3 minutes)

*Can also be used for evaluation

3. Identify specials in given ads. (C-K)		*3. View double-page newspaper ad held up by teacher and name the featured specials. (2–3 minutes)
4. Give examples of premiums that influence shoppers to make food purchases. (C-C)	4. *Premiums that influence shoppers* –Coupons –Games like bingo –Products sold at discount such as dishes, flatware, encyclopedias –Food samples in stores	4. Describe premiums that have influenced people in your family and other individuals when they have been planning food purchases. (4–5 minutes)
5. Summarize advantages and disadvantages of shopping in stores that offer trading stamps. (C-C)	5. *Trading stamps—advantages* –Accumulate goods you choose at redemption centers. –Many staple items cost no more. –Increases volume of sales in store. –Increases likelihood that numerous products are available at store. –Some stores allow you to use them to reduce cost of purchases. *Trading stamps—disadvantages* –Some items cost more because someone must pay for the stamps. –Takes time to put stamps in books. –Redemption center may be inaccessible. –Stamps stick to other items and dye runs.	5. Share results of interview done for homework in which at least one person was asked, "Do you shop for food in stores where trading stamps are given? Why or why not?" Discuss advantages and disadvantages of shopping where stamps are available. (8–10 minutes)

6. Explain the advantages of preparing a shopping list. (C-C)	6. *Advantages of shopping list* –Lessens impulse buying –Saves time –Promotes advance meal planning –Serves as a reminder –Helps capitalize on ads, specials, and premiums	6. View pantomime done by one or two classmates of a consumer shopping for food without a list. *Discuss the advantages of using a list when shopping for food. (8–10 minutes)
7. Point out factors contributing to consumer skill in planning food purchases. (C-An)	7. *Factors contributing to consumer skill in planning food purchases* (skit analysis) Kim and Pat considered: –Coupons –Trading stamps –Prices –Store location –Ads –Specials Kim and Pat did not consider –Planning very far ahead for puchases –Being hungry leading to impulse buying –Having a shopping list	7. View skit, "Kim and Pat Go Shopping." (Skit attached.) Compile a list of factors the characters do and do not consider in planning food purchases.

SKIT FOR SAMPLE LESSON PLAN

"Kim and Pat Go Shopping"

KIM: We'd better go shopping for food for dinner tonight.

PAT: Yes, I'm starving!

KIM: Got something special in mind for dinner?

PAT: No, anything that looks good. Where shall we go shopping?

KIM: Supertown Market gives purple polka-dot trading stamps. We almost have enough of those stamps to fill another book.

PAT: Aren't prices higher there?

KIM: Maybe. Where do you think we should go?

PAT: Let's try that new place, the Super Savings Store. It's nearer than Supertown Market, too.

KIM: Oh, yeah. They've advertised they're giving double off on coupons this week. I'll take the coupons we have. Are you ready?

PAT: Let's go. Maybe we can buy enough food for tomorrow too.

Summary/closure

Have a student interview another student on a mock T.V. talk show. (5–6 minutes)

Questions for interviewer:

1. Why should you as a consumer pay attention to ads and specials?
2. What benefits might trading stamps and premiums offer to consumers?
3. When might trading stamps and premiums be a disadvantage to consumers?
4. Why should a consumer develop a shopping list?

Generalization: Consumer skills in planning for food purchases are enhanced when consideration is given to the use of ads, specials, trading stamps, premiums, and shopping lists.

Teaching materials

- Poster showing ways to identify specials
- Double-page newspaper ad
- Skit script "Kim and Pat Go Shopping"

Evaluation

See starred learning experiences and summary/closure.

Assignment

For today: Interview at least one person and ask the question: "Do you shop for food in stores where trading stamps are given? Why, or why not?" Write the answer on a paper to be turned in.
For next class period: None

If the component parts of the lesson plan are capitalized or underscored, the plan is easier to use. To save time, some teachers make multiple copies of the lesson-plan format. Then they fill in the component parts as individual lessons are planned. A substitute teacher would find it helpful to know both the course and the unit for which the lesson is planned because this gives some indication of the type of students that may be in the class and their subject-matter background. Because the times at which class periods begin and end vary in different schools, it is essential that a substitute teacher have this information. The major concept(s) and broad terminal objective(s) are taken directly from the unit plan.

Introduction/Establishing Set

opening

The introduction should be appropriate for the age and ability level of the students, get the attention of the class, be related to the topic, stimulate thinking about it, and provide for a smooth transition into the body of the lesson. For these reasons, set is usually more effective when it is planned carefully than when it is haphazard. Of course, sometimes you will get a better idea at the last moment than the one you had planned to use. You can usually change your approach, but it may be impossible to think at the last minute of a stimulating way to begin.

Having a carefully planned introduction contributes to your security and allows you to think about the students rather than about what you will say and do. See page 54 for the discussion about establishing set.

Specific Objectives

Specific or daily objectives lead up to the level of learning of the terminal or broad objective but do not exceed this level. Since it sometimes takes several days to achieve a broad objective, the specific objectives for some days may fall several levels below that of the terminal objective. There may be several objectives at the same level that relate to different subconcepts.

It is also possible occasionally to skip a level of learning. As the content or a subconcept changes, the specific objectives may revert to lower levels of learning again. Hence, daily objectives could go in this order: C-K, C-K, C-C, C-An, C-E, C-K, C-C, C-An, C-An, and C-E.

In the sample lesson plan, the first three objectives are at the C-K level, then there are three at the C-C level. One of these C-C objectives relates to premiums, one to trading stamps, and one to shopping lists. The C-Ap level was skipped. The last daily objective may or may not reach the level of the terminal objective. In the sample given, the last specific objective and the terminal objective are identical.

Because the three domains of learning interrelate, specific objectives may shift from one domain to another. An objective from one domain may be used to complete the sequential order of objectives in another domain such as C-K, C-C, A-V, and C-An. Because a level is occasionally skipped, a sequence such as this is also possible: C-K, C-C, P-GR, P-M, and C-E.

Content Notes

The content notes provide the basic subject matter of the lesson. The content notes include the points you want to be sure are covered. Notes are *written* so no content is overlooked and omitted. It is easier to make note of key points and examples before class than it is to think of them while teaching. There are many forms for making content notes. Usually key points can be used for reference more easily than complete sentences in paragraph form. Sometimes it is appropriate to formulate key questions and to jot down points you want to be sure are brought out in the responses.

Content notes relate directly to each subconcept that is suggested in each specific objective. Occasionally one component of content notes pertains to the subconcepts included in two specific objectives. In the sample lesson plan, the content notes labeled *2* and *3* cover points related to specials *and* ads. These subconcepts are referred to in two objectives. There are no content notes for Objective 8 because ads, specials, stamps, and the like were covered previously.

Some sources for content notes include textbooks, professional journals, popular magazines, newspapers, and commercial teaching materials. Your own notes from college courses may also be a valuable source.

Learning Experiences

Learning experiences are the activities in which students take part so that they are able to achieve the specified behavioral objectives. Every objective has at least one learning experience indicating what the students will *do*. Sometimes two activities are planned to provide for attainment of one objective. Sometimes alternative learning experiences are suggested from which students may choose.

Remember that learning experiences correlate with their behavioral objectives in levels of learning, although they may begin with components that are at lower levels of learning.

The specific objectives, content notes, and learning experiences interrelate. The three-column format illustrates this interdependence, but you may prefer another lesson-plan form in which the specific objectives, content notes, and learning experiences are written vertically and in sequence.

When listing learning experiences, it is helpful to include the specific media and teaching methods that will be used. Obviously, some learning experiences will require more planning than others. Sometimes an idea that is better than those that have been planned will come to the teacher or to a student spontaneously. In such a case, it may be wise to depart from the lesson plan, at least in part. Teachers who are secure in their knowledge of the subject matter are able to be flexible about how it will be presented. Teachers who are insecure about their knowledge of the subject matter or their teaching ability are more likely to be rigid and afraid of what will happen if they depart from previously made plans.

Summary/Closure

The summary or closure ties the lesson together by helping students formulate generalizations about the content that has been covered. See pages 58 and 59 for the discussion about closure.

Teaching Materials and Resources

Listing the teaching materials needed for a lesson helps you to organize your thinking and plan ahead. A substitute teacher would find it extremely helpful to have a list of the media such as posters, filmstrips, and case studies to be used in the lesson.

Resources include student or teacher references such as texts, curriculum guides, and written materials distributed by commercial concerns. It is helpful to include resources and references so that, if the lesson plan is to be used again at a later date, the subject matter can be reviewed quickly and easily.

Evaluation

Some learning experiences serve to evaluate student achievement. It is helpful to indicate, perhaps with an asterisk as in the sample lesson plan, the activities that serve this purpose. By doing this, it is easy to note the objectives that remain to be evaluated. The objectives that have been formulated will, in turn, influence the methods and levels of evaluation used.

Assignment

The daily lesson plan may or may not include a student assignment to be done during class time or outside class. It could be a project, small-group assignment, survey, experiment, observation, or almost any other form of learning activity. Assignments to be used as a basis for evaluating student achievement should be directly related to the behavioral objectives that have been established.

TEACHING SKILLS 5

Teaching skills are specific and identifiable techniques and tools that teachers use to derive maximum value from the lessons they have planned. Only the most important teaching skills are described in this chapter. They include:

- Establishing set
- Using appropriate frames of reference
- Illustrating with examples
- Reinforcing subject matter
- Reinforcing behavior
- Questioning that includes
    - Using higher-level questions
    - Using probing questions
    - Using student-initiated questions
    - Balancing student participation
    - Timing
- Using silence
- Pacing
- Recognizing and obtaining attending behavior
- Achieving closure

If you develop expertise in using these teaching skills, the others should be easy for you. Effective questioning skills are so important in the teaching process that all of Chapter 7 has been devoted to questioning.

ESTABLISHING SET

In education, the term *set* refers to establishing rapport with students as a lesson or class period begins. Establishing set refers to introducing a lesson, but it may encompass more than that. Set may be enhanced by establishing direct eye contact with students and by talking with them as they enter the room, by making sincere comments that reflect your concern for them, and by asking questions that show your interest. There is a direct correlation between effectiveness in establishing set and the effectiveness of a total lesson. When you succeed in creating a positive attitude at the beginning of the lesson, students are more likely to be involved and interested throughout. Similarly, when students are involved in a lesson from the beginning, they are likely to participate willingly throughout the class period.

Reaction to a lesson is likely to be negative when a teacher begins by saying, "Today *I'm* going to tell you *all* about . . ." This gives students the impression the lesson is going to be boring and very teacher-oriented. Students want to feel included from the beginning. In a teacher-dominated classroom you hear lots of words and phrases like *I want you to, tell me*, and *my*. In a student-oriented classroom you are more likely to hear *let's, we*, and *our*.

When teachers dominate lessons at the beginning by doing all the talking, students are often reluctant to participate and feel awkward and self-conscious when asked a question 20 or 30 minutes after class has begun. Students realize that when they have not talked for some time, their voices may sound shaky and hesitant when they do speak.

You do not need an elaborate introduction that takes a long time to prepare. It may consist of a thought-provoking rhetorical question you ask while looking right at the students to show your interest in their reactions. You might use an analogy to show the relationship between the topic for the day and some current or historical event, or you might refer to a bulletin board, display, or exhibit. You can stimulate interest by having materials relating to the main concept of the lesson in a paper bag or on a tray that is covered with a towel to create an element of surprise. If you are going to use a poster, turn it toward the wall until you need it in the lesson.

In a lesson on grooming or health, you could pretend to be taking the students' picture with a camera. As the students sit up straight, you might say, "We would all feel so much better if we always looked as we do when we're having our picture taken." In a lesson on the significance of food, you might begin by serving a small snack and then leading into a discussion of the many reasons people eat what they do. For a lesson on personal characteristics for employability, you might drop an effervescent headache remedy into a clear glass containing water. Relate the bubbling action to friendliness, enthusiasm, and good health required for success on the job. You could also use this idea to introduce a lesson on nutrition, energy conservation, or patterns of physical activity and fatigue. Occasionally you can scramble one word denoting the main topic of the lesson on the board to create interest. You need to plan for establishing set, but you do not need to have an elaborate and time-consuming activity.

USING APPROPRIATE FRAMES OF REFERENCE

Frames of reference provide several different points of view through which students gain an understanding of content. Because a subject is better understood when it is presented from different points of view, such a procedure is more effective than using only one. For example, fashion merchandising becomes more meaningful to students when it is seen from the points of view of the garment designer, fabric manufacturer, assembly-line production staff, wholesale distributor, retailer, and fashion coordinator. The key to this teaching skill is the word *appropriate*. You identify many possible frames of reference that can be used in instruction and then make judicious selections from among them, depending on the needs and interests of the class.

ILLUSTRATING WITH EXAMPLES

Examples are used to clarify, verify, and substantiate concepts. Here are some ways to use examples effectively:

- Start with simple examples and progress to more complex ones.
- Begin with examples relevant to students' experiences and knowledge.
- Build on students' verbal contributions by giving examples to clarify points students have made and to add depth of subject matter.
- Relate examples to the principles being taught or the guidelines being covered.
- Check to see if the objectives of the lesson have been achieved, by asking students to give examples that illustrate the main points.

REINFORCING SUBJECT MATTER

The purpose of this skill is to further clarify major concepts, generalizations, principles, and key words. You can use repetition effectively to focus, highlight, and direct attention to points that need emphasis. However, students feel belittled and bored when teachers cover subject matter verbatim a second time and with the same media and teaching methods. Varying instructional strategies usually enhances the reinforcement of content. For example, principles of design may be covered in home furnishings and reinforced in clothing selection, table setting, and flower arranging. With each conceptual area, different visual media and verbal examples would be used, and students would participate in different learning experiences and build on previous ones.

REINFORCING BEHAVIOR

Your positive reaction to desired student behavior is an integral part of your role as a teacher and facilitator of classroom learning. You can give reinforcement nonverbally through smiling and nodding or verbally with words of support. Praise is often a single word such as "Good," "Fine," or "Exactly." Sometimes you can simply say, "Go on. This is interesting." or, "Tell us more about your idea." Reinforcement is also given by repeating those students' answers that contribute positively to the lesson. When a learner makes a worthwhile comment, you may paraphrase the statement, restate the idea more simply and concisely, or summarize what has been said. Both verbal and nonverbal reinforcement reflect concern for students' feelings. It is important to give reinforcement in a variety of ways because students react differently to various types of support.

QUESTIONING

The learning value derived from using an educational game, showing a filmstrip, participating in a sociodrama, reading an assignment, or taking part in *any* educational activity depends to a very high degree on your questioning skills. Five general questioning skills are discussed here. See Chapter 7 for more detailed coverage of questioning.

Using Higher-Level Questions

Higher-level questions cannot be answered from memory alone. They call for explaining, using, analyzing, synthesizing, or evaluating rules, guidelines, or principles rather than stating them. Higher-level questions can seldom be answered with only one word. Beginning questions with *how*, *what*, and *why* generally fosters thinking at levels above recall, or cognitive knowledge.

Using Probing Questions

When teachers probe, they ask questions that require students to go beyond superficial *first answer* responses. You do this when you:

- Ask students for more information or what their replies mean.
- Require students to justify or defend their responses.
- Refocus the students' or class's attention on a related issue.
- Prompt students or give them hints.
- Bring other students into the discussion by getting them to respond to the first student's reply.

Using Student-Initiated Questions

If the classroom environment is nonthreatening and students are interested and motivated, they will usually ask questions that can be used to enhance a lesson. Replying to students' questions can add depth to the subject matter of a lesson. However, replying to students' questions at length should meet the needs and interests of a sufficient number to justify the time spent doing this. Teachers need to be careful not to let students' questions and their own responses extend beyond the point of educationally diminishing returns. In answering a question, be careful not to look at and speak only to the student who asked the question, but rather maintain eye contact and talk with the entire class to keep the students' attention. So that your answer has maximum value, repeat the question or ask the student to do this.

Students often ask questions that lead their teachers into talking about topics different from those related to the purpose of the lesson. Sometimes students delight in seeing how long they can keep their teachers off the subject. Students realize that they cannot be held responsible for material that was never covered in class. Limited discussion about topics not included in the curriculum can add interest and serve as a motivating force, but avoid topics that are too personal, that are *highly* controversial, or that stimulate extremely emotional reactions. Issues that might be acceptable topics for classroom discussion in one school may be totally unacceptable in another school. You need to sense the appropriate time to conclude the talk about irrelevant topics. You might say, "This is all very interesting, but let's get back to what we were saying about. . . ." Sometimes you may avoid being sidetracked by making a comment such as, "That's an interesting question, but we need to continue our discussion about. . . ."

Balancing Student Participation

You need to be aware of which students have contributed to a discussion and which have not, so you can include the nonparticipating students. You should provide the opportunity for most of the class to participate. Use a random order to call on students rather than going around the room in a set pattern up and down rows.

Timing

As a beginning teacher you may be tempted to answer your own questions rather than give students sufficient time to think of their own responses. In the absence of a response, you may provide a hint to the answer. Perhaps you would feel comfortable saying something like "Let me put it another way," or "I guess I didn't make the question clear," before rephrasing it or changing it to incorporate a lower level of learning.

USING SILENCE

Many teachers are frightened by silences or pauses in classroom discussions. Because they feel uncomfortable, they tend to fill silences by talking unnecessarily or by making sounds such as "umm." Silence can be a powerful tool in the teaching-learning process because it can provide students with the opportunity to think about what has transpired. You can use pauses effectively after the following:

- Introductory comments that encourage students to think about their answers.
- Questions asked of students to give them time to think about their answers.

- Questions from a student directed to another student verbally or by a look or gesture.
- Student responses that foster additional remarks from other students.

PACING

Pacing refers to making a smooth transition from one part of a lesson to another and to balancing the amount of intellectually difficult material presented at one time. You should plan the transition to link one concept to another and to move students from one activity to another. When pacing is effective, students have time to absorb the information, but the lesson does not drag. You should be careful not to cover too many *weighty* cognitive concepts at one time, because students need to be provided with the opportunity to analyze and synthesize. For example, if you planned to cover hue, value, intensity, temperature, force, and color schemes in a ninth grade class in one day, there would be too little time for the students to grasp the material. There also should be several opportunities during a lesson for evaluation and student-initiated questions and comments.

RECOGNIZING AND OBTAINING ATTENDING BEHAVIOR

Successful and experienced teachers use visual cues that indicate student reactions such as interest, boredom, comprehension, and confusion. A facial expression, the direction of the eyes, the tilt of the head, and body posture offer messages that make it possible for skilled teachers to evaluate their performance according to students' reactions. Doodling, yawning, twisting hair, and swinging feet are signs that might indicate it is time to modify the lesson by varying the pace, changing the activity, or introducing a different method of teaching.

ACHIEVING CLOSURE

Closure helps students formulate generalizations. It is appropriate when the major concepts, purposes, principles, or particular portions of a lesson have been covered so that students can relate new knowledge to past knowledge. Closure is more than a quick summary of the material covered in a lesson. In addition to pulling together major points and helping students see the relationships among concepts, closure provides students with a feeling of achievement. Closure is not limited to the end of a lesson. You can provide closure at specific points within a lesson to help students see where they have been, where they are, and/or where they are going. Questions such as these are helpful in closing lessons:

"How does what we've been talking about relate to . . . ?"
"What does this mean to you in your life today?"
"How can you use this information in the future?"

good?

In addition to using specific techniques skillfully, you can vary the environment to enhance learning. You increase student interest when you change the seating arrangement and the appearance of the classroom. You can use different accessories or rearrange them, make a new bulletin board or display, and use a fresh teaching method. Sometimes you can hold class in another room or have the students sit on the floor during a class discussion.

Although creating interest through variety is usually not identified as a specific teaching skill, it does enhance the teaching-learning process. When you vary your habitual patterns, student attention often increases. For example, you can vary your interaction style or the way in which you move around the room, or even your appearance. A new hair style or fashion worn by the teacher may serve to heighten student interest in content areas completely unrelated to personal appearance. A variety of media, materials, and methods of teaching is also important in creating and maintaining student interest.

Teaching skills are tools of the trade—and they are also tricks of the trade, in the legitimate sense that they make one teacher succeed where another, equally informed and well-intentioned, fails. The skills can be summarized at length, as in the preceding; but their secret comes down largely to the art of communication, or *interchange*. Learning is not a one-way street. Teaching skills are the things that facilitate the transfer of knowledge from teacher to student, but the feedback generated in the process is also a constant and invaluable guide to the teacher in reaching the desired target.

EVALUATION 6

Teachers who want to evaluate their students' achievement fairly and honestly provide a broad base on which to determine final grades. A variety of evaluative methods is fairer because different students do well on different types of measures. A variety of evaluative methods gives all students an opportunity to do well occasionally. Thus, student achievement may be based on homework assignments, work done in class, projects, reports, laboratory experiences, self-evaluative instruments, and tests. The proportional weight given to each evaluation in determining the composite grade should be made clear to students so that they can establish priorities.

USING TESTS

In addition to determining grades, test results can also be used to analyze students' strong and weak points, to provide a basis for initiating a conference or counseling session, and to help students see the relationships among the concepts covered in the text. Teachers can also use test scores to determine which topics they have covered most adequately and which methods of teaching they have used most effectively.

The frequency of testing depends on the concepts being covered. When only one or two tests are given in a course, undue emphasis may be placed upon them. It is a good idea to give tests at the beginning of the class period. When students are told they will be given a test at the end of the period, they are likely to spend class time in worrying or cramming rather than paying attention to the business at hand. Surprise or pop tests foster student resentment against both the teacher and the subject matter, and increase the probability that students will cheat. Although not all students will study for announced tests, students should have the option of deciding this for themselves. Furthermore, one of the purposes of giving a test is to encourage students to review and clarify concepts. Obviously, the purpose will not be served if the students do not know that they are going to have a test.

Since cheating is a difficult problem to handle, take precautions to minimize its occurrence. See pages 220–221 for specific suggestions for coping with this problem. As a test score increases in importance in determining a final term grade, the likelihood that students will cheat also increases. Therefore, you want to provide opportunities for self-evaluation and to figure term grades on a broad base of quizzes, assignments, reports, and projects. Pressure to cheat is lessened when students realize that neither one very high test score nor one very low score will have a great impact on their overall averages.

GUIDELINES FOR CONSTRUCTING ACHIEVEMENT TESTS

The following guidelines relate to writing variations of teacher-made achievement tests. Specifics that pertain exclusively to constructing a particular type of test item precede the examples given for different possibilities.

1. As you write test questions, keep a tally to be sure the behavioral objectives are covered in proportion to the instructional emphasis given to each. Also check to see that achievement of each objective is measured so that some test questions come up to the level of learning of the corresponding objective. However, none of the test questions for a given objective should exceed the level of learning of that objective.
2. Similar types of test items should be grouped together. For example, all simple two-response true-and-false questions should be grouped in one section of the test, and all multiple choice questions of the one-correct-answer type should be grouped in another section. Write separate directions for each section. This organizes the test so that students do not have to keep changing their orientation and thinking process from question to question. Within each section, arrange items so they are grouped by subject matter.
3. Write test items so that an obvious pattern of answers does not emerge, such as *true, true, false, true, true, false*, and so forth. At the same time, questions ought to progress in difficulty, beginning with easier questions. This enables students to experience an initial success that may motivate them to proceed through the test with a positive attitude. Difficult items usually take longer to answer. Students may have a tendency to devote so much time to answering harder questions that little or no time remains to complete the test.
4. Word test items and directions clearly and concisely. If the vocabulary is too difficult, the item may be assessing whether the students understand the

meaning of specific words rather than the concepts involved. On the other hand, when the vocabulary is too simple and monotonous, students may be insulted or bored and, consequently, make careless errors. Test-wise students or ones who are particularly adept in syntax will have a decided advantage if there are grammatical clues that give away the right answer. This possibility can be eliminated by using "a (an)" and "(s)" with nouns and verbs where plurals or verb tenses could indicate the correct responses.

5. It is important that both visual and verbal examples used in class and statements from the text do not reappear on a test precisely as they were originally presented. Using the exact wording of the textbook or the same pictures or samples used in class does nothing to determine whether students can interpret, apply, or analyze subject matter.
6. Use quantitative statements in place of qualitative ones whenever possible because they are clearer. Words like *more, less, sometimes, often, seldom, generally,* and *usually* may be interpreted in various ways by different students.
7. If you have to use negative statements, call attention to the negative word by underlining or capitalizing it. Avoid negative statements if at all possible.
8. Avoid parenthetical clauses and phrases. Although your intent in placing additional material in parentheses may be to clarify by giving an example, in actuality this might cause confusion.
9. Complete each question on one page. If you continue an item onto the succeeding page, this may confuse students and cause unnecessary paper shuffling.
10. Plan the test so the majority of students have enough time to finish. Objective items tend to provide more extensive sampling per unit of time than do essay questions. However, objective tests have a tendency to become highly factual and to place a premium on memory alone, whereas essay questions provide an opportunity for students to organize and express their thoughts. The subject matter and objectives will affect the types of questions used.
11. Indicate clearly the point value of each test item. This can help students determine the amount of time and effort they should allow for completing their responses.
12. Be sure each test question is independent of all other questions on the test. Answering a question correctly should not depend on having answered a previous question correctly.
13. Check to be sure that the answers to questions are not inadvertently provided in other items on the test.
14. Give a point of reference for attitudes, theories, and philosophies. For example, instead of stating, "Experience is the best teacher," you might write, "John Dewey believed that ideas must be judged by experience."
15. The scoring of tests is simplified when questions are arranged and written so that answers can be checked easily and quickly. Responses to objective questions can be written to the left of each item so that you can place an answer key next to the answer column for rapid scoring. You might want to use a separate answer sheet when tests are longer than one or two pages.

True-and-False Items

Because true-and-false questions are fairly easy to write, they are frequently used in tests. However, caution should be observed in constructing true-and-false items so that they will be clearly understood and guessing will be minimized. There should be approximately the same number of true items as false items. When almost all the answers are either true or false, students may become more concerned with an answer pattern than with the content of the items.

The letters *t* and *f* can be easily confused; therefore, use + for true and 0 for false to save time in grading and to avoid potential arguments when tests are returned. It takes more time to read *true* and *false* when the students write out these words. Or you might want to provide an answer column and direct students to circle either T or F.

Correction-type responses and responses that require giving reasons for false answers minimize guessing better than simple two-response items. They also give you a better assessment of student learning.

The following examples show different types of true-false items. The level of learning progresses from knowledge to comprehension to analysis. Many educators erroneously believe that objective test items can be written only at the knowledge level.

True-False—simple two-response choice (with knowledge-level example)

Directions: If the statement is true, place a + in the blank to the left of the item. If the statement is false, place a 0 in the blank.

__+__ 1. Advance meal planning contributes to wise consumer planning.

__+__ 2. The selection of the grade of a food product depends upon its intended use.

__0__ 3. Federal regulations require that recipes be given on the labels of canned food products.

True-False—correction-type response (with knowledge-level example)

Directions: If the item is true, write + in the answer column. If it is false, correct it by writing, in the space provided at the left, the word you would substitute for the underlined word to make it a true statement.

__+__ 1. Most of the design principles we use were developed by the ancient <u>Greeks.</u>

__proportion__ 2. A large design in a fabric to be used for draperies in a small room is an example of poor <u>balance.</u>

__transition__ 3. Curved lines that create rhythm are referred to as <u>opposition.</u>

True-False—series of statements based on a given situation (with comprehension-level example)

Directions: Mary and Bob have bought an old house that needs redecorating. The rooms in the house are small. Mary and Bob want to make these rooms appear larger through effective decorating.

The following is a list of changes they are considering. If the change would make a room appear larger, put a + in the blank to the left of the statement. If the change would make the room appear smaller, put a 0 in the blank.

___0___ 1. Use dark colors on the walls.
___0___ 2. Use intense colors on the walls.
___+___ 3. Paint the baseboard, molding, and woodwork the same color as the walls.
___0___ 4. Paint each room a different color.
___+___ 5. Use mirrors for wall decorations.
___+___ 6. Choose furniture that is small in scale.

True-False—with reasons for false answers (with comprehension-level example)

Directions: If the statement is true, place a + in the blank to the left. If the item is false, place a 0 in the blank and then, below the item, give the reason why it is false. Credit will be given only if the reason you supply is correct—true and to the point. You do not have to give reasons for items marked true.

___+___ 1. On a limited budget, it is more practical to buy furniture that is open-stock than that which is custom-made.
___+___ 2. Other things being equal, wood veneer of seven ply will be more durable than solid wood.
___0___ 3. Scotchguard is a finish applied to upholstery fabric that helps to minimize color fading. *It helps fabric to resist soil and stains.*

True-False—analogy (with analysis-level example)

Directions: If the analogy is true, circle the letter *t* in the answer column. If the analogy is false, circle the letter *f*.

(t) f 1. Vitamin A is to night blindness as vitamin D is to rickets.
t (f) 2. Iron is to milk as vitamin A is to carrots.
(t) f 3. Vitamin C is to healthy gums as calcium is to strong bones.

Multiple choice items usually consist of an introductory statement or question, called the *stem,* followed by a series of words, phrases, or sentences that are called *alternatives.* The stem should consist of a completed idea, not just a single word. All the multiple choice stems in one group should be in the form of either a question or an incomplete statement. Use four to seven plausible alternatives below each stem. Each multiple choice question in one section of the test should have the same number of alternatives for a unified effect. The correct alternatives, as well as the distractors, or incorrect responses, need to be homogeneous in content and form. Distractors should seem plausible or they become *giveaways* and affect the validity of a test. Remember, too, that when students are in doubt, they frequently select the longest choice. Use alternatives such as "all of the above," "none of the above," "two of the above," and so forth infrequently. This type of response is often confusing and can increase the probability of guessing correctly.

The first three types of multiple choice items are illustrated with knowledge-level questions. The last three use analysis-level questions.

Multiple choice—single best answer

Directions: In the blank to the left of each item, write the letter corresponding to the *one* answer that best completes each statement.

__b__ 1. Dry a 100 percent wool sweater:
- a. In the sun.
- b. On a flat surface.
- c. In a dryer.
- d. Near a heat outlet.
- e. On a hanger.

Multiple choice—one incorrect answer

Directions: Circle the letter of the *one* item that *incorrectly* completes each statement.

1. Fortified whole milk is a good source of:
- (a.) Vitamin C.
- b. Phosphorus.
- c. Calcium.
- d. Vitamin A.
- e. Vitamin D.

Multiple choice—variable number of answers

Directions: For every item that correctly answers the question, black out the corresponding letter(s). All, some, or none of the answers may be correct.

1. Which of the following foods contain vitamin C?
   a̸. Citrus fruit
   b. Eggs
   c. Milk
   d̸. Bell peppers
   e̸. White potatoes

Multiple choice—one-answer analogy

Directions: Black out the letter corresponding to the word that *best* completes the sentence.

1. Strength is to nylon as heat resistance is to:
   a. Acetate.
   b. Cotton.
   ¢. Linen.
   d. Polyester.
   e. Rayon.

Multiple choice—most inclusive item without stem

Directions: Circle the letter that corresponds to the most *inclusive* item in each group. In other words, choose the item that includes all the others listed in that particular group.

1. a. Educational background
   b. Job experiences
   c. Organizational affiliations
   d. References
   (e.) Résumé
2. a. Chef
   b. Caterer
   c. Food laboratory tester
   (d.) Food-service semiprofessional employee
   e. Dietitian's assistant

Multiple choice—most dissimilar item without stem

Directions: In the blank to the left, write the letter corresponding to the one item in each group that is *not* associated with the others listed. In other words, choose the item that is dissimilar to the others in the group.

__d__ 1. a. Flying a kite
b. Riding a bicycle
c. Jumping rope
d. Modeling with clay
e. Playing on a jungle gym

__a__ 2. a. Assembling and gluing model airplanes
b. Playing with toy trucks in a sandbox
c. Putting together wooden puzzles
d. Building with blocks
e. Playing with push-pull toys

Matching Items

Matching tests are used to show the association of or relationship between two elements such as words and definitions, events and persons, examples and principles, or causes and effects.

The matching test typically consists of two columns. Each column should be homogeneous in form and content. For example, items referring to the function of nutrients should not be mixed in the same column with those indicating the best sources of nutrients. Columns should be labeled according to content.

It is recommended that from five to ten items be used in a matching question. When possible, place the longer items in the left-hand column and the shorter responses in the right-hand column. This helps students identify the correct answer quickly. Responses in the right-hand column should be arranged in some logical order such as alphabetically, numerically, or chronologically. This also reduces time spent in locating a correct answer.

The chances of guessing may be reduced by providing a greater number of responses than items or by allowing for response alternatives to be used more than once. However, avoid using one response more than three times or the validity of the test might be affected. This should be specified in the directions in order to minimize confusion for students. Grading is quicker when responses are recorded as numbers rather than letters because numbers are easier to read.

Matching—identifying illustrations

Directions: Match the illustrations in Column A with the terms in Column B. Use terms in Column B only once.

COLUMN A

Illustrations

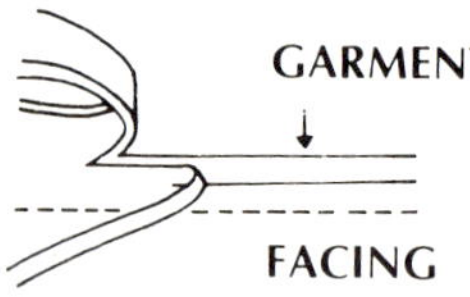

__2__ a.

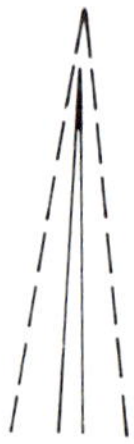

__4__ b.

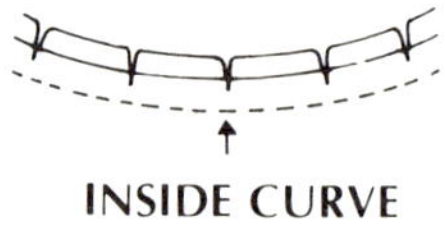

__1__ c.

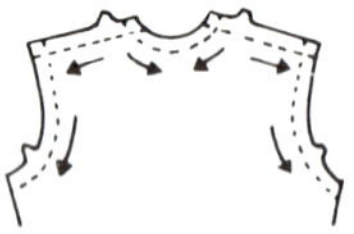

__5__ d.

__7__ e.

COLUMN B

Terms

1. Clipping and grading
2. Grading
3. Hemming
4. Slashing
5. Staystitching
6. Trimming
7. Understitching

Matching—definitions

Directions: For each function in Column A, locate the nutrient in Column B associated with it. Place the number corresponding to the best choice in the blank to the left of each item in Column A. Use a number only once. (10 points)

	COLUMN A *Primary Functions*	COLUMN B *Nutrients*
9	a. Keeps gums healthy; aids healing of skin injuries	1. Calcium 2. Iodine
8	b. Helps prevent night blindness	3. Iron
6	c. Builds and maintains body tissues	4. Niacin
7	d. Steadies nerves; aids digestion	5. Phosphorus
1	e. Builds strong bones and teeth	6. Protein
10	f. Regulates the deposit of minerals in bones and teeth; prevents rickets	7. Thiamine 8. Vitamin A
2	g. Prevents goiter	9. Vitamin C
3	h. Helps form hemoglobin in red blood cells	10. Vitamin D

Completion Items

Fill-in-the-blank, or completion, items are statements in which one or more words are omitted. One-word or single-expression answers such as *credit rating, installment loan,* and *bait and stitch* are preferred. They tend to be more objective than answers written in phrases or sentences. Only a significant word should be omitted from the sentence; the resulting blank should occur at or near the end of the statement. In that way, the major thought is presented before the blank appears. It is necessary to achieve a balance between providing too little information and too much, so that completion items are truly discriminating. All blanks should be of uniform length throughout the test so that students will not be encouraged to respond to an item because of the presumed length of the omitted word.

Scoring can be facilitated by using numbers or question marks in the blanks within the sentences and by placing response blanks to the left of the completion items to form an answer column.

Completion—incomplete sentences

Directions: Fill in the blank to the left of each sentence with the *best* word or words to complete the statement.

credit union 1. An institution that offers limited cash installment loans only to its members is a(n) (1).

banks 2. The majority of noninstallment cash loans is provided by (2).

percentage rate 3. The amount of interest you pay in a finance charge is determined by the annual (3).

Completion—analogy

Directions: Fill in the blank to the left of each sentence with the *best* word or words to complete the statement.

blue 1. Violet is to yellow as orange is to (?).

red 2. Green and orange are to purple as yellow and blue are to (?).

analogous 3. Pink and red are to a monochromatic color scheme as yellow, yellow-green, and green are to a(n) (?) color scheme.

Identification Items

The identification test item typically requires the student to label or locate parts of a diagram or to give specific information about a picture or an object. Pictures, diagrams, and actual objects are more vivid than verbal descriptions and provide interest and variation in testing procedures.

Sketches and diagrams should be drawn clearly and large enough to be seen easily. It is important that lines and numbers indicating various parts of a diagram are easy to understand. Illustrations used for testing should be different from those that were used in class. Directions about how students are to proceed should be clear and explicit.

Identification—passing around articles

Identification tests can also be designed so that actual food products, kitchen utensils, small equipment, sewing machine attachments, samples of clothing-construction techniques, or pictures are passed from one student to another in a planned-sequential order. Gauge when it is time to say "pass" by ascertaining when most of the students have completed the identification on which they are working. An essential in using this technique is to be certain that all students understand that they must *pass* at the designated time. Otherwise, some students will accumulate articles while others will not have any to work on. A variety of rotation systems for passing articles can be used. There should be the same number of items (or only a very few more) as there are students taking the test. To begin, each student should be given either one or two articles. Students should be reminded that items may not necessarily be received in numerical order and that they must write their responses in the correct places on their test papers. After the rotation, the items may be placed on a table so that one student at a time can reexamine them.

This technique lends itself to many variations. Numbered swatches of fabric might be passed for identification by their common names. Pictures representing various periods of furniture design could be mounted, numbered, and used in a similar manner. A question that applies to a large number of items might be asked, such as "What is wrong with each of the following?" Students would respond to samples such as these when the items were passed around: staystitching on a seam line; staystitching continuous around a neckline; a dart marked on the right side of fabric; notches cut inward; pins placed on the cutting line of a pattern; a pattern pinned off-grain; a pattern placed on selvage instead of a fold.

Essay Questions

Essay questions can be used to evaluate a student's ability to use higher mental processes. These processes include: interpreting information, applying rules and principles, analyzing causes and effects, evaluating and developing an original plan. In addition to controlling student guessing to a greater extent than some types of test items, essay questions may more closely approximate the use of information and skills in life situations.

Essay questions are relatively easy to construct, but they do require considerable time for the students to respond and for the teacher to grade. Essay questions are often criticized for having a limited sampling of subject matter, an inconsistency or subjectivity in scoring, and a premium placed on quantity rather than quality of response. These weaknesses can be minimized through the use of several techniques.

Guidelines for writing essay questions

1. State short-answer and essay questions so that they can be graded objectively. This necessitates stating them so that students who are prepared know what is expected in the answer. For example, if students are asked to "discuss the Basic Four food groups," they might respond in a variety of ways. But if they are asked to "analyze the dietary intake record below, according to the Basic Four food groups and the basic nutrients provided by each food group," students should know how to respond, and you can establish objective criteria to evaluate their answers. An answer key that you develop as you make out the test should include the major points that a student is expected to cover and the relative weight or point value of each.
2. Balance the difficulty level of questions so that sufficiently prepared students can complete their answers in the allotted time.
3. Require students to answer all items. When students have the option of answering three out of four questions, one student may not know anything about the problem he or she has omitted while another student may have been prepared to answer all the questions. Obviously, this test would not determine both students' comprehension of the subject matter fairly or to the same degree.
4. Keep in mind that a lengthy response does not necessarily represent comprehension of the subject matter or a high level of thinking. A brief answer may result from recalling material or thinking analytically and critically.
5. Grade the content of an essay question without regard to handwriting, spelling, or grammar. You might assign these a separate grade.
6. Read the first answer on all the papers and check it according to the established criteria for grading. Group the papers according to the adequacy of the response. Then reread and assign point values to the first question on all the students' papers. Repeat with the second question on all papers, and so forth.

Sample essay questions

It is easy to develop essay questions incorporating levels of thinking above the knowledge level. For example:

- Describe the differences between guidance and discipline. (Cognitive-Comprehension)
- Make a complete nutrition label for one of these food products:

  box of enriched cereal

  can of dietetic peaches

  food bar as meal substitute

You may use an RDA chart to help you.* (Cognitive-Application)
- Analyze the blueprint on display for factors relating to high and low building costs. (Cognitive-Analysis)
- Develop an instrument for rating television programs for children. (Cognitive-Synthesis)
- Evaluate this spending plan for the family situation described below. (Cognitive-Evaluation)

Home economics education students might be offered a choice of concepts for writing a lesson plan. The objective in this example would be to determine the students' ability to plan for teaching rather than to determine the students' knowledge of a given topic. Students could choose the subject matter they know best in demonstrating their ability to plan lessons.

TESTS FOR STUDENTS WITH LIMITED READING ABILITY

Students who read at a level far below their grade placement are penalized when emphasis is placed upon traditional pencil-and-paper methods of evaluation. However, when test questions are read to these students and their responses are based on visual stimuli, many of them are not at a disadvantage. Oral questions should be asked as concisely as possible and repeated more than once. Test materials can include photos, drawings, models, or actual items. Students may be asked for simple oral or written responses, or they may be required to give reasons for their answers. Written responses can best be handled with an answer sheet constructed so that students have only to check off a correct item or write in a number, letter, word, or short phrase.

Practical tests and lab work are appropriate for measuring skills in areas such as food preparation, clothing construction, and child care. The most important point to remember in using these types of tests is that definite criteria must be established so that the results can be scored in objective terms. Well-developed checklists and rating scales are appropriate for measuring student performance on a skill test or on work done in a laboratory experience.

Sample Tests for Poor Readers

The following are examples of test items that could be answered easily by poor readers who know the subject matter.

*You should not offer students a choice of essay questions, but you can provide choices within an essay item when the alternatives are unrelated to the major purpose of the question. In this example, the crucial element is to apply what is known about nutrition labels in general rather than what is known about the nutritional content of a specific food item.

Quantity food preparation

Number from 1 to ______ on your paper. Write the letter of the beater that best answers the questions.

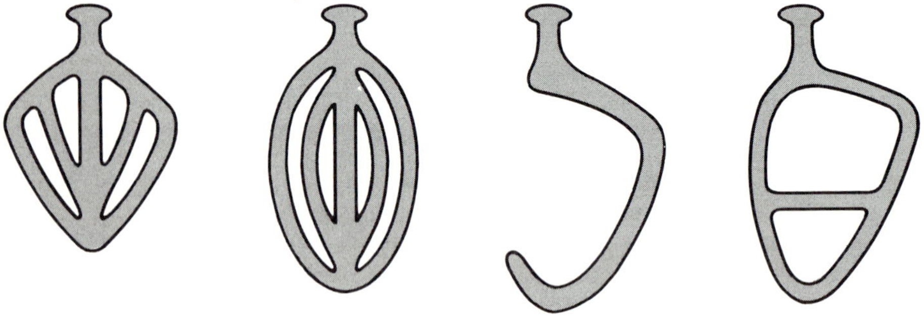

A B C D

1. Which beater would be used for beating egg whites?
2. Which beater would be used for mixing bread dough?
3. Which beater would be used for mashing potatoes?

Number from 1 to ______ on your paper. Write the letter corresponding to the muffin that best answers the question.

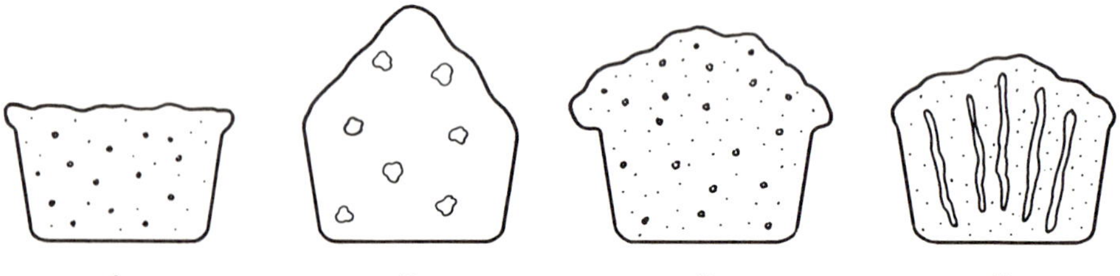

A B C D

1. Which muffin was mixed correctly?
2. Which muffin was mixed too much?
3. Which muffin was baked in an oven that was too hot?

Table setting

Simulated table settings can be sketched, drawn, or pictured on large pieces of construction paper, poster board, or transparencies, so that they can be viewed simultaneously by the entire class. The questions can be asked orally. Student responses are recorded on answer sheets.

1. Write the number showing the correct place for a water glass.

2. Write the number of the item that is in the wrong place.

Table manners

Directions: Circle the one in each pair that is correct.

1.

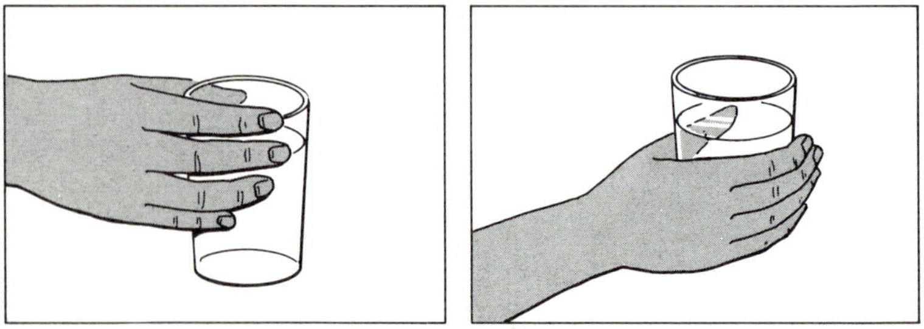

2.

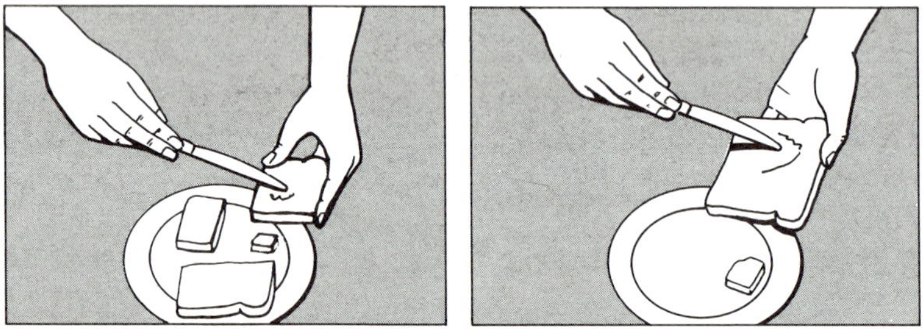

SCORECARDS, CHECKLISTS, AND RATING SCALES

Scorecards, checklists, and rating scales can be used by students to evaluate themselves or their peers and by teachers to evaluate students' work. Often there is value in having both the teacher and students use the same device to judge the same product or performance and then to compare their evaluations.

A wide variety of scorecards, checklists, and rating scales can be found in textbooks, periodicals, and commercial publications. It is also a relatively easy matter for teachers to develop their own scorecards and checklists. However, constructing a rating scale is much more difficult and time-consuming. A valuable learning experience consists in having teacher and students work together to develop instruments for evaluation other than rating scales.

Scorecards and Checklists

The terms *scorecard* and *checklist* can be used interchangeably. However, scorecards are more often used to rate the quality of a single item as one home canned product, a single toy, or a clothing-construction technique. Checklists tend to include a greater number of subconcepts for consideration than are included on a scorecard. Both refer to an evaluation instrument consisting of a list of qualities to be considered and checked off or questions to be answered with a simple yes-or-no response. Scorecards and checklists are adaptable for use in the cognitive, affective, and psychomotor domains in all areas of home economics. Their chief limitation is that they have no descriptions of quality or provisions for making interim ratings. The primary advantage of scorecards and checklists is that their use requires students to think about the factors listed for consideration.

Rating Scales

Rating scales are a more highly refined measuring instrument than scorecards or checklists because rating scales include descriptions of various levels of quality. This provides for rating on a continuum. The descriptions, against which work is judged, are usually given at three quality levels. Care must be taken that each level includes all the aspects described in every other level.

Rating scale—evaluating a clothing-construction project

If you were going to use rating scales to judge clothing-construction projects, you could develop an instrument for each of the techniques used: marking, stay-stitching, sewing darts, and so forth. When each technique is evaluated as it is finished, points can be recorded and later cumulated to determine a final grade at the completion of the project. Both you and the students know how well their work is progressing, and steps can be taken to improve the quality, if needed.

One of the techniques to be evaluated in most clothing-construction projects would be hemming. Three levels of quality might be described this way:

HEM

1	2 3	4 5	Points
Stitching			
Conspicuous and/or uneven stitching.	A few stitches show on right side and some uneven.	Inconspicuous, even stitching.	_____
Choice of stitch			
Unsuitable choice of stitch for fabric.	Not the best stitch for fabric.	Suitable choice of stitch for fabric.	_____
Depth of hem			
Should be considerably deeper or narrower. Uneven in depth.	Should be somewhat deeper or narrower. Some variance in depth.	Appropriate depth for garment. Same depth all around.	_____
Ease of fullness			
Fullness eased off-grain and/or tucked.	Fullness eased slightly off-grain and/or some tucks.	Fullness eased with grain and no tucks.	_____
Appearance when hanging			
Hangs unevenly.	Hangs fairly evenly.	Hangs evenly.	_____
		TOTAL	_____

A scale in which three descriptive levels are used permits rating on a five-point continuum. In the previous example, the description of quality for each aspect ranges from unfavorable (left) to favorable (right). If the hem being evaluated had some of the characteristics described as highly desirable in the right-hand column and some of the characteristics described in the middle column, the point value assigned would probably be 4. When only two levels are described, a three-point continuum is appropriate. Blanks should be provided to indicate the number of points assigned to each feature that is evaluated and for the total score.

Combination checklist-rating scale—evaluating a group report

A rating device can have characteristics of both a checklist and a rating scale. Subconcepts, questions, or statements are listed that the evaluator rates by assigning numerical scores based on a range of point values, or on a continuum.

Directions: Rate each statement below, as it relates to your group's oral report, by placing the number of the word or words that best describes it in the space provided. Briefly explain or support your rating in the space below each statement.

SCALE:

Excellent	Very Good	Adequate	Fair	Poor
5	4	3	2	1

Criteria:

__________ 1. Variety of resources were used to prepare report.
__________ 2. Material presented was accurate and up-to-date.
__________ 3. Statements could be verified through facts or statistics given or by sources of information cited.
__________ 4. Information was presented in a logical sequence.
__________ 5. Subject matter was covered adequately for the time allowed.
__________ 6. Provision was made for class members to become involved.
__________ 7. Everyone could hear presentation.
__________ 8. Visuals, if any, were made neatly and could be seen easily by the entire class.
__________ 9. A demonstration, if used, could be seen by everyone.
__________ 10. Group members contributed equally in preparing report.
__________ 11. Group members participated equally in oral presentation.
__________ 12. Class seemed interested in presentation.

__________ TOTAL

Evaluating a Laboratory Meal

The remainder of this chapter consists of a checklist and a rating scale for evaluating laboratory meals. They consider essentially the same qualities, although the emphasis is somewhat different in each. However, it should be noted that a rating scale encompasses greater depth of subject matter and necessitates the use of a higher level of thinking to make selections on the continuum. The evaluators are forced to think about their reasons for making certain ratings.

Checklist

Directions: Evaluate your group's laboratory experience by answering each of the following questions and checking the appropriate column.

Did we:	YES	NO
1. Plan a well-balanced meal?	______	______
2. Stay within our budget?	______	______
3. Use any foods that are out of season?	______	______
4. Forget to order any food when planning?	______	______
5. Have enough to eat?	______	______
6. Have food left over?	______	______
7. Plan for all the tasks we needed to do?	______	______
8. Need equipment we had not planned for?	______	______
9. Use more dishes and utensils than we needed?	______	______
10. Wash utensils as we cooked?	______	______
11. Keep the counter top neat and clean as we worked?	______	______
12. Waste any food in preparation or cooking?	______	______
13. Have all the food ready at the same time?	______	______
14. Serve the meal at the appointed time?	______	______
15. Waste time in preparing the meal?	______	______
16. Serve an appealing and appetizing meal?	______	______
17. Prepare food that tasted good?	______	______
18. Set the table attractively?	______	______
19. Forget anything that should have been on the table?	______	______
20. Use acceptable table manners?	______	______
21. Include everyone in the table conversation?	______	______
22. Leave the cupboards and our lab section in order?	______	______
23. Hand in our bills and written plans on time?	______	______
24. Work well together as a group?	______	______
25. Share fairly the amount of work to be done?	______	______

Rating scale

Directions: Rate your laboratory experience on each of the factors listed by placing 1, 2, 3, 4, or 5 in the blank to the right. If the quality corresponds to the description in the first column, assign 1 point; if described in the second column, give 3 points; if it falls between the two, record 2. Add these points to determine the total score.

A. MENU

	1	2	3	4	5	
1. Use of Time	Meal elaborate. Not prepared easily in time available.		Meal somewhat complicated. Prepared in time but workers rushed.		Meal simple. Easily prepared in time available.	______
2. Cost	Excessive. Foods out of season and expensive.		Moderate. Some unnecessary expense involved.		Reasonable. No extra or unreasonable expense involved.	______
3. Contrasts	Little or no contrast in color, texture, flavor, temperature.		Some contrast in color, texture, flavor, temperature.		Good contrast in color, texture, flavor, and temperature.	______
4. Suitability	Food preparation too difficult and involved unavailable equipment.		Food preparation suitable for student abilities or available equipment but not for both.		Food preparation suitable for both student abilities and available equipment.	______
5. Nutritive Value	Menu not very nutritious. Did not include enough foods from the Basic Four food groups.		Menu included some of the Basic Four. A few items could have been substituted for less nutritious foods.		All groups of the Basic Four included. Meal was very nutritious and well balanced.	______

B. WORK PLAN				
6. Time Schedule	Time needed to complete tasks not indicated, inaccurate, or unrealistic.	Time needed to complete tasks indicated fairly realistically.	Time needed to complete all tasks given accurately.	______
7. Sequence of Tasks	Sequence not given or illogical.	Logical sequence given for part of work such as preparation, service, or cleanup.	Logical sequence given for all tasks.	______
8. Division of Tasks	Division of tasks among group members unfair or not clearly indicated.	Division of tasks indicated but somewhat unequal or lacking in detail.	Fair and equitable division of tasks indicated for each member of the group.	______
C. MARKET ORDER				
9. Lists	Did not include all foods needed, quantities not stated or unsuitable.	Most of foods needed included, quantities questionable for number served.	All foods needed included in realistic quantities.	______
10. Cost	Not given, given for only part of the foods, or inaccurate.	Cost of foods fairly accurate, cost of meal not summarized.	Costs given, summarized, reasonable, within budget.	______
			TOTAL	______

EFFECTIVE QUESTIONING 7

Skillful questioning is one of the most important keys to a stimulating teaching-learning situation. You can ask questions that help students to explore ideas and to work toward satisfactory solutions to relevant problems or you can ask questions that require only knowledge of specific facts. Information is easily forgotten, but developing thinking processes through significant questions that probe for solutions can make an important contribution to the students' education.

Some educators are able to formulate good questions without a great deal of forethought. This usually results from having practiced effective questioning techniques. However, many teachers find it helpful to formulate questions before class either by writing them in their lesson plans or by jotting down key words to remind them of the questions they intend to ask. By doing this, you can more effectively guide students toward attaining the planned objectives of a lesson. Notes on significant, preplanned questions also serve to limit the number of questions that relate to minutiae rather than to important concepts and generalizations.

ASKING QUESTIONS AT APPROPRIATE LEVELS OF THINKING

Effective questions place the burden of thinking on the students. Questions can represent the limited levels of thinking such as recalling or recognizing specifics, or the higher and more challenging levels such as comprehending, applying, analyzing, synthesizing, and evaluating ideas. Generally, it is wise to ask questions at different levels of thinking. The proportion asked at each level depends on the objectives of the lesson. If one of the objectives is to recall cognitive information, then you will ask some questions that focus on remembering and recognizing facts. However, because one of the major purposes of education is to help students apply knowledge and develop critical thinking skills, it is hoped that you will plan both objectives and questions that incorporate the higher levels of learning. Questions that require only one-word answers or a simple "yes" or "no" response seldom involve higher levels of thinking, unless they are followed by comments such as "Please *defend* your point of view" or "Please *explain* that to us." Following up on students' replies by asking "Why?" usually fosters analysis-level thinking. If it is possible to answer a question with a "yes" or "no," many students will take advantage of that and not give any further explanation.

Some examples of questions involving higher levels of thinking are: What is an example that illustrates the meaning of the word *compassion*? (Comprehension); How can the principles of meat cookery be applied to the demonstration we just saw? (Application); What may be the real problems in this situation? (Analysis); If you were given this responsibility, what are all of the actions you would consider taking? (Synthesis); and What decision would be the most satisfactory one for you? Why? (Evaluation).

The sequence of questions asked should be logical and provide continuity in the lesson. The sequence also depends on the subject matter and the background of the students. One approach is to begin with easy questions and move toward more complicated ones. This is effective when the content is complex or when students have difficulty working with abstract ideas. Being able to answer easy questions at first gives students a feeling of confidence, security, and achievement. This may contribute to a positive attitude toward the learning situation and may also affect their desire and determination to be successful in answering more difficult questions.

An example of questions ranging from a basic to an advanced level would be: What are the fibers we have studied? (Knowledge); What important characteristics does each of them have? (Knowledge); If you were to purchase a carpet for a heavy-traffic area in your home, what fiber would be the best to use? (Application); and Why is this fiber better for this situation than others you might choose? (Analysis).

Another type of questioning sequence is directed toward a problem-solving or a discovery approach to learning. In this case, questioning serves to encourage students to examine the parts of a whole, to clarify a problem, and to ask their own relevant questions.

In order to work toward problem-solving or discovery learning, a teacher might ask: How would you describe the experimental approach we used? (Comprehension); What might have caused this? (Analysis); and How can you prove your theory? (Synthesis). Asking questions such as these encourages students to engage in thinking above the recall level by testing their powers of observation and calling on them to give proof of their theories.

Encouraging Student Participation

Some of the guidelines for effective questioning suggested in this chapter can be implemented immediately. You may need to practice other techniques before they become natural and spontaneous for you.

1. Students should have sufficient background to answer questions successfully. It can be very discouraging to say, "I don't know." A sense of timing is important so that the lesson is developed to the point of enabling students to answer questions intelligently. Matching the difficulty of the question level to individual student ability is helpful. Success in classroom discussions is more likely to be attained and students are more likely to feel a sense of achievement when simpler questions are given to marginal students and challenging questions are asked of more intellectually capable students.
2. Questions need to be clearly worded. A question like "What do you think about this?" often receives no response or a poor response because students cannot understand the indefinite wording. More structure is offered when the teacher asks, "Why do you agree or disagree with Kim's decision?" It is best to avoid asking "what about" or "how about" questions because they are too vague and too broad.
3. Variation in wording questions helps create interest. A few of the phrases you can use to begin questions are: "What might," "Why is there," "Which of," and "If you had." However, avoid introductory words such as "Can anyone give *me*" or "Who can tell *me*," because these phrases tend to discourage participation. Use *us* instead of *me*. "Please share with *us*" elicits a more favorable reaction than "Please tell *me*." The latter sounds as if the student should do something just to please the teacher. Or, simply ask the question without the preface. For example, when you begin a question with "Would you like to," you are encouraging nonparticipation by setting the student up to think "No, I wouldn't like to . . ."
4. Directing questions to the entire class, pausing, and then calling on a student by name will help keep class members alert to the discussion and will encourage them to formulate answers. When a student's name is designated before the question is asked, others realize they probably will not be called on to respond. However, it may be desirable to reverse this order when a particular student's attention has been diverted and the teacher wants to bring the student back into the discussion quickly without calling public attention to his or her lack of concentration.
5. Do not call on students by going up and down rows or around a circle in a set pattern. When students know that they will not be asked questions until several others have been called upon, they are less likely to pay attention. However, there is no point in calling on students when their nonverbal cues indicate an inability to answer satisfactorily.

Teacher Responses

If you are animated and interested, you are more likely to obtain student participation than if you do not show these characteristics. In addition to being enthusiastic, there are specific response techniques you can use and behaviors you can develop that encourage meaningful student involvement.

1. Vary reinforcement given for correct answers to encourage student participation. If you overuse expressions such as "OK," they become monotonous and distracting. Besides, replying with "OK" is like saying, "I heard you." It is a neutral response rather than positive reinforcement and does little to encourage students to participate further or contribute again. Although words like "Right" and "Good" convey positive reactions, if overused these words lose their reinforcement value and sound like "canned", or mechanical, responses. See page 55 for a discussion of reinforcing behavior. Students often become so conscious of teachers' repeated use of certain words or phrases that they listen for them and actually begin to count the number of times they are said. When this happens, students do not hear *what* is being said but rather only *how* it is being communicated. (Other annoying habits, such as pacing back and forth or fingering glasses, hair, or accessories, are also distracting to students.)

   Reinforcement can be given to students by saying: "That's a good answer." "Nice contribution, Pat." "I hadn't thought about it that way." Occasionally paraphrasing students' answers adds variety. Extending students' answers by adding an additional thought or providing nonverbal acceptance such as a nod of the head also provides positive reinforcement. Skillful teachers can often alter students' answers slightly, so they are more meaningful and acceptable but still give students the feeling that they have made a valuable contribution.
2. Try to avoid telling students, "No, that's wrong," because this kind of remark stifles participation. Students are reluctant to answer questions if they think they might be rebuked. You can indicate that an answer is incorrect, without damaging a student's self-concept, by saying something such as "The question may not have been clear," or "Part of your answer is right, but . . ." or "That's an interesting thought; however, you may remember . . ." It is also discouraging to be told by a teacher: "I have something else in mind," "I'm thinking of another point," or "There's another answer that is right, too." Replies like these make students feel as if they are playing a guessing game and have to read the teacher's mind. The impression is given that there is only one preconceived and precisely correct answer. In actuality, there may be many responses that are right or partially right. Students often think of excellent points that their teachers had never considered.
3. When you follow students' answers with additional probing questions, participation is usually increased. You might ask students to clarify answers, with questions such as "What is an example to illustrate that?" or "What might have caused that to happen?" When you follow up on students' responses this way,

students are encouraged to expand their remarks and to justify their answers. This provides additional clarification for the class, and you have increased your opportunity to evaluate students' contributions.

4. When a student is unable to respond to a question, you might direct another question to the same student. You can reword the original question or provide a clue to assist the student in answering. For example, your initial question might have been "Why did Tony behave that way?" If no student response is received, you can reword the question: "Suppose you were Tony. What might have prompted you to act that way?" Or, "In what ways is this situation similar to a situation we discussed yesterday?" By assisting or guiding students toward correct responses, you can help them feel successful. In this way, students also learn that they are expected to participate in class discussions.
5. Breadth of subject matter is developed when you bring additional students into the discussion by asking them to respond to the same question just answered by another. In this way, a variety of viewpoints can be presented so that all sides of a topic are explored. You might ask, "What can be added to John's answer, Sandra?" or "What is another side of the issue, Mary?"

Teachers who answer their own questions or interrupt students' answers do not allow students to engage in independent thinking. Often this is done to advance the discussion, but it can lead to a monopolization of class time by the teacher. Students become conditioned not to listen, and future communication may be jeopardized.

The type of questions you ask and the way you ask them reflects your competence as an instructor. Skillful questioning techniques provide the basis for using all methods of teaching effectively. Showing a film, reading a skit, or seeing a demonstration may be nothing more than entertainment unless it is followed by thought-provoking questions that foster higher levels of thinking.

LEADING DISCUSSIONS 8

A stimulating discussion does not take place just because you announce that the class is going to have one. Plans for a really worthwhile discussion have to be thought through in advance. A discussion is enhanced if the members have a common goal that they select by mutual agreement or through compromise. It is important that every discussion participant respects the rights of all the others. In addition, the overall atmosphere and physical arrangements must be conducive to a comfortable exchange of opinions, ideas, and experiences.

Numerous benefits result from well-conducted classroom discussions. Students learn to listen to other viewpoints and thus broaden their perspectives. They gain skill in tackling an issue rather than in attacking the person discussing the issue. Exposure to a stimulating and "safe" climate for discussion helps participants develop greater sensitivity in communicating with others. There are few substitutes for the satisfaction of a frank, thoughtful, and relevant exchange of ideas.

SELECTING A DISCUSSION TOPIC

Selecting the topic for a classroom discussion requires great care to ensure that it is relevant to the students' lifestyles and is understood by everyone in the group. You may want to encourage students to present problems they hope to solve and subjects they want to discuss. Worthwhile topics offer several facets to explore and also provide opportunities for a variety of viewpoints and perspectives. Discussion topics should be related to a group's real interests, concerns, needs, and experiences.

INITIATING A DISCUSSION

You can initiate the main theme of a discussion in a variety of ways. You can provide the needed stimulus through clearly worded and provocative questions that relate to previous experiences of group members, an interesting movie, a stimulating story or article, or an exciting presentation of pertinent data. The problem should be clearly stated, and every member should have sufficient information and background to be able to make a positive contribution. If students lack sufficient knowledge or experience relating to the topic, the discussion may be meaningless or even damaging and prejudicial. A stimulating discussion is also based on a firm foundation of student interest and a classroom climate that invites participation. A comfortable, informal atmosphere in which spontaneous humor might surface at any moment is the type of environment that nurtures honest expressions of feeling and opinion.

LEADING A DISCUSSION

As a discussion leader, you need to serve as a model of behavior for the students as you listen, encourage student involvement, display interest in the opinions of each individual, maintain good eye contact with everyone in the group, and keep the discussion going through a variety of means. You should avoid monopolizing the conversation, but sometimes you will have to provide direction and guidance. You must be prepared, when necessary, to summarize the main points, make supportive and encouraging comments, or ask pertinent questions. Such sensitivity can prevent the discussion from bogging down or being monopolized by one or two students.

In your role as a discussion leader, more than in any other role you assume as a teacher, you must be able to think on your feet. At times you may have to rephrase the ideas of the group in clearer and simpler language. However, you should be careful not to impose your own ideas and values on the class and may have to restrain a desire to express your own feelings and opinions. It is sometimes difficult to let others do the talking, especially when you disagree with what they are saying. Above all, as a discussion leader you must keep emotions under control.

Responsibilities in Leading a Discussion

The leader's main responsibilities are keeping the discussion going and involving everyone, if possible. You must watch facial expressions for signs of interest, desire to contribute, and waning attention. You need to be sensitive to nonverbal cues such as swinging feet, stares directed at the window or clock, and doodling—evidence of lack of interest. Keep distractions to a minimum to encourage students to pay attention and to participate.

You may want to make periodic summaries, and usually you will be responsible for concluding the discussion. Doing this can take the form of asking the participants to identify the main points, to explain how their ideas or opinions may have changed, or to predict how the discussion could affect students' future behavior.

SEATING ARRANGEMENTS

Experience demonstrates that the people sitting nearest the teacher or discussion leader are the most active participants. People outside this limited area may be hesitant to contribute unless they are tactfully brought into the discussion.

Various seating arrangements can either promote or inhibit communication among group members. It is desirable to have students facing each other. In this way both verbal and nonverbal cues can be detected and acted upon to assist in the discussion process. In most situations, it is better to sit with the students. It is usually better not to stand over the group or behind a podium or desk. Psychologically, this tends to place you in an unapproachable and authoritarian position and diminishes the participation and leadership that can emerge from the group members.

PARTICIPANTS IN CLASS DISCUSSIONS

It often takes time for groups to develop the kind of rapport necessary for truly democratic and effective discussions. It is important that leaders do not push members too much, but rather give them time to become adjusted to one another and to the classroom environment. Discussion leaders should expect and encourage variety in the group response. Individuality, within limits, should be supported.

Some quiet people prefer to let others do the talking and still may be participating silently. Yet, they may find it difficult to express themselves and consequently become self-conscious in a group of their peers. These individuals may be encouraged to contribute if they are involved in a friendly conversation on a one-to-one basis before or outside class. Questions should be asked of them that require the expression of an idea or opinion rather than a simple "yes," "no," or other one-word answer.

People who monopolize a discussion talk too much and too long and often depart from the subject. They may talk excessively because they are nervous and insecure. Their comments often pertain to personal concerns and interests. In time, others in the group become inattentive or bored and may direct some of their resentment toward the leader.

Allow overparticipators a reasonable amount of time to talk and then ask for others' ideas. A comment such as "Thank you—now let's hear from someone else" has to be made with great tact. In extreme cases it may be necessary to direct questions deliberately to those who are not participating, by calling on them by name, or to allow another student to interrupt the nonstop talker.

You can often satisfy the need for attention of students who tend to dominate discussions if you use methods that contribute to the progress of the class. One is to ask students to move chairs into a semicircle prior to the discussion. You can also ask them to operate equipment that adds a dimension to the discussion, show visual media and other teaching materials, or write points on the board as they are made.

The secure teacher enjoys a good laugh as much as the students. However, when joking has reached the point of interfering with the purposes of a discussion, the teacher who has the respect of students should have no trouble in redirecting their attention. It may be effective to say something like, "That was good for a laugh. Now let's get serious again because this topic is important to all of us."

Any form of humor that is clearly intended to embarrass a group member should be stopped immediately. This usually can best be done by not making an issue of the incident, for that will probably aggravate the situation. Often a frown or some other nonverbal communication indicating disapproval is sufficient to get your message to the offender.

SMALL-GROUP DISCUSSIONS

Small-group discussions in the classroom are important in promoting communication. Students who are reluctant to speak out when in larger groups often participate when in smaller groups. The total group's viewpoints and experiences are expanded and enriched thereby. At the same time, a larger percentage of the students actually contribute and discover that they, as individuals, can be part of a democratic process of decision making based on compromise and mutual agreement.

Cautions in Forming Small Groups

Teachers are responsible for knowing the class as a whole and as a body comprising distinct individual personalities. This background knowledge is important in helping teachers decide when to use discussion methods appropriate to small groups and how to form such groups. Teachers may designate group memberships or allow students to form their own groups. The second course has many disadvantages. Students may be inclined to form their small groups on a basis of friendship. As a result, the intellectual stars, the "I don't cares," the class clowns, and those with various common interests tend to cluster together. The viewpoints expressed and the work produced by such groups may be limited considerably. You can avoid this by using other methods of group selection.

Quick ways to form groups

One of the simplest ways to form small groups is to ask students to number off consecutively. The highest number called should be the same as the total number of members desired in a group. Doing this will achieve a more random assignment of group members. Organizing students according to their birth months or zodiac signs is another possibility. Listing students alphabetically by first names and using appropriate cutoff points for group formation will also avoid using the traditional last-name method of grouping. If a variety of methods is used over a period of time, students will benefit from having worked with most of their classmates.

Group building

To use the group-building approach, tell students to number off by two's ("one, two, one, two," and so forth) until everyone has a number. The students who are "ones" go to one side of the room and those who are "twos" go to the other side. Each "one" is instructed to invite a "two" to join him or her, thus forming pairs. The invited partner should be someone the student does not know or does not know well. When all students have been paired, each pair invites another to join them. If possible, the invitation should go to students not closely known by those extending it. If groups larger than four are desired, this process can be repeated.

This exercise serves as a means of forming groups with members who have never, or perhaps infrequently, worked together. Members gain a feeling of togetherness as a result of mutual decision making in extending and accepting or declining invitations.

Groups formed in this fashion can work effectively on problems that profit from having participants with differing backgrounds and viewpoints. Some examples of these group activities are solving management problems, choosing and preparing for careers, and adjusting to changing male and female roles. This method of group building is especially useful for getting members of newly formed classes better acquainted.

Related objects

From a broad subject such as food and nutrition or clothing and textiles, select a group of objects that can be classified in subgroups related to common function. The items chosen depend on the purpose for which a particular small group was formed. A variety of kitchen utensils can serve as the basis for grouping students to discuss problems related to food preparation, kitchen equipment, or work simplification and time management. The objects chosen to serve as a basis for designating group membership are limited only by one's imagination and resources.

The number of objects used should equal the number of people in the class, and the objects should be chosen so that some serve the same function. The number of student subgroups for the class activity should be the same as the number of subgroups that can be formed by using the objects. After you have displayed all the objects on a table or counter top, tell the students to select one. Then instruct the participants to compare their items and to divide themselves into groups of three or four persons having objects with a common purpose. When the basis for classification is obvious to the students, groups tend to form quickly.

This exercise produces interaction among class members and stimulates thought on an analytical level. At this point, the students should be prepared to work at a task or problem or on assigned questions.

Puzzle cutups

Different media, such as related pictures cut from magazines, may also be used to form groups. Choose pictures related to the specific area under investigation.

The pictures may be used without a backing material or they can be attached to something lightweight—a file folder, cardboard, or construction paper. Cut each picture into jigsaw-shaped puzzle pieces. The number of pieces will depend on the desired size of the small groups. One picture is needed for each group.

To organize the class into groups, scramble the puzzle pieces and place them on any flat surface. Then, instruct students to select one piece and locate the classmates who have other pieces that will complete that picture. Through such matching, groups soon form. The teacher can assign specific activities or discussion questions to each group or instruct the groups to turn their pictures over and read the questions on the reverse side.

Activities in child development, as it relates to housing and home furnishings, might use illustrations of different types of housing (individually owned homes, duplexes, mobile homes, apartments), furniture styles, and interior color schemes. Pictures representing various kinds of stores, types of store displays, or various forms of advertisements could provide a stimulating beginning for small-group discussions of consumer economics.

Facilitating Small-Group Discussions

After groups have been formed, teachers can use a variety of methods to promote discussion and interaction. Inner and outer circles, brainstorming, and buzz sessions are some that help to involve students in small groups.

Inner and outer circles

In this exercise, several small groups of ten to twelve students can be formed (and operate simultaneously) or one group of ten to twelve can participate while the rest act as observers. In either case, directions for one or more groups are given by the teacher from the floor. The purposes of this exercise are to have students listen to others, to give them an opportunity to express their thoughts in a concise manner, and to have them summarize or react to what is said by others.

This is a timed exercise using incomplete sentences or questions relating to specific subjects. To begin the exercise, half of the group is asked to take chairs and form a close circle. The remaining students form a circle around the outside in order to watch and listen carefully to the discussion taking place in the inner circle.

Before the exercise begins, the students in the outside circle are told not to participate in the discussion while they are in that position. The students in the inner circle are instructed to monitor the discussion and to provide as much opportunity as possible for each member to participate.

The inner circle is given the first statement or question and instructed to discuss it for 4 minutes. At the end of that period, the students in the inner and outer circles exchange positions. The students in the new inner circle are asked to react to what they heard the first group say. Two minutes is allowed for this. Then this same inner circle responds to the original statement or a new one for 4 minutes. Positions are again reversed and students now in the inner circle are told to react, in a 2-minute period, to any previous statements with which they agreed or disagreed. This process continues until the students respond to all the statements.

After the exercise is over, you may want to have students express their feelings as you ask specific questions. For example, did the students feel under great pressure to contribute to the discussion? What kind of interaction was there among group members? What were their feelings about silent periods? How did they feel when they heard themselves quoted?

Brainstorming

The personalities of the participants and the ultimate question to be resolved determine whether it is feasible to conduct this activity in large or small groups. Either can be effective if the participants realize that their ideas will not be criticized. In fact, the first step in brainstorming is to gather a quantity of ideas without considering their quality.

An example may be to list suggestions for the theme of an annual employer appreciation banquet or an open house for parents of young children in the cooperative program. As ideas are suggested, the teacher or a student writes them so that they can be seen by everyone. After all ideas are expressed, the participants vote to determine the two or three they like best. Then these are discussed in detail; the advantages and disadvantages of each idea are explored. After this, another vote establishes the *one* idea students think is best. Such a procedure increases the likelihood that the group will be reasonably satisfied with the decision.

If brainstorming is done in small groups, each group may present the two or three ideas it considers its best. After the best of each small group's ideas are listed, an elimination process may be carried out by a vote of all students.

Brainstorming is not designed for use in situations that point obviously to one best solution. Nor is the outcome predetermined by the teacher or student leader. In other words, the group works together democratically to arrive at *a* solution, not at *the* solution.

Buzz sessions

The term *buzz session* is commonly applied by teachers to the activity of students working in small discussion groups. Three, four, or five students is the most desirable number. If there are fewer, there may not be enough interaction; if there are more, some students may be reluctant to express their ideas and opinions. And the purpose of this form of activity is to maximize student participation.

It is the teacher's responsibility to go from group to group to offer help and to give encouragement. If the teacher is aware of students' progress, she or he will sense the right time to give a warning such as "Take only another minute or two to wind up your discussion." Generally, it is advisable to call time while the students are still enthusiastic about their topics, before their attention wanders.

Buzz groups may be used to formulate replies to letters found in advice columns of newspapers; to offer solutions to situations presented in case studies; to plan menus, time schedules, and market orders; and to develop role plays and skits. Almost anything that can be done in a class-size group can be done equally well or perhaps better in a buzz group. However, there must be enough depth of subject matter in the chosen topics to warrant the time involved. If the solutions to be suggested or decisions to be reached are not sufficiently thought-provoking, the time spent in buzz sessions may be wasted.

Student discussion leaders

When students serve as small-group discussion leaders on a rotating basis, they have an opportunity to share the teacher's responsibility and develop leadership potential.

At the beginning of the school year, or before small discussion groups are organized, it is desirable to have the class talk about the role of the discussion leader and the qualities of a good discussion. Guidelines for both can be established, and a duplicated sheet summarizing important points to remember can be given to students. The sheet serves as a reference for all students. It also gives discussion leaders a basis for evaluating how well they are fulfilling their roles.

The student discussion leader can assist the group by:

1. Talking when it is necessary to initiate and guide the discussion, but without monopolizing it.
2. Maintaining an atmosphere that is positive, stimulating, and enjoyable.
3. Being responsive to the contributions of all members.
4. Listening to what is said and maintaining good eye contact with participants.
5. Watching the faces and body positions of group members for additional communication cues and using the cues to help each member participate as fully as possible.
6. Keeping the goal of the activity continually in mind so that the discussion stays on target; doing this skillfully may require that the leader ask questions and summarize when appropriate.

STRUCTURED DISCUSSION TECHNIQUES

The purpose of a panel discussion, debate, symposium, or forum is to bring together different ideas and opinions on various aspects of one subject. The audience hears thoughts and opinions that should help each member analyze a timely problem. Although summarizing the material presented is an important part of each of these techniques, the listener is expected to draw personal conclusions from the information presented by forming conclusions, to some degree, independently of the group.

In all these activities, the only people formally involved are the teacher or designated leader and part of the class, but all may participate in follow-up discussions and activities. The success of each depends upon careful planning, preparation, and organization.

Panel Discussion

The panel serves to air views relating to a selected topic rather than to arrive at any one decision. The moderator introduces the subject and calls on one of the members to lead off. Each panel member, or a small group of students or guests, gives a brief (3 to 5 minutes), prepared but informal talk that is usually presented in the form of a question. After each speaker has presented a viewpoint, he or she is free to react to and ask questions of the others.

Following this informal exchange, the moderator usually opens the program to audience participation. The moderator must guide the direction of the discussion, keep it on the topic or on closely related ones, and then summarize the main ideas and the principal sides of the issues.

If a panel discussion is unsuccessful, it is usually because the members have not studied the issue thoroughly or because the topic is too narrow in scope to allow for discussion in depth. Some questions that are appropriate for panel discussions follow:

- What are desirable qualities in an employee?
- Are teenagers today more mature than those of previous generations?
- What should a father's role be in today's world?
- What are some community services that are available to help families?

Debate

In a debate, the participants are trying to persuade others. Therefore, the topic must be one about which there are fixed positions or definite "for" and "against" viewpoints to be argued. These issues are debated by teams of students who take opposing sides.

A debate begins when one member of the pro team gives reasons for favoring the issue; then a member of the con team gives a case for being against it. This procedure continues until each team member has had an opportunity to present evidence and supporting facts. Each should select the strongest possible arguments, make reference to statistics, and quote experts where relevant. This will give authority to the debaters' remarks.

After the prepared speeches, team members have a chance to respond to the statements of their opponents. During this exchange, a new issue cannot be brought up but new supportive material may be used. Debaters need to investigate the topic thoroughly beforehand so that they can answer questions and defend remarks they and their teammates make. The chair or moderator summarizes briefly, mentioning only the highlights. A class discussion may follow the debate.

A debate topic is given in the form of a positive or negative statement.

Controversial issues such as the following lend themselves to debate techniques:

- Women have been (or have not been) liberated.
- Parenthood should be (or should not be) licensed.
- Abortion should be (or should not be) available on demand.
- One year of full-time employment should be (or should not be) required of all freshmen before admission to college.

Symposium

In a symposium there is one problem under investigation, and each participant is qualified to present one aspect of it. Usually the participant's expertise has been gained through personal experience. Speakers are given specified lengths of time for their presentations, and after all of these the participants exchange ideas or ask questions of one another. Following this exploration of viewpoints by the speakers, the class may also enter into the discussion. The symposium, when used correctly, ensures that several aspects of the topic will be presented and, consequently, that the audience gains an overall view of the subject.

The teacher, student leader, or chairperson has the responsibility of introducing the participants and their subjects within the general topic, of summarizing after all the prepared talks have been given, and of leading the ensuing discussion among the speakers. Some topics suitable for symposiums follow:

CAREERS IN HOME ECONOMICS: Speakers who are employed in semiprofessional and professional areas of home economics could be asked to tell about needed skills and abilities, desirable personality traits, educational requirements, duties and responsibilities, salaries, and chances for advancement in their respective fields.

MOTHERS MANAGE THEIR RESOURCES DIFFERENTLY: A mother who is not employed outside the home, one who works part time, and one who has full-time employment could share ideas about how they use their money, time, and energy differently to meet their individual and family needs.

MEETING THE NEEDS OF EXCEPTIONAL CHILDREN: It may be possible to ask parents and siblings of mentally retarded, physically handicapped, or intellectually gifted children to discuss how they meet the special needs of these family members.

ONE-PARENT FAMILIES: Both male and female representatives from Parents Without Partners may be asked to tell about the problems they have encountered and the solutions they have found most satisfactory in rearing children alone. Students who live with only one parent may also be willing to give their viewpoints on this topic.

Forum

In a forum, two, or occasionally three, speakers offer different points of view about a somewhat controversial issue. A forum is more formal than a panel discussion because the participants do not interact with each other after the prepared speeches, but rather answer questions posed by the class or audience. Listeners have an opportunity to express their own ideas and to ask the forum participants to react to them. The moderator must be adept in changing the direction of the dialogue if it becomes dull, if one or two individuals monopolize it, or if the discourse becomes irrelevant. The moderator summarizes briefly and clearly by reiterating the major contributions.

A forum may be used effectively to introduce a new topic because the speakers are well informed about the topic. The audience is encouraged and expected to ask questions. This does not necessitate their having a very extensive knowledge of the subject matter. Some possible topics for a forum are:

- Men's roles have changed more in the last decade than women's roles.
- People should avoid eating foods to which preservatives have been added.
- Financial problems are the leading causes of marital failure today.
- Cohabitation has more disadvantages than advantages.

EVALUATING CLASS DISCUSSIONS

Teachers can make improvements in leading meaningful class discussions by periodically thinking about and answering the following questions:

1. Was the discussion carefully planned so progress could be made toward meeting stated objectives?
   a. Was the discussion focused on worthwhile objectives that were clear to the participants and accepted by them as important?
   b. Did the students help determine the objectives and/or discussion topic?
   c. Was the approach to the topic stimulating and challenging?
   d. Did the discussion move fast enough to be interesting but slow enough to provide for sound, analytical thinking?
   e. Were the physical arrangements of the room managed to promote student participation?
2. Was the discussion appropriate for the students involved?
   a. Did the discussion present a true-life problem or a situation that was relevant and meaningful to the group?
   b. Was the discussion related to concepts or topics that had been covered previously?
   c. Did the class members have the background information and experience necessary to make valuable and purposeful contributions?

d. Was the vocabulary and language used appropriate for the group?
e. Was there adequate discussion on essential ideas to arrive at some broad generalizations?

3. Were students helped to arrive at their own conclusions and to make their own decisions?
   a. Were students led to explore all sides of the issue?
   b. Were they encouraged to support their conclusions with evidence?
   c. Were they guided to explore the bases for their beliefs and values?
   d. Were they led to consider the possible consequences of their decisions?
4. Were interpersonal relationships supportive and conducive to student participation?
   a. Was there evidence of friendliness, acceptance, sincerity, and mutual cooperation?
   b. Did students seem to feel free to express their ideas and to defend their beliefs?
   c. Were ideas that students initiated treated seriously?
   d. Was it possible, when students digressed from the purposes of the discussion, to refocus their attention without hurting their feelings?
   e. Did at least three-fourths of the group participate?
5. Were the students given an opportunity to evaluate their growth and gain a sense of progress?
   a. Were students led to formulate generalizations that related to previously established objectives?
   b. Was the discussion summarized clearly and concisely?

It is advantageous to you as a teacher to gain feedback from your students to help you evaluate and improve your teaching competence. You can occasionally ask students to answer the preceding questions for the purpose of evaluating a class discussion. The questions can be reworded so the word *you* is substituted for the word *student*. Be sure to let students know that you appreciate their comments and input by thanking them for their participation in the evaluation process, by using their ideas when feasible, or by explaining why you cannot use a particular suggestion that has been offered.

CASE STUDIES 9

Case studies provide a vehicle for involving students in solving problems that may be similar to those they face in their lives. If problem situations seem realistic to students, they are likely to be willing to discuss them in class. Providing a common basis for discussion is preferable to talking in class about students' personal problems or publicly discussing personal and family situations. Through case studies, students may obtain additional insight into the various facets of their lives and acquire experience in considering their personal problems in objective ways.

Students are encouraged to use the higher levels of thinking by analyzing the situations provided and by planning creative solutions to the problems presented.

Case studies can be used in many ways. They can be read aloud by the teacher or students, or presented by means of an audiotape or videotape and analyzed in a class discussion. Case studies can be duplicated for each student, who is then asked to write answers to the questions provided. Different students' responses would be kept anonymous and could be presented to the entire class for analysis and comparison. Case studies can be analyzed in small groups. Each group might have the same case or the groups might have different studies to analyze. In either situation, the small groups' conclusions and recommendations can be shared with the entire class to provide the basis for further discussion.

The format of case studies may be varied by using narratives, letters, log or diary entries, and dialogue excerpts. The studies will vary in length depending on the type of problem presented, the amount of information to be provided, and the attention span of the students.

Newspaper advice-column letters and magazine articles often provide appropriate case study material. When the teacher or students write the case studies, it is motivating to use the names of local places such as streets, schools, and shopping centers to make the situations seem more relevant and meaningful. Published case studies can also be localized by making substitutions for the proper nouns used in the original story.

Case studies may be open-ended or they may include the outcome or decision that was made. The follow-up activities or questions asked about the situations are actually as important as the case studies themselves. Regardless of whether the ending is provided, case studies can be examined for alternative solutions, along with predictions of possible outcomes. When the material is used in this way, students are given experience in critical thinking and decision-making.

The questions used to help students analyze case studies are extremely important. An effective technique for maximizing the value of this method of teaching is to give students points to look for in the case studies, or to provide them with follow-up discussion questions before reading about the situations. There are four steps in the decision-making process that students can use in analyzing the case studies provided in this chapter:

1. Identifying the problem—What exactly is the problem? What additional information is needed?
2. Identifying alternative solutions to the problem—What are all the possible solutions?
3. Examining and weighing the consequences of the possible solutions—What might happen if this is done? What might happen if another alternative is chosen?
4. Deciding on a solution—Of all the alternatives, which provides the best solution? Why? In view of all the consequences, why is this the best thing to do?

Following are four case studies appropriate for students at various maturity levels and from varying socioeconomic backgrounds. At the end of each case study there are suggested discussion questions that follow the problem-solving format.

Transportation Problems

The following case study presents problems that many teenagers face because it involves financing education after high school, having a job, and obtaining transportation.

James wants to be in a cooperative education program during his senior year in high school next year because he needs to work at least 40 hours a week. Working only after regular school hours, he would have a maximum of 25 hours of employment per week—a schedule that would not enable him to earn enough money or save enough to attend the local community college the year after his graduation from high school.

If James enrolls in the cooperative program, he will need transportation to his job located several miles from school. He would have to go to work right after his fourth-period class, but there is no school bus or public transportation available at that hour.

James has thought about buying a motorcycle, a used car, or a small and economical new car. James will work all summer near his home before he needs a vehicle for transportation in the fall when school starts. He feels he could save enough money to pay cash for a low-horsepower motorcycle or an older-model used car by the time he would need it. However, the idea of riding a motorcycle to school and work on cold winter days is very unappealing to James. He also realizes that he could have mechanical trouble with a high-mileage used car and that both his own mechanical skills and his time to do major repairs are limited.

Follow-up questions

1. Identifying the problem:
   a. What seems to be James's major problem and concern?
   b. What problems have emerged that are related to his primary concern?
   c. What additional information do you need in order to make decisions about the problems described here?
2. Identifying alternative solutions:
   a. What are several possible solutions to each of the identified problems?
   b. What are several possible solutions that James has overlooked?
3. Examining and weighing the consequences of the solutions:
   a. If James postpones going to college, what might happen?
   b. If James buys a new car, using an installment loan, what might happen?
   c. What might happen if, in turn, each of the other possible alternative solutions is chosen?
4. Deciding on a solution:
   a. What do you think James should do first? Next?
   b. Why do you think these are the best solutions to James's problems?

A Decision

The next case study concerns problems of friendship, truthfulness, and behavior of senior high school students. It is presented in the form of a dialogue between two friends.

Barbie was walking home from school with Judy, one of her best friends. Judy said, "Where's Peg? I didn't see her in school today."

"I—uh—don't know. She's hardly ever absent. I tried calling her yesterday, but no one was home. I guess the family went to church and to Peg's grandmother's house for the day. I was really frantic to talk to her. I've got to get a story straight. I'm really sorry I ever got involved. You're lucky your family went out of town this weekend or she probably would have had you spending the night at my house, and you'd have been involved too. I know we're all good friends, but sometimes Peg does the darndest things!"

"What did I manage to miss getting involved in? Why on earth are you being so mysterious?" Judy stopped for a minute and gave Barbie a quizzical look.

"Well, it all started last Thursday when Peg said she was spending Saturday night at my house—but not actually staying there. I was supposed to be her excuse. Well, I couldn't back out because she had already told her mother she was staying with me. She said that she didn't know what else to do and knew I wouldn't mind. Any other time she has spent the night, no one ever called."

"You're going to tell me her mother called you," Judy said. "I feel it in my bones."

"Right, she sure did. I had to think fast, so I told her that Peg went bowling with Jimmy and that she'd be in a little later. I told her I'd be glad to take a message, but she said it was OK. It was something about the next day and it could wait. I'm glad no one in my family heard me on the phone."

"Where was she? She didn't go to that all-night party, did she?" Barbie nodded. "Oh, for heaven's sake, we told her to quit thinking about that. I've heard some of the stories about those kids' escapades. I've thought about it and I've thought about going too. It sounded like fun at the time. You know that Mary got pregnant last year after one of those parties. She dropped out of school.

"If it had been me, Barbie, I would have told Peg on Thursday, when she first mentioned it, that I wouldn't be a part of it."

"Well, maybe you're right, but what will I do if her mother finds out that she never came to my house at all Saturday night?"

Follow-up questions

1. Identifying the problem:
   a. What conflicts are Barbie and Peg facing?
   b. Are there any other issues involved? If so, what are they?
   c. What additional information might help to clarify the problem?
2. Identifying alternative solutions:
   a. Did Barbie and Peg make the right decisions in the beginning? Why or why not? What else could they have done at that time?
   b. What can they do now?
3. Examining and weighing the consequences:
   a. What might have happened if Barbie and Peg had made other decisions in the beginning?
   b. What are the possible consequences of any decision they might make now?
4. Deciding on a solution:
   a. Under the circumstances, what would be the wisest decision? Why?
   b. Are there other solutions that would be equally satisfactory? What are they? Why are they satisfactory solutions?

Letter to a Friend

The following case study, involving the decision of a mother to work and provide for the care of her preschool child, is written in the form of a letter. After the students have considered this situation, using the decision-making approach, the solution they consider best could be written in the form of a return letter.

Dear Martha,

It's been a while since I have written to you, but time seems to pass quickly. I've had some things on my mind lately, and I'll have to use that as my excuse for not writing.

It seems as if we have some big decisions to make in our family. I have been thinking about going back to work again. Johnny is three years old now, and we are considering having him attend a day-care center or possibly having him stay with another family during the daytime.

Tom isn't very enthusiastic about my returning to work. However, I don't want to turn down a good opportunity to become active in the business world again. I have missed working very much. In addition, the extra money would come in handy. There are so many things we could do for Johnny with the added income.

I guess there isn't much I need to tell you since you are already a working mother. That's why I needed to write to you now, Martha. I know you have Janie in a day-care center. We have been trying to decide between having Johnny stay with a very competent person who has taken care of some of my friends' children or putting him in a day-care center. There are several centers in town—some of which have very good reputations.

Martha, have you been satisfied with keeping Janie in the day-care center? We want to be sure Johnny gets the best care possible. There's a lot to consider, and we want to make a wise decision. Perhaps you can share some of your experiences with us and give us a few guidelines about what to look for and ask about as we check into child-care facilities.

Well, enough of this for now. I hope everything is going well. Give my best to Jim, and give a big hug to Janie for me.

Love,
Suzie

Follow-up questions

How could Martha respond to Suzie's letter?

1. Identifying the problem:
   a. What is the problem Suzie is facing?
   b. What additional information would one need in order to help Suzie and Tom make a decision?
2. Identifying alternative solutions:
   a. Should Suzie return to work? Why or why not?
   b. If Suzie returns to work, what should be her and Tom's considerations in selecting a private home or day-care center where Johnny could stay during the hours that both parents work?
3. Examining and weighing the consequences of the solutions:
   a. What would be the possible advantages of each solution suggested?
   b. What would be the disadvantages of each solution suggested?

4. Deciding on a solution:
   a. Which of the suggested solutions would seem to be the most suitable one? Why?
   b. If you were Martha, how would you respond to Suzie's letter?

The Counselor's Record

The final case study of Kenneth Jones is written briefly in the form of a record kept by the school counselor. It deals with the decision of a rural high school student who is considering dropping out of school in order to help support his family.

February 1—Office sent Kenneth Jones to me after he went there requesting withdrawal from school. Ken was offered a well-paying job helping with the construction of a dam.

He stated that father was not working because of a serious accident that occurred on the job at a fertilizer factory near Blimpton. Father will be hospitalized for several months and cannot return to work for a period of time after that. Papers have been filed for workman's compensation, but will not become effective for some time.

Mother is at home and not employed. Previously worked part time at county hospital. Older brother and sister, both married, in their middle twenties, work to support their families—not much money there.

Talked for a while about possibilities of Ken's remaining in school. Asked him to come see me the next day after we had both thought about it awhile; suggested he bring mother with him tomorrow.

February 2—Checked Ken's school record early in A.M. Has junior standing; grade average is C+. Record showed no major problems while in school. Wish there were some way to help him stay in school. He seemed determined to leave and help support family.

Follow-up questions

What alternatives do you think the school counselor should have suggested to Ken? Some of the following questions may help students think the problem through:

1. Identifying the problem:
   a. What are the factors influencing Ken's decision to leave school?
   b. What additional information might help to clarify the problem?
2. Identifying alternative solutions:
   a. What are some alternative solutions Ken ought to think of before he leaves school? Is there any way the family could get additional money now?
   b. If Ken did leave school now, do you think he would ever complete high school? Why or why not?

3. Examining and weighing the consequences of the solution:
   a. What would be the consequences of the alternative solutions suggested for Ken? What would he gain? What would he lose?
   b. What are some problems in the world of work and in private life that may be faced by people who have not completed high school?
4. Deciding on a solution:
   a. Under the circumstances, which decision would you make if you were Ken? Why?
   b. If you were the counselor, how would you try to help Ken?

Case studies can be adapted to meet the needs and interests of every class, and offer a wide range of opportunities for teaching higher-level cognitive and affective skills.

SIMULATED EXPERIENCES 10

As a teaching aid, the term *simulated experiences* applies to a variety of means for taking subject matter off the printed page and bringing it to life, chiefly in the form of small-scale dramas, or slices of life. The major simulated experiences described in this chapter include *skits*, in which students take part in problem situations by reading lines from prepared scripts; *sociodramas*, which emphasize interpersonal relationships for which only a very sketchy outline is provided; and *role playing*, which involves the acting out of roles that are defined in part by convention and students' existing knowledge of the types of characters they portray, even though there may be no formal dramatic framework, as in a skit. Through simulated experiences, students discover meaning that a textbook can only state; the difference is that between doing and merely being told about doing, a case of action speaking far louder than printed words. In the highly improvised sociodramas, moreover, one is not only involved but involved on one's own terms—free to interpret the assigned role by drawing from one's own experience. So subject matter could hardly be made more relevant, on a personal level.

SKITS

Using skits in classroom teaching provides an excellent opportunity to involve students actively, to add variety to classroom teaching, and to plan meaningful follow-up activities ahead of time. If teachers write or distribute the skit themselves, they have an opportunity to include slower learners by asking them to read the parts with fewer and easier lines. It is advisable to give out scripts to students in the skit a day or two in advance of the time they will be used. By doing this, students have an opportunity to read the lines several times and are able to give a smoother and more meaningful reading in class. A stand-in may be chosen to become familiar with the skit in case one of the actors is absent on the appointed day.

Teachers may want to change the names in a skit to fit the local situation—to use the names of students in the class, the name of their school, and the names of commercial concerns in the local community. This heightens student interest and may make the situation seem more realistic and pertinent.

Using props also adds interest. When skits are first used in a particular class, teachers may supply or suggest the props. Later, students can be encouraged to bring them.

When teachers are familiar with the contents of a skit, they are in a position to give the class points to look for, to suggest topics that may be discussed after it is read, and to suggest follow-up activities in advance. This kind of guidance helps students see the purpose and relevance of the skit.

Teachers can encourage students to plan their own follow-up activities. Planning stimulates analytical thinking, increases student interest and participation, and serves to motivate students to higher levels of achievement. Of course the points to look for, the discussion questions, and the class activities will depend upon previous learning and the students' interests, needs, abilities, and maturity.

This Communication Will Self-Destruct . . .

The following skit could be used in a home and family living course or in any other home economics class in which interpersonal relationships are emphasized.

Characters: Toby and Dana, who may be friends or husband and wife

Setting: Toby and Dana's kitchen

TOBY: What time will you be ready for dinner?

DANA: In just a minute.

TOBY: Dinner is almost ready.

DANA: I'll be there as soon as I can.

TOBY: Dinner is ready. I'm dishing up.

DANA: Hold it. I'm almost through.

TOBY: How can I hold dinner? It will get cold—or burn.

DANA: I'm hurrying.

TOBY: Do you know how much time I spent cooking this meal? I was trying to please you.

DANA: You are *so* impatient!

TOBY: Me? You're selfish! All you think of is yourself. You're just like your mother.

DANA: Well, now, I consider that a compliment. It's certainly better than being like *your* mother.

TOBY: Now, what's wrong with *my* mother?

DANA: She's nosy.

TOBY: Now, just one minute. I think you . . .

Behavioral objectives

- Identify barriers to effective communication.
- Give examples of barriers to effective communication.
- Explain how a destructive argument differs from a constructive argument.
- Point out barriers to effective communication in the foregoing dialogue.

Points to look for

- Being too vague
- Using poor timing
- Arguing destructively
- Giving criticism poorly
- Lacking consideration for another person

Discussion questions

- What could Dana have done to avoid the argument?
- Was Toby unreasonable? Why, or why not?
- What did Toby say that led this conversation into a destructive argument?
- What issues came into the argument that were not related to the main topic?
- How did both Toby and Dana use poor timing in this situation?
- How could both Toby and Dana have handled the situation more effectively?

How to Lose a Job Before Getting One

The following skit could be used in a class on gainful employment or career education, or in a comprehensive class on personal development.

Sometimes exaggerating a scene will add humor to a situation and help clarify the basic ideas. Satire may help students identify the main points being illustrated in a skit. This type of humor usually appeals to junior and senior high school students.

Characters: Ms. Wilson, personnel manager for Eatmore Restaurant, and Betsy Smith, an interviewee at the restaurant for a job as a waitress

Setting: Ms. Wilson's office, where Betsy has just arrived—15 minutes late, chewing gum, and dressed in a very tight and revealing outfit

BETSY: Gee, Ms. uh, uh. Is it Martin or Wilson? Oh yes, I remember, it's Ms. Wilson, right? Sorry to be late to tell you all about myself, but I got a huge run in my hose and, of course, I had to go back and get a different pair. You know, the panty hose they put on the market these days isn't worth . . .

MS. WILSON: Yes, I understand, Ms. Smith. Now, I have your application in front of me and would like to talk to you about some of your answers and about why you want to work for us. Your Social Security number was left off your application. Do you have a Social Security card, Ms. Smith?

BETSY: Oh, yeah. Well, you see, I was in such a hurry when I filled out the application that I didn't have time to find it. I changed purses; you know what that means!

MS. WILSON: I see. Do you have your card with you now?

BETSY: I think so. (She digs at length through the items in her purse, taking some of them out and putting them on Ms. Wilson's desk. She finally finds the card.) Yeah, here it is!

MS. WILSON: Thank you. Now, it says here that you graduated from high school, but it is very difficult to read the name of the school.

BETSY: Oh, gosh, I sure did have trouble with that! I didn't see that it said to print until after I'd already filled in all that other old stuff. So I had to mark it out. I graduated—just barely—from Central High School. My mom was so surprised and pleased.

MS. WILSON: Everything else seems to be here. Tell me, Ms. Smith, why would you like to work here with us?

BETSY: Oh, I don't know. I guess it's the only thing open now, and a person gets in the habit of eating, you know. (She laughs boisterously.) Besides, I heard the pay was pretty good here, huh?

MS. WILSON: What do you think would be a fair salary for your work?

BETSY: Well, I used to work for the Good Food Restaurant down the street; they're awful people to work for. You have to keep your hair tied up all the time. And the people that manage the place are impossible. Sometimes I'd have to stay ten or fifteen minutes after closing time to help them clean up. Sometimes they didn't pay me for the extra time, either. They paid me $300 a month and that wasn't enough for all I had to put up with. I was the best waitress they had, but they just didn't realize it or appreciate me!

MS. WILSON: Thank you for coming in for an interview, Ms. Smith. As soon as we've made a decision, we'll call you. Don't bother calling us. If we need you, we will get in touch with you. Good-bye.

BETSY: Thanks a lot. Oh, if you can't get me at home, I'll probably be at City Hospital. My Aunt Mary is going to have her gall bladder out. She's . . .

MS. WILSON: I'm very sorry to hear that. Now, Ms. Smith, my secretary will show you out. Good-bye.

Discussion questions

These questions could be given to the students before the skit is read:

- What did Betsy do that created a poor impression? How could she have made a more favorable first impression?
- Why would an employer be unlikely to hire Betsy?
- What traits did Betsy show in this scene that indicate that she may be a poor employment risk?
- What traits are desired of employees in any type of work? How may a person reveal some of these characteristics during a brief interview?
- Why should prospective employees refrain from asking about salary early in an interview? How could they bring up the subject without being too obvious or direct about it?
- Why is it inadvisable to criticize previous employers?
- How can people answer questions honestly and fairly without hurting their chances of getting a job?

Classroom activities

- Reenact this scene showing how Betsy could improve her chances of getting this job.
- Write minidramas planting good and poor features of job interviews, such as being on time (neither late nor early), having necessary information available, and asking appropriate questions. Identify the features of each interview situation that would create a favorable and an unfavorable impression. Discuss which interviewee would be most likely to land the job and why.
- Draw stick-figure or cartoon posters showing proper and improper interview techniques.
- From a grab bag, select the name of a job in which teenagers are likely to seek and find employment. For each job, list appropriate and meaningful questions that the interviewee might ask the employer to increase the likelihood of getting the job.
- Practice filling out job applications. Discuss why each item of information is requested. List points to follow in filling out applications to help "sell" oneself.
- Suggest appropriate attire to wear when applying for various types of work. Discuss why the clothing worn for one kind of job interview may be inappropriate for another.
- Give examples of questions interviewers might ask prospective employees applying for a variety of jobs.

Camera-Shy

Many concepts related to consumer education can be introduced, using the following skit. Those that will be covered depend upon the students' previous experiences and the depth in which consumer buying will be studied. Some concepts that are suggested by the skit, entitled *Camera-Shy*, are the following:

1. Selling techniques
2. Types of selling
   a. Door-to-door
   b. Catalog
   c. Stores
      1. Department
      2. Specialty
      3. Discount
3. Comparative shopping
4. Credit
   a. Types
   b. Costs
   c. Contracts
5. Consumer protection

Through the discussion and activities following the skit, the teacher may guide students into formulating generalizations similar to these:

1. Selling techniques may be effective in persuading consumers to buy, or in dissuading them.
2. Consumers have a choice in deciding where and from whom to buy.
3. People who plan expenditures are more likely to derive satisfaction from them than people who do not plan.
4. Buying on credit costs money but allows consumers to use goods and services while paying for them.
5. Laws and government regulations cannot protect individuals in all aspects of consumer buying.

Characters: Bernard Brown, a high school senior
Mr. John Blabb, a high-pressure camera salesperson

Setting: The front doorway of Bernard's home

MR. BLABB: Hi, sucker—I mean, sir. Congratulations. I have heard that you're graduating from high school this spring. I'm John Blabb, and a representative from Classy Camera Company. Of course, you've heard of our wonderful and outstanding company, haven't you? Well, of course, you have.

BERNARD: Well . . . er . . . I might . . .

MR. BLABB (Interrupting): Great! Our company has a very special offer and it is only available to graduating seniors. You may be wondering why we're offering such a fabulous buy. At Classy Camera, we feel that you deserve a little something extra as a graduate-to-be.

BERNARD: That's nice. What are you . . .?

MR. BLABB (Interrupting again): We're offering a marvelous, fully automatic camera at a cost you simply wouldn't believe. I'm sure that you'll want to start to develop your skills as a photographer and record the important coming events in your life.

BERNARD: But, I wasn't planning to learn photography. I don't even know how to focus a camera.

MR. BLABB: I was just coming to that. For a very limited time only, we are offering a free course in photography with the purchase of our camera and a few necessary accessories. You're probably thinking, "How can those nice people afford to do that?" Well, we feel that high school graduates deserve a reward and gift for their great accomplishment.

BERNARD: Oh, that's nice, but what would I have to . . .

MR. BLABB: Here's our Classy Camera catalog. We're offering combinations of cameras and accessories in the sets numbered seven and eleven. They are only $89.98. Think of all that for eighty-nine dollars. Set thirteen is really a super buy. Monthly payments are so easy—just $5.49 a month—less than 20 cents a day. Just think of that bargain!

BERNARD: When would I get my photography course?

MR. BLABB: It will be scheduled when you receive your camera set. Due to a delivery—but your wait will be well worth it. Now, if you'll just sign here and indicate which of the camera sets you prefer, I'll get your order off immediately. In fact, if you hurry, I can make the next mail pickup.

BERNARD: I think that I like this one best, but . . .

MR. BLABB: Good, just check it—no, I'll be glad to check it for you. Have you signed the agreement? Good, good! I must hurry so you'll be sure to get in on this great deal and receive your camera on time. Good-bye, Mr. Brown.

BERNARD: Good-bye—and thank you.

Discussion questions

- What techniques did Mr. Blabb use that helped him make this sale? What other techniques are sometimes used to persuade people to make purchases they had not planned?
- What should Bernard have found out before signing the contract agreement?
- What responsibilities do consumers assume by signing contracts to buy on credit?
- What are some of the advantages and disadvantages of using credit?
- What does this expression mean: "It is just as important to know how to spend money as it is to know how to earn it"?

Follow-up activities

- Plan and give sales talks in an attempt to persuade class members to buy particular products. Use typical selling techniques and subtle methods of persuasion. Analyze the sales pitch used in each mock situation to determine what was said that might influence a consumer to buy the item. Discuss what might have influenced the consumer not to buy the product.
- Write a short story or make a tape describing the misfortunes of an individual or a family that has overextended its credit obligations. Suggest solutions to the problems described.
- Collect and discuss magazine and newspaper articles that seem to support the concept of a cashless society.
- Compare the cost of buying a variety of products on credit in several local business concerns.

Creating your Own Skit

A skit reading will be nothing more than a reading unless the teacher provides opportunities for making it a meaningful experience. Students often enjoy writing their own skits and may lead the follow-up discussion as well. This has the advantage of involving all class members, of including topics that are of real concern to students, and of showing them that their contributions are worthwhile and important.

Skits in which the lines are more or less spontaneous may also be presented to the class. The plot, the first line for each character and the essence of the dialogue are planned in a general way by class members working together in small groups. A skit of this type could be used in studying various nutrients. Each group of students could select a specific nutrient and, through a short drama, illustrate the following about it:

1. Historical interest and/or discovery
2. Deficiency symptoms
3. Sources
    a. Foods
    b. Others

The teacher will need to provide reference materials and resources to enable students to look up appropriate information to include in this type of skit. A typical skit emphasizing vitamin C may include a scene from Vasco da Gama's trip from Portugal around Africa to India, on which 62 percent of the crew died of scurvy. Later, on the first English expedition to the East Indies, three of four ship captains saw their crews so disabled by scurvy that they were barely able to navigate. The fourth ship, whose daily ration included doses of lemon juice, was untouched by the disease. Soon all British sailors were required to drink lime or lemon juice, and eventually they became known as limeys.

In the skit about vitamin D, it could be brought out that George Washington, who escaped the more serious and crippling effects of rickets, lost his teeth early in adulthood and had to replace them with wooden pegs. Nor were women, as a group, spared such misfortune. To include information about the history, deficiency symptoms, and food sources of vitamin A, the students could act out a scene in which early Greeks, troubled by night blindness, were told by Hippocrates to eat liver dipped in honey. Later, fishermen blinded by the sun glaring on the water ate the livers of codfish and sea gulls to improve their sight. The Greeks and fishermen were not only preventing night blindness but were contributing to their health by getting enough vitamin A, which had been stored in the livers of animals for future use.

In the skit about riboflavin, which promotes growth, it could be shown that the average American man and woman today are several inches taller than their ancestors. By bringing out interesting facts such as these, you will help students remember the material better, and they will see that what is studied in home economics really does influence one's life.

SOCIODRAMAS

In skits, the participants read the parts and portray the roles of the characters that are delineated for them. In sociodramas, the students are free to interpret roles as they actually feel and perceive them. Since the dialogue is spontaneous and unrehearsed, participants usually react as they really would in similar situations. Sociodramas are used when studying problems related to personal or social relations, family living, or any area of human development involving interpersonal relationships.

The primary advantage that sociodramas have over skits is that they take little or no preparation time before class. Skits must be written or at least, in most cases, duplicated and distributed. Since a sociodrama is an extemporaneous portrayal of a situation in which only the first few lines and the general plot or theme are planned, what the participants say and do cannot be anticipated. Therefore, one distinct disadvantage of sociodramas is that the follow-up cannot be planned in advance. Only very general guidelines such as these can be given ahead of time:

- What seem to be some of the underlying and basic causes of conflict between the characters as they are seen in this scene?
- Which of the reactions and behaviors shown by the characters are typical of mature and immature individuals?
- What are some ways in which this situation could be improved?

How to Use Sociodramas

One principle of using sociodramas in the classroom is that a student should never be forced to be in one. Participation should be completely voluntary. However, when teachers know their students well, they can sense which ones would like to take part despite their hesitancy to say so publicly. These students may be encouraged and cajoled into participating with just the right lighthearted approach. The teacher may say something like, "Who will be the younger brother? Nobody? Oh, come on, Mark, I imagine you could play the part of a ten-year-old boy very well!" (This would be particularly appropriate if Mark really has a brother about this age.) If Mark declines this personal invitation, the teacher could reply, "Well, we'll just have the sociodrama without a younger brother." This would be preferable to making a student feel self-conscious and uncomfortable. The first time a sociodrama is used, the class "hams" may be the only volunteers. However, after two or three successful sociodramas, the more reserved and retiring students are likely to want to take part too.

A sociodrama depicts a situation involving interpersonal conflict. In order to include episodes that will be most meaningful to the class members, the teacher could ask, "What are some problems students your age may have at home in getting along with other family members?" Of course, this would be a better and more ethical question than "What are some problems you have in getting along with your family?" Actually, most of the time the impersonal question will result in the same response but will lessen the likelihood that the class period will become a "show and tell" session of family secrets.

A typical ninth-grade class may list problem areas such as these:

- Using the telephone
- Sharing a bathroom
- Having to take care of younger brothers and sisters
- Doing chores around the home
- Disagreeing with parents about dating
- Setting curfews

A student could write on the chalkboard the ideas suggested by class members. Then the students can vote for the two or three items that they believe are most likely to be sources of conflict. Those that receive the most votes would logically be the concerns to be included in the sociodramas.

The class may decide which and how many family members should be portrayed. After the volunteer cast is selected, the teacher will take the participants into a corner of the room, into an adjoining room, or into the hallway near the open classroom door—to any place where there is some degree of privacy but where the teacher can also be near enough to know what the rest of the class is doing. Actually, this planning session will take only a few moments because the participants decide only how the drama will begin and plan just a few of the opening lines. From then on, the dialogue and action should be spontaneous; the students say and do what comes naturally to them.

Teachers have a key responsibility in stopping sociodramas as soon as they sense that the participants are straining for their lines and before the action becomes tedious. The teacher may say something like, "Thank you. Let's stop here and talk about this situation."

Follow-Up

If no discussion follows the sociodrama, it will become only a means of entertaining the class. The purpose of the follow-up is to lead the students in formulating generalizations that can guide them in solving problems similar to those depicted in the drama. The students can be given guidance in many ways. The participants may be asked to analyze the feelings and emotions they experienced during the enactment of the scene. Then, through skillful questioning, the teacher may lead the students to a better understanding of others' responses and reactions.

After a discussion of how the situation might have been handled better, another scene could be dramatized, incorporating the suggestions for improvement. The same players or another group of students could take part in the replay.

Students may reverse roles to gain greater empathy for the feelings of others. For example, the person who played the part of a teenager in the first dramatization may play the part of a parent in the next one.

Advantages of Sociodramas

A sociodrama provides students with an enjoyable and common experience on which to base a meaningful discussion and follow-up activities. In addition, teachers gain valuable insight into their students' maturity levels because the participants in a sociodrama are likely to reflect the emotions they really feel in similar situations. Students also see that others have problems very much like their own. If not used too often, sociodramas add variety and interest to classroom teaching.

Cautions in Using Sociodramas

On rare occasions, the teacher may want to stop a sociodrama because the participants become very emotional about their roles or they become overly self-conscious. Self-consciousness often manifests itself in giggling. This is most likely to happen if the problem situation being acted out is one about which the students feel embarrassment. If this problem persists, the teacher may not want to use this method of teaching at all. However, it is recommended that the teacher use the technique several times before discarding it because it has many advantages. If teachers are enthusiastic and excited about using sociodramas, this will undoubtedly be reflected in their students' attitudes toward them.

Variations

Several unique ways of creating situations for sociodramas are available to teachers. One possibility is that they, or students, could read or tell a short story. Class members could then act out the ending of the dramatization based on this material, without prior discussion of how it will or should end.

Another variation is to use pictures of people who are obviously involved in interpersonal problem situations. Students can enact the scenes as they sense and feel them. Of course, the follow-up discussions described previously will enable these dramatizations to become the bases for meaningful learning experiences.

ROLE PLAYING

Most educators do not make a distinction between sociodramas and role playing. However, as the terms are used in this book, there is one difference. In sociodramas, students interpret the parts being played in the way they actually feel them or desire to play them. There is not even a subtle suggestion that a role should be interpreted any certain way. However, in role playing, students are more likely to feel a commitment to portray a character's role in a way that matches what is expected of a person in that particular situation.

For example, when role-playing a situation in which one student is serving food to another, the students undoubtedly sense that there is a correct and an incorrect procedure to follow. The players may purposely plant errors in their ways of serving and being served, but there is still the knowledge that there are right and wrong ways. Another example might center on a consumer thinking about making an expensive purchase using credit. In this situation there would be an expected pattern of behavior including certain questions the student knows should be asked.

Other situations typically used in role playing may involve baby-sitters asking parents for specific information and prospective consumers asking salespeople questions about specific features of certain products. Situations such as these are usually acted out with maximum benefit after students have gained some background knowledge about the topic.

PHOTO SITUATIONS

In photo situations, pictures provide the common basis for discussion. In other words, a discussion is built upon what students feel about and read into a picture. Usually, but not necessarily, the pictures depict interpersonal relationships.

The picture needs to be large enough for the entire group to see easily. If necessary, it can be enlarged. For this purpose, an overhead projector may be used, or the teacher may move around the room with the picture. If the picture is available in multiple copies of a book or periodical, all the students can view it at the same time. After students analyze the scene, the teacher can start a discussion by asking pertinent questions. The examples on pages 118 and 119 illustrate how photo situations can be used:

Photo situations require that the teacher ask questions based on student responses. For instance, in the example on page 118, a student may have replied to the first question by saying, "The child pleaded with his mother not to leave." The teacher could develop this idea by asking an additional, more probing question to carry the thought further, such as "What are some ways of helping children to feel secure so that they are able to cope better when a parent leaves the house?"

The success of skits, sociodramas, role playing, and photo situations as methods of teaching depend primarily upon the teacher's ability to ask significant, relevant, and thought-provoking questions that promote meaningful discussions.

Michael Kagan/Monkmeyer

- What may have occurred prior to this scene?
- How could this situation be handled? If it were to occur often, how could it then be handled?
- Describe the feelings and conflicts that the parent may be experiencing.

Sybil Shelton/Monkmeyer

- What may be taking place?
- What feelings may the teenager be trying to express? Describe the feelings the parents may be experiencing.
- What do you expect the outcome of this situation to be? Why?
- What nonspoken messages are being given by the parents? By the teenager?

MULTIMEDIA APPROACHES 11

Various media can be used in the classroom to introduce, reinforce, summarize, or highlight material and to stimulate interest in the home economics curriculum.

CHALKBOARDS

Chalkboards in the form of slates date back to the time of the oldest schoolhouse in America, and stories about Abraham Lincoln "cipherin' " on his slate are well known. Today, some form of the chalkboard can still be found in almost every classroom. If at all possible, needed material should be put on the chalkboard before class. Teachers lose contact with the class when they turn their backs to write on the board, and if the process takes very long, students may become bored and inattentive.

The chalkboard can be used most effectively during class time by writing only key words or ideas on it. Most teachers can do this by turning only slightly away from part of the class. Having students write on the board can also be an effective way of engaging them in various problem-solving situations. If extensive material has been put on the board before class time, it can be covered by pulling down a screen hung above the chalkboard. By doing this, students will not be distracted by the material before it is to be used, and information can be revealed a little at a time by moving the screen up at appropriate intervals. Thus, students are not likely to be overwhelmed by seeing a lot of writing all at once, and they will not become distracted by reading ahead.

The chalkboard is an excellent place to put reminders that need to be availablc for several days. These may include vocabulary lists to which words are added as they are used, behavioral objectives to be accomplished over a short period of time, dates of school events such as FHA/HERO meetings, or assignments with due dates.

FLIP CHARTS

It takes considerably longer to put written material in a flip chart than on a chalkboard, but flip charts are fairly durable and can be used indefinitely. Because of their durability and the time and money involved in making them, it is advisable to use flip charts with subject matter that is relatively stable. Principles of furniture arrangement or the Basic Four food groups are practical for a flip chart; clothing fads or changing fashions would make such a chart obsolete in a relatively short time. Pictures, cartoons, or sketches can be used in flip charts to add interest but they must be large enough to be seen throughout the classroom. Different colors should be used to emphasize important words. (Avoid yellow—it doesn't show up well.)

Selecting and Making Flip Charts

1. Use a large pad with a spiral edge. The pages turn more easily and are less likely to tear than those that are stapled, glued, or taped.
2. If the flip chart is to contain writing, select the kind with ruled lines printed lightly on the pages. This eliminates the need for ruling guidelines in pencil and then having to erase them.
3. Be sure the writing is large enough to be read easily at the greatest distance from which it will be viewed. Measure carefully and rough out lightly in pencil what is to be written. By doing this, the ends of lines will not be crowded and few words will have to be divided.
4. Do not put too much writing on any one page. A large amount of written material that is cluttered and lacks variety does not encourage anyone to read it.
5. Put a protective sheet of paper between the page on which writing is being done and the next page, so that ink will not leak through.
6. Use the flip chart on an easel or other brace where it is high enough to be seen by everyone in the room. Place it so the pages can be turned without having to move the flip chart.
7. Number pages near the lower edge of each sheet and make an index on the cover of the flip chart including the pages devoted to each topic. This may eliminate wasting class time and boring students by unnecessarily flipping through pages to locate certain sections.
8. Affix your name to the outside cover so the flip chart will not be misplaced and can be identified readily when stored with those belonging to others.

The use of a flannel-board display such as this can help students understand the effect of lines in clothing on apparent body size.

FLANNEL BOARDS

A wider range of illustrative materials can be used with a flannel board than with a flip chart or chalkboard. Visuals for a flannel board can be prepared in advance so that they are ready when needed. Once made, items can be filed and used many times over. It is efficient to keep flannel-board materials and accompanying notes or lesson plans together in large, heavy envelopes that have been marked clearly on the outside to identify their contents.

The flannel board and the articles on it can be moved from place to place, providing a high degree of flexibility that some other media lack. Items can be rearranged for comparisons, they can be added sequentially, and they can be taken away. Therefore, a whole process or any part of it can be reconstructed. Charts, diagrams, and graphs can be built as learning proceeds. Thus, materials can be used to suit the immediate needs of the situation.

Making Flannel Boards

Cotton flannel, because it is inexpensive, is usually used to cover lightweight plywood, very heavy cardboard, or composition board. Actually, any napped or fuzzy fabric such as velvet, corduroy, or felt can be stretched tautly to cover the board and taped or tacked securely on the wrong side of the board. It is also possible to sew two pieces of flannel together, perhaps of different colors, in pillowcase fashion, and to slip the board inside so it fits snugly. This provides a reversible flannel board of different colors with a case that can easily be removed for cleaning. A flannel board measuring approximately 30 by 40 inches is of sufficient size to be seen by an audience of 150 to 175 people. A board of this size is not difficult to move about, although a somewhat smaller one might be equally suitable for classroom use. But if the board is too small, the variety of ways in which it can be used is limited.

Preparing the Illustrations

Magazine pictures should be glued or cemented, with a product that will not leave buckles or ripples when dry, to a background such as construction paper or very lightweight poster board. Magazine paper is too lightweight and flimsy to be used without backing, and unmounted illustrations of this kind create an unfinished appearance. Care should be taken not to use backing materials that will be too heavy to stay on the flannel board securely. Other illustrations that do not need framing, such as figures from pattern catalogs, can be backed with old file folders.

At least one-half of the back of the mounted illustrations should be covered with a napped fabric. The fabric should be glued with the napped side up. When the prepared article is placed against the flannel board, it will stay in place because the two napped surfaces have an affinity for each other. For added assurance that the materials will stay in place when positioned, they can be stroked gently with an *upward* motion of the hand, and the board can be tilted backward slightly.

To clarify concepts through visual stimuli

As with all media, the educational value of flannel boards depends upon the teaching skills employed in using them. Flannel boards can help students who do not verbalize well to clarify concepts through visual stimuli. For example, pictures of foods of different colors, textures, and temperatures can be used to teach principles of meal planning. Silhouettes of objects like vases, bowls, candlesticks, plaques, and plants can be effective in demonstrating formal and informal balance, lack of balance, emphasis, pleasing proportions, and various types of rhythm. Students can use the flannel-board illustrations to practice and criticize their own arrangements.

Students may study the theoretical relationship between line and design in dress and the apparent size of the body without being able to visualize specific lines in actual garments. For that reason, a flannel board of pattern-catalog silhouettes can be very helpful in clarifying these concepts. Students can be asked to group pictures of garments from one side of the board with the lines displayed on the other side. Students can also be asked to point out garments appropriate for different body types, to analyze the effects of color and texture on apparent body size, to determine which garments could be recycled to be fashionable, and to suggest ways to accessorize the clothes for a variety of effects.

To illustrate sequences or progressions

Flannel boards are especially effective for showing a sequential series or progression of events. Principles of furniture arrangement can be illustrated by placing the various pieces until an entire room or home exemplifies pleasing balance, appropriate groupings, and workable traffic patterns. Felt can be cut to scale and used without any backing to represent various items of furniture. Rooms can be marked off with tape or strips of fabric pinned in place to indicate walls, windows, and doors. If desired, a yardstick and soft lead pencil can be used to mark off 1-inch squares on the background flannel.

A flannel board makes an excellent medium for explaining the color wheel. Poster board can be cut in the shape of numerals and colored to show the primary, secondary, and tertiary hues. As the colors are defined, the numbers can be put in place—1 for the primary colors, 2 for the secondary colors, and 3 for the tertiary colors. Color harmonies can be illustrated with markers. Later, the numerals can be replaced with colored circles so that students can arrange them without the help of the numbers.

To reinforce, introduce, or summarize subject matter

Flannel boards are effective for introducing, reinforcing, and summarizing subject matter. One could be titled "What Is a Parent?" As terms like teacher, counselor, nurse, personal shopper, recreation leader, cook, gardener, and chauffeur are mentioned, appropriate pictures can be put on the flannel board. When students think of roles for which there are as yet no illustrations, they can be asked to bring representative pictures to class to add to the flannel-board collection.

Another flannel board, to which illustrations can be added as students suggest ideas, might be titled, "Mr. Blueprint, Consider Our Needs." Pictures or sketches representing things to consider when planning a home can be placed around a blueprint or house plan. A piggy bank or play money can be used to represent finances; families with many, one or two, or no children can represent size of family; and a young couple and an older couple can represent age of family members.

A jigsaw puzzle can be employed to review cuts of meat by using two colors of construction paper, flannel, or felt for the tender and less tender portions. The pieces can be fitted together in the shape of a cow. As each cut of meat is placed, it can be discussed in relation to the anatomy, development, and movement of the animal.

Principles of commercial buffet-food service, such as a salad bar, can be illustrated by using cutouts to represent dinnerware, specific food items, dressings, and other accompaniments. Later, small groups of students could be given different menus and asked to illustrate appropriate table settings for these menus on the flannel board. Cutouts of plates, utensils, and other necessary pieces can be traced from the actual items.

By adding, shifting, and removing parts of a flannel board, the teacher will be able to clarify concepts. Students can work individually or in small groups with flannel-board illustrations to experiment until the best solution to a problem is demonstrated.

BULLETIN BOARDS

Bulletin boards can be effective in supplementing classroom teaching, emphasizing certain areas of subject matter, teaching by themselves, creating interest in a topic, and making a classroom more attractive. However, these objectives will be realized only if the bulletin-board display attracts attention. A bulletin board that is left up more than two weeks will have little, if any, educational value. Ideally, bulletin boards or parts of them are changed about once a week. Current events, community celebrations, important school events, or contemporary verbal expressions may provide timely themes.

Newspaper and magazine advertisements often stimulate ideas for creative and catchy bulletin boards. Games such as football and chess may provide a frame of reference for conveying an idea. For example, the slogans *Cheer for . . .* or *Team up for . . .* with an illustration of a megaphone, or *Make the Best Move* with the silhouette of a chess figure or a checkerboard background, could be used in many ways.

Tips for Saving Time

Making bulletin boards can be a valuable learning experience for students working individually or in small groups. Looking for pictures of foods representing each of the Basic Four food groups can be a meaningful activity for younger students, while making step-by-step displays that show various clothing-construction techniques, with written descriptions, may be appropriate for more advanced students. Finding pictures that illustrate warm and cool color combinations, formal and informal balance, and different principles of design can be a worthwhile learning experience, and students' examples can be used to create attractive bulletin boards.

Magazine pictures should be mounted for a professional and finished appearance. Unmounted pictures tend to look messy and *tacky*. Pin marks that make pictures look worn can be avoided by placing pins or small tacks so they brace the illustration rather than make a hole in it. The pins near the lower corners are slanted upward and the pins near the upper corners are slanted downward. Tacks can be inserted so that the cap portion, rather than the nail-like part, holds the paper firmly in place. Tape can be rolled in loops, with the adhesive side out, and used on the back of lightweight illustrations to fasten them to the bulletin board. This gives a neat appearance and can create a three-dimensional effect if the pictures are not flattened against the background surface.

Cutouts, silhouettes, cartoon characters, and large line drawings can be made easily by utilizing an opaque projector. The poster board on which a picture is to be drawn is fastened to the wall or bulletin board. The opaque projector is moved forward or backward until the desired size of the image is obtained. The picture is traced directly on the poster board and can be cut out later, if desired. It is also possible to use transparencies with an overhead projector for the purpose of providing images to trace. Children's coloring books are excellent sources of simple line drawings, especially of animals.

It may be possible for students to make lettering or captions for an assignment in an art class that could be used later in a home economics class. Ready-made letters are relatively inexpensive and come in a variety of sizes, colors, and styles. To make lettering straight, a very light guideline can be penciled on the bulletin-board background, a yardstick can be pinned in place and the letters lined up with it, or a string can be fastened across the board to form a straight edge.

Color

Color is important in creating mood, providing associations, and strengthening the theme or message of a bulletin board. Pastels would be more appropriate than harsh colors for a bulletin board entitled *Everybody Loves a Baby*. Yellow, white, and clear bright colors are more appropriate than tan or gray for conveying the idea of cleanliness. Green and red or orange and black suggest specific seasons of the year. Certainly, "stop" written in red and "go" written in green are more effective than they would be in other colors.

Usually it is desirable to use only three main colors: one for the background, one for the lettering, and one for the illustration mountings. Of course, pictures will contain a variety of colors, but the effect of these will be small in proportion to the basic colors of the display. When large areas have too many colors, the bulletin board is likely to lack unity.

Principles of Design

The most effective display is simple and uncluttered, with a clear message. It is better to rotate illustrations than to use too many at one time. A bulletin board should provide interesting treatment of space and a variety of shapes to attract attention. This usually calls for unequal proportions. Informal balance is generally more eye-catching than symmetry.

A variety of textures can add interest. Background materials may be burlap, felt, tissue paper, corrugated cardboard, or any other substance that will add textural variety without detracting from the primary purpose of the bulletin board. Real objects like empty milk and egg cartons, cereal boxes, and other containers can be tacked in place from the inside. Small brushes and mirrors, clothing accessories, kitchen utensils, and doll furniture are just a few of the items that can be used to add a three-dimensional effect.

Lettering

The lettering should be easy to read and in keeping with the theme. A word in the caption may be written in a different lettering to emphasize a point. Block letters would be appropriate for a bulletin board on children's toys, while delicate script would be better for a display of different types of invitations and replies. The following examples illustrate lettering that strengthen and weaken the message.

Lettering should be easy to render. Obviously, cutting out individual letters is very time-consuming. However, if this is done, letters can be saved, and eventually a substantial file can be accumulated. Storing each of the twenty-six letters and various punctuation symbols in a separate envelope, folder, or box makes them easier to locate when they are needed.

Captions

Bulletin board captions can do much to attract attention, create interest, motivate students, and reinforce subject matter that has been covered by other methods. Popular song titles, advertising slogans, proverbs, or contemporary expressions can be used. Captions might capitalize on a play on words, current events, or special lettering. A bulletin board can also be made without a caption, encouraging students to suggest a suitable title. Teachers can ask students to suggest labels for parts of the bulletin board, thus using it for a learning experience. Many of the bulletin-board ideas that follow could be used this way.

Captions—letters for emphasis

YOU **AUTO** CONSERVE FUEL: Use students' driving and car-maintenance tips for conserving gas. Cartoons might be used to illustrate these points.

GOOD GROOMING FROM A TO Z: Use colorful construction paper to make the letter *Z* large enough to cover most of the bulletin board. Center the *Z* under the title and mount pictures showing well-groomed boys and girls or grooming aids across the top and bottom and down the center of the letter.

BOWL THEM ꓤƎɅO: Use the cutout of a bowling ball. Mount fashionable-looking garments on construction-paper bowling pins that seem to be flying in various directions.

STAIRWAY TO: Adapt this caption to career education, good grooming, better use of resources, or any other topic. Position each letter on a different "step" so that it leads into the main title.

Captions—plays on words

NO "LION," GOOD GROOMING COUNTS: Write *hair, nails,* and *clothes* in appropriate spaces around a picture of a lion or a toy lion. Put the word *clothes* near the animal's tail, to which a pert ribbon or bow tie has been fastened.

GET READY, GET SET, SEW!: Display patterns, showing the number of pieces, that would be appropriate for a first clothing-construction project. This caption could also be used with a display of items needed for an approaching unit in clothing construction.

WHAT TYPE OF LEARNER ARE YOU?

- Are you a (*Tack up a strainer*)? Keeps important material?
- Are you a (*Tack up a sponge*)? Soaks up a lot?

- Are you a (*Tack up a sifter*)? Blends knowledge together?
- Are you a (*Tack up a corer*)? Gets at the core of the matter?
- Are you a (*Tack up a chopper*)? Cuts up a lot?
- Are you a (*Tack up an egg beater*)? Gets things mixed up?
- Are you a (*Tack up a funnel*)? Goes in one ear and out the other?

GIVE A HOOT. DON'T POLLUTE: Mount a cutout of an owl. Use pictures that show lack of concern for the environment and ecology, such as cans thrown along a highway, a crowded room full of people and cigarette and cigar smoke, and a campfire left unattended.

PROTEIN MOO-O-VES YOU: Picture a cow in the center of the board. Place illustrations of meat, poultry, fish, egg, and milk products around it.

Captions—seasons and holidays as themes

DON'T GET SPOOKED: Drape a sheet in the form of a ghost and pin it to the background of the bulletin board. Use terms appropriate for the situation, such as "Study for test Oct. 13," "Hand in home experience progress report Monday," or "Complete notebook by Friday."

MARCH IN WITH SPRING FASHIONS: Use the silhouette of a drum or drummer on one side of the board. On the other side mount pictures of garments appropriate for a spring clothing-construction project.

Captions—titles with multiple uses

SEEDS WORTH SOWING: Outline the bulletin board with packages of plant seeds. In the center of the board, develop ideas for various concepts. For example, in consumer education, include: staying informed, reading tags and labels, determining quality and quantity, paying promptly, keeping records, and handling merchandise carefully. For career education, use words such as: honesty, loyalty, dependability, resourcefulness, independence.

HAPPINESS IS . . . USING YOUR MONEY WISELY . . . HAVING A JOB: Use a happy-looking cartoon character. Arrange items around it that are things for which teenagers like to spend their money—snack foods, clothes, makeup—or use items pertaining to the world of work, such as a job-application form, Social Security card, paycheck stub, income tax return.

DEVELOP GOOD HABITS: Outline the bulletin board with an old film or filmstrip. In the center, mount pictures illustrating the topic. For grooming include: brushing teeth, washing face, shampooing hair, caring for clothes, and choosing food wisely. For management, use pictures illustrating desirable study habits such as: good light, TV and radio off, working at a table or desk, sufficient sleep, and scheduling work.

TOOLS OF THE TRADE: Mount actual items or illustrations of the tools necessary for completing a certain task or job. For clothing construction, mount sewing equipment such as a measuring tape, tracing wheel, carbon paper, seam guide, and zipper foot. In food preparation, you might include measuring spoons and cups, spatulas, peelers, and other small equipment.

GUIDEPOSTS IN BUYING: Mount a large posted sign in the center of the board. Change the label on the sign to indicate the area of study and arrange appropriate pictures or models around it. For instance, when the guidepost says "insurance," use replicas of a home, car, and hospital to illustrate kinds of insurance; play money or dollar signs to illustrate the cost; a calendar to illustrate length of coverage, and so forth.

STEPPING-STONES TO ... KEYS TO ... OR FOOTSTEPS TO ...: Use cutouts of stones, keys, or footprints to mount words and pictures appropriate for the specific theme. For example: for *Good Health* use Basic Four, cleanliness, rest, exercise. For *Happy Family Living* use words such as security, understanding, affection, common goals.

OPEN THE DOOR TO ...: Place a simple silhouette of a door in the center of the display. Around it mount large keys cut from construction paper. Give the keys labels relating to topics such as grooming, health, and careers. In a cooperative program, words such as courtesy, dependability, respect, cheerfulness, and loyalty might be used.

DON'T FIDDLE AROUND: Use a picture or sketch of a fiddle or violin as the center of the board. For a display on decision making or management, write the steps in problem solving on pieces of paper mounted around the fiddle. This idea could be used for an FHA/HERO chapter membership drive. Add *Join FHA/HERO* and pictures of chapter activities from previous years. The theme could also be used as a reminder to *Bring Your Materials Monday* for a clothing construction project and to display the items needed.

Some other titles and illustrations that can be used to remind students of school events, important dates, and assignments, or to join school groups are: *Don't Forget*—with a silhouette of an elephant; *Don't Poke Around*—with a picture of a turtle; *Count Down For*—with a cutout of a rocket; *Hop to It*—with a sketch of a rabbit; and *Be Wise*—with a drawing of an owl.

Captions—introducing Home Economics

At the beginning of the term, a bulletin board can be used to convey the idea that home economics encompasses a wide variety of subject matter, to encourage participation in FHA/HERO and other activities, or to foster interest in home economics-related careers. The following bulletin boards could be used to serve such purposes:

WE'LL BE BUSY AS BEES: On the horizontal layers of a simulated beehive, list the conceptual areas of home economics that will be covered. Place cutouts of bees around the hive. This idea would be suitable for use with elementary or middle-school students.

FOCUS ON . . . : Use the silhouette of a camera, and mount and label pictures depicting child development, home management, family living, consumer education, and other areas of home economics.

SOMETHING TO CROW ABOUT—HOME ECONOMICS: Use a sketch of a rooster that seems to be telling the good news about areas of home economics to be studied.

DIAL A CAREER IN HOME ECONOMICS: Use a cutout of a telephone dial or a game spinner. Around it place pictures of people in home economics-related occupations.

BE ONE OF THE BUNCH . . . JOIN FHA/HERO: Make a bunch of grapes from purple felt or construction paper. A green stem and a few leaves can be added for interest.

SEW UP A CAREER IN HOME ECONOMICS: Make the caption with heavy yarn or broken lines to suggest stitches, or "sew" the words into a backing using heavy yarn. Use pictures to depict various career opportunities in home economics or to show areas in which students are working if the class is part of a cooperative program.

Captions—subject-matter areas in Home Economics

ALWAYS BE CLEAN: Display various articles or pictures of items that are associated with cleanliness, good grooming, and/or sanitary food preparation.

MANAGEMENT MENACES IN THE HOME: Mark off the bulletin board to look like a house. Arrange scissors, poison labels, matches, medicine containers, a frayed electrical cord, and other appropriate items or pictures of them in each room of the house.

S ensible
S afety
S afeguards: Display articles and pictures of items such as a knife, racks, labels for poisons, and repaired electrical cords.

BETTER SAFE THAN SORRY: Use a picture of a teddy bear wearing a bandage or a sling. Around it mount suitable line drawings showing children playing in the street, electrical cords and fans within children's reach, a child playing with a potentially dangerous item, or other appropriate scenes.

Food and nutrition

GET UP CROWING: Mount a picture of a rooster crowing about the attractive breakfast illustrated.

AIM FOR GOOD NUTRITION: Mount an arrow and the facsimile of a bulls-eye. On the circles of the target, write the Basic Four food groups or the nutrients—vitamins, minerals, proteins, fats, and carbohydrates.

BE WISE ABOUT THE EGGS-SENTIALS: Use a picture of an owl hooting about the nutritive value of appealing egg dishes.

Clothing and textiles

ONE BUYS THE COMMONPLACE BUT YOU CREATE THE ORIGINAL: Have the students take turns displaying the patterns, fabrics, and notions they have chosen for a sewing project.

Super
Swift
Sewing: Use pictures or pattern envelopes of easy-to-make or *jiffy* garments with few pattern pieces. Also tack up swatches of fabric that require a minimum amount of work.

TENDER CARE MEANS LONGER WEAR: Use pictures or real items illustrating the subcaptions: save and read hangtags, repair immediately, store properly, follow washing instructions, remove spots and stains quickly.

THE GUIDE SHEET—YOUR MAP TO CLOTHING CONSTRUCTION: Separate and label parts of the guide sheet such as views, layouts, and steps in construction.

Consumer education

IT'S IN THE BAG: Tack up a large paper bag with "Spending Plan" written across it. On each of three packages, wrapped like gifts and protruding from the top of the bag, write *resources*, *expenses*, and *savings*.

TIMELY TIPS: Mount a facsimile of a clock. Around it place pictures or captions relating to concepts such as maintaining a good credit rating, shopping for interest rates, and comparing goods, prices, and guarantees.

THERE'S MORE TO CREDIT . . . THAN SIGNING YOUR NAME: Write the word *credit* in green or red letters, using the opposite color for the rest of the words. Use a cutout of a wallet and a picture of a person who looks as if an agreement is being signed. If such a picture cannot be found, a contract could be used instead. Mount mock dollar bills so that they look as if they are flying out of the wallet.

Child development

WANTED! BABY-SITTER: Mount a mirror under the title. List qualities necessary for successful baby-sitting. Complete the bulletin board with "Do You Qualify?"

PLAY IS THE BUSINESS OF CHILDREN: Mount pictures of children playing quiet and active games, cutting and pasting, painting, listening to stories, playing with clay.

PUZZLED ABOUT TOY SELECTION?: Mount pictures of toys on construction paper cut in the abstract shapes of puzzle pieces. Complete with suggestions or guidelines for choosing toys.

Personal development

MAKING A HOUSE A HOME: Use a floor plan or outline of a house in the center. Around it mount pictures depicting scenes such as family members enjoying a meal together; parents giving their children tender, loving care; children playing; a child caring for a pet; a family entertaining friends.

YOUR COLORFUL ENVIRONMENT: Tack up an artist's palette. Around it, place large simulated dabs of paint labeled with words such as home, neighborhood, family, friends, church, recreation. Utilize labels suggested by class members.

CASH IN ON A GOOD PERSONALITY: Simulate a cash register. On rectangles made to look like dollar bills coming out of the drawer of the register, write appropriate words suggested by class members, such as: friendliness, loyalty, sincerity.

TRANSPARENCIES

Transparencies are easy to make and store in regular file folders, are readily available commercially, can be shown in a well-lit room, allow the teacher to face the class while showing them, and can be projected as large or small as desired by simply moving the projector backward or forward and focusing it. Overlays, up to about five or six sheets, can be used to build a concept sequentially. For example, a series of centrifugal circles can be placed, one at a time, to show how love grows and broadens as an individual matures. To facilitate their use, overlays can be taped together in sequence on one edge or fastened into a cardboard frame.

Making Transparencies

Transparencies can be made easily with clear, stiff plastic such as that bought by the yard or as x-ray film that is unusable for that purpose. Plastic project-folders measuring 8½ by 11 inches are inexpensive and can be split in half to provide two sheets. Felt-tipped pens, grease pencils, or special pens marketed for making transparencies can be used to write and draw on the plastic. Most colors, except occasionally yellow, reproduce and project satisfactorily. Because grease pencil rubs off easily, it is used when the material on a transparency will be removed. Grease pencil may be advantageous when figuring problems such as interest rates because the writing can be erased quickly and easily by rubbing it with a tissue or soft cloth, and then other problems can be worked on the same sheet of acetate. The transparent sheets of plastic are also ideal for tracing pictures and sketches.

Another type of transparency, which is considerably more expensive, is made by passing a sheet of acetate and the original through a heat-sensitive machine that is designed for making transparencies. This particular process transfers the image on the original to the acetate by etching it. Special sheets of acetate, marketed specifically for use with this machine, must be used for making transparencies.

Any carbon-based product such as newsprint, typewriting, or soft pencil makes an excellent medium for transferring material from paper to transparency. India ink works well, but most ballpoint pens do not copy. If a typewriter ribbon is worn or if it is not carbon-based, typing can be done by inserting a piece of carbon paper in backwards against the sheet being typed. This mirror image will process especially well. Elite and pica type are usually too small to project well unless they are shown on a very large screen. Primary type, sometimes called sight-saver or bulletin-board type, is much larger and excellent for making transparencies.

Color

Color is not transmitted from paper to acetate through transparency processing, but can be added to the etched transparency with markers, special pens, tapes, and adhesives produced specifically for this purpose. It is advisable to check the colors of tapes and adhesives by projecting small samples because colors do not always project the same as they look in the package. Acetate sheets for transparencies can be purchased in several colors so that the entire background will be viewed in one solid hue. This can add variety to presentations and may be helpful in categorizing concepts or organizing material into subtopics.

Because transparencies are rather expensive, you may want to reproduce as much material on one sheet as possible, even if all of it will not be shown at the same time. Material relating to different concepts or for use with different classes may be fastened to a background sheet of paper with transparent tape, which will be invisible after processing. These small transparency items can be cut apart and the pieces can be slipped (temporarily) into clear plastic folders for projection. This process can help to cut down on cost without creating an overcrowded and cluttered visual.

Many commercial companies sell transparencies and paper master copies. Commercial transparencies are usually framed, which helps keep them flat and easy to handle and provides a place to write notes. However, frames can make the transparencies rather large for storage in regular file folders.

Ideas for Transparencies

In studying textiles, cartoons or stick-figure sketches make effective transparencies for portraying the characteristics of various fibers. For clothing construction, the back of a pattern envelope can be reproduced to show a large group how required yardage is determined and to point out other pertinent information. Newspaper ads can be made into transparencies for use in studying consumer education.

Some topics that can be handled easily and effectively with transparencies are:

- *Child Development.* Transparencies and overlays could be used to evaluate how clothing features, eating utensils, closet arrangements, bathroom accessories, and furniture can foster or hinder independence and self-reliance in young children.
- *Grooming.* Overlays can be used to show the effects of different hairstyles on various face shapes. A series of overlays can also be used to illustrate application techniques and effects of makeup.
- *Design.* Overlays of various landscaping could be used to illustrate the principle

of placing large shrubbery at structural points and the effect of too many centers of interest.

- *Housing.* Floor plans of small homes with identical dimensions can be used with different overlays to illustrate satisfactory and unsatisfactory room and furniture arrangements, provisions for privacy and storage, and traffic patterns.
- *Management.* Sketches containing potentially hazardous conditions and ways of eliminating them can be identified and discussed by the viewers.

SLIDES

A teacher can use slides in the order that best suits the needs of a particular group, make comments about the slides as they are shown, and ask and answer questions while they are being viewed. A teacher with little skill in photography can take slide pictures or make them. The beautiful and true colors in slide projections make slides especially effective in portraying natural scenes and color harmonies. Slides are an excellent medium for showing detail in close-ups of period furniture, storage arrangements, and window decorations.

One of the most outstanding advantages of slides is that they can be used to show items of interest in the local community, such as architectural styles and features, people at work in home economics-related careers, and home-experience projects. Using slides of local scenes has great motivational value because students can identify with what they are seeing. Viewing pictures of others' home experiences may stimulate students to think of meaningful projects of their own and increase their desire to do well on the projects they choose.

Slides can be synchronized with audiotapes for a rather formal presentation. Although the tape recorder can be stopped at any time, this method may stifle a spontaneous exchange between teacher and students.

Processed slides can become quite costly but instant slides made from transparencies are inexpensive. These can be used for titles and headings, simple line drawings, and brief written directions. To make instant slides, mark a sheet of paper into rectangles measuring 1⅜ inches in width and ⅞ inch in height. Write, type, or sketch the material needed for a slide within these boundaries. Be sure to use a medium that will etch well and then process through a transparency-producing machine. Cut the rectangles apart, leaving a margin of sufficient size to place the slides in frames. The frames can be from commercially processed slides that are unusable, although frames designed specifically for making instant slides can be purchased. Keep in mind that the heat from the projector lamp can cause this type of slide to become distorted or to burn if projected for too long.

Slides are placed in a carrousel or slide holder so that the pictures are upside down and the wrong sides are facing the direction in which they will be projected. Care should be taken to ensure that slides will be projected correctly because confusion and wasted time may result when slides have to be arranged as they are shown. It is easy to preview slides with a small hand projector designed for this purpose. The preview session provides an excellent opportunity for planning the commentary and the answers to questions that will be asked during the presentation.

FILMS

A film should always be previewed before it is shown in class, unless it is familiar from prior use. This is necessary if teachers are to give students guidance for viewing it, in the form of questions that will be discussed later, points to look for, or planned follow-up activities. Without any orientation to the film, students may respond to it as entertainment and overlook its educational value. This orientation is particularly important if the clothing styles, car models, and background furnishings to be seen are out-of-date. If teachers admit these things ahead of time, but also point out that the subject matter is still valid and reliable, students will be more likely to view the film in a positive manner. Of course, a certain amount of preoccupation with outdated fashions is to be expected. Everyone should be able to enjoy a good laugh from seeing them if this does not overshadow the more desirable aspects of the film. The countdown numbers can be another distraction. If at all possible, begin showing the film at the title frame to avoid them.

Advantages of Films

Films are particularly useful for showing sequential events or stages that in actuality have considerable time lapses between them, such as developmental levels of children or steps in clothing construction, food preparation, or housekeeping. Movies also provide a common experience on which to base a discussion about interpersonal relationships. Films can be especially valuable in providing students with experiences that they would not ordinarily have, otherwise. For example, a film might show how a certain food is used around the world or how clothing styles reflect various worldwide cultures. Often, films can be stopped so that students can predict the outcome and then compare their ideas with those of the film producers. Films, unlike filmstrips, do not lend themselves well to skipping sections, although they can be shown in parts, perhaps on two consecutive days, to permit some intervening discussion.

Sources of Films

Educational films are readily available from a wide variety of sources. A school district may have a media library from which films can be borrowed. Professional organizations, universities, and nonprofit associations often lend, rent, or sell educational films. They are also available, usually for the payment of postage, from companies whose major purpose is to distribute media produced by commercial business concerns. Naturally, media financed by large companies will contain some reference to their products. However, this seldom creates a problem, and students can be asked to suggest other brand-name products with similar characteristics. When borrowing or renting films, it is the teacher's professional responsibility to see that they are returned promptly since schedules for their use are usually made many months ahead. If media are kept longer than planned, others may be inconvenienced and disappointed. When scheduling films, it is important to keep in mind that they have to be shown in a darkened room. This may present a problem in a school that is not air-conditioned if the weather is hot in the early fall or late spring. Blackout shades prevent the circulation of air through open windows.

Efficient teachers keep annotated bibliographies of films that have been used so they can be shown in the future without previewing. Index cards cataloged into general subject-matter areas can be used to file valuable information such as the name of the film, source, rental fee, length, grade levels and courses for which it is appropriate, evaluation of the film, guide questions, and follow-up learning experiences. It is a wise practice to keep a record of films previewed and judged not good enough for use, so that these will not be reordered in the future.

FILMSTRIPS

Filmstrips can provide the basis for building a meaningful lesson. They can be previewed easily, shown in part or whole, depending on class needs, and reexamined with a minimum of effort. Filmstrips are suitable for use with large and small audiences. They can provide close-up views of work that might be difficult to see clearly in a live demonstration. The medium can also cut down on the cost and time involved in an actual demonstration. Students can catch up easily, after an absence, by viewing a filmstrip individually or in a small group. A room does not have to be darkened to see a filmstrip, but it is desirable to show it in dim light. Manuals or teacher's guides and student materials that provide additional information are frequently available. Filmstrips are easy to store. They are made in a wide variety of subject areas and are often made available to schools without charge by commercial concerns. They can also be purchased at reasonable cost from various textbook and media publishers.

Filmstrips are available with and without sound. Silent filmstrips may have captions on each frame and/or a written script to be read. Records and tapes can be synchronized with filmstrips to provide continuous sound. These sound filmstrips require the use of a record player or tape recorder in addition to the filmstrip projector. A filmstrip is inserted in the projector upside down as it comes off the roll.

Although filmstrips have many advantages, they are not without limitations. Frames are in a fixed order and cannot be rearranged unless they are cut apart and made into slides. Filmstrips are not easily repaired. Those that are free usually contain elements of commercialism.

As with films, the teacher should in some way point out to the students the purposes for which a filmstrip is being viewed and its relevance to other learning. As with slides, the teacher can ask and answer questions and lead a limited discussion as frames are shown. Students can be asked to read the captions aloud. They are more likely to remain attentive when called on in a random order. Some students may enjoy participating by operating the projector.

Outdated commercial filmstrips can be used to make personalized ones. Soak the old filmstrip in a solution of half liquid bleach and half water for about 10 minutes. Then use a soft rag to rub off the original images. Allow the clear film to dry. Write or draw on it with a pen suitable for making transparencies, or use a grease pencil if the material is not to be used again. Sprinkle the filmstrip with talc, powder, toothpaste, or corn starch if you have difficulty with the ink adhering. Four holes arranged vertically on the filmstrip constitute one frame. Because this space is so limited, use only very simple line drawings and messages with few words and letters. Students enjoy these filmstrips when they relate to a school event or local activity. Students can make filmstrips to accompany their oral reports.

AUDIOTAPES

Audiotapes and recorders can be used by teachers and students for class presentations and special projects. Tapes can be synchronized to be used with slides, filmstrips, transparencies, exhibits, and displays. They can also be coordinated with examples of step-by-step procedures such as many of those used in clothing construction, food preparation, or craft making. Tapes are particularly well suited to conducting interviews and can make an immediate experience of an interview with a special person who cannot come to school.

Tapes are often an integral part of individualized study units, such as modules, learning packages, and programmed instruction. They also provide an easy method of reviewing previously covered material.

EXHIBITS

Making an exhibit can be a class endeavor, a small-group project, or an FHA/HERO activity. Exhibits can serve to provide educational information, to create interest in home economics activities, to interpret the program to others, and to bring favorable publicity to the department. Making a display can help students develop creativity, a sense of responsibility, the ability to work well with others, and leadership skills.

Places Exhibits Can Be Used

In the classroom, an exhibit may be used to show students' work. Although the types of projects exhibited by students may differ over a period of time, everyone should have an opportunity to display an assignment at some time.

There are often showcases that can be used for exhibits in the hallways, the main office, or a lobby of the school. Displays can be planned for Parent-Teacher Association (PTA) meetings, back-to-school nights, and the school or public library. A city hall or county courthouse may have facilities for showing exhibits. Museums often welcome displays made by students.

Sometimes store windows can be used. A local furniture store may provide excellent opportunities for students studying home furnishings to create room arrangements and to decorate display areas and windows. A local jewelry store or china shop might provide space and materials for a table-setting display. Students' home projects can be exhibited at a local fair where the home economics department may have a special booth.

Making Effective Exhibits

An exhibit should have only one theme, simply communicated. Writing is kept to a minimum with only enough key words to convey the message clearly. A few large items attract attention better than many small ones. It is desirable to use real objects, but if that is impossible, models are preferable to pictures. The colors and background used should strengthen the theme of the display and attract attention without being overwhelming. Sometimes the effectiveness of an exhibit can be increased if the viewer is permitted to touch the item on display.

Some ideas for exhibits in which real objects can be used are:

- Children's clothing with growth features and alterations, or home-sewn children's clothing
- Toys and books for children of various ages
- Low-cost, high-nutrition foods
- Home-experience projects such as refinished furniture and homemade furnishings
- Home accessories made from inexpensive or recycled materials

Well-planned, attractive, and effective exhibits can help bring status to the individuals and groups that prepared them as well as to the department. There is much potential value in exhibits for changing the traditional image of home economics and for establishing good public relations. If teachers avail themselves of every opportunity to inform others about home economics, the discipline will continue to grow in numbers and prestige.

GAMES FOR LEARNING 12

The types of games that can be used in teaching range from those that are simple and can be played within a relatively short period of time to those that are complex and time-consuming. All games require some degree of knowledge and many games involve a certain amount of chance. Chance enters into games when cards are drawn; when rewards are granted and penalties imposed, as in board games; or when dice, spinning wheels, or similar devices are used.

Simulation games are currently popular. They serve to isolate a portion of a life situation from its complex environment. The simulation is designed so that the players can experience some of the daily responsibilities, decisions, consequences, and pressures inherent in life or in a given situation. Through these means, people are helped to make decisions, to approach problems in a new way, and to explore areas that are new to them without suffering the consequences one is likely to encounter in life.

Since students either play according to predetermined rules or establish the guidelines themselves, the teacher is no longer the authority or judicial figure. Games, then, are one form of student-directed learning.

When implementing games in the classroom, caution must be taken so that winning does not become more important than learning. Games should not dominate the curriculum. As with other methods of instruction, if games are overused, they become ineffective.

Games that are used for reinforcement of information previously covered can be fairly uncomplicated. Commonly known card games, TV quiz shows, popular board games, and word games that involve decision-making experiences are somewhat more difficult to devise because they are more comprehensive and complicated. However, a number of well-known board games can be or have been adapted for educational use. A variety of games is available today. Many of these games are designed to simulate life situations in areas relating to consumer issues, interpersonal relationships and the clarification of values and goals.

It is very important that the purpose and the rules of the game be clearly stated and understood by all players. If the rules are written, the students can begin the game themselves, and they have a reference immediately available if a question should arise. When a player's response to a question is challenged, textbooks, periodicals, or appropriate charts and tables should be available for students to check the accuracy of the answer.

The teaching power of a game is limited only by the instructor's imagination and ability to plan meaningful follow-up questions or activities. The games and the follow-up activities can help students find pleasure in learning and, therefore, serve as a means of motivation. Following is a discussion of some noncommercial games that are especially suited to the home economics classroom.

MATCH 'EM

Match 'em is an easy game to assemble and to explain to students. The purpose of the game is to identify common equivalent measures used in food preparation when dividing or increasing a recipe.

A set of thirty playing cards is needed. Old playing cards can be backed with colored paper, or construction paper can be cut up in card-size pieces or 3-by-5-inch index cards can be used. A measurement is written on each card. For example, one card may have one-half cup and another card eight tablespoons. The finished deck must include fifteen sets of equivalents.

Directions: Lay all playing cards face down on the table. Turn two cards face up on each play. If the cards are equivalent measurements (not identical), the two cards are placed in a stack in front of the player. If the cards are equivalents, the student gets another turn. If a player does not turn up two equivalents, the next player takes a turn. When all of the cards are matched, the matches should be checked against an answer sheet. The student with the greatest number of matches wins.

CARD GAMES

Familiar card games can be used as a form of student-directed review. The rules can be simple or complex depending on the specific learning objectives for the lesson. After a card game has been played, students may want to change the rules to provide variety. The game becomes more interesting as student involvement is increased.

To play the card games described in this chapter, make a deck of 52 cards with pictures of various foods or garments that illustrate different lines, colors, and textures. Pictures of architectural and furniture styles can also be used, but it may be necessary to have some duplicates of the styles. You can use the same general style more than once, but use different pictures. You could also make 52 cards by writing on them characteristics or brief descriptions of children at various age levels; different fibers; and a variety of clothing, architecture, and furniture styles. To show how card games can be used as an educational learning experience, the area of food and nutrition has been selected for illustrative purposes here. Pictures of foods that are good sources of one or more of the following nutrients can be used: protein, fat, carbohydrate, vitamin A, B-complex vitamins, vitamin C, iron, and calcium. Some empty-calorie foods may be included. Two wild cards might be added for variety, making a total of fifty-four cards.

Cards can be made by cutting pictures of food from magazines and attaching them to small index cards. If multiple sets of cards are desired, labeled sketches of foods should be drawn in rectangles of playing-card size on a ditto or stencil master sheet. After these sheets have been duplicated, the individual pictures are cut out and attached to a firm backing.

Each of the game variations described here could be adapted to other content areas such as these:

Child development—developmental characteristics of a certain age group such as a four-year-old:

- playing in small groups with three or four friends
- beginning to share possessions and toys with "special" friends
- asking for things instead of snatching them
- seeking approval with comments such as "I'm good, aren't I?"

Textiles—characteristics of a certain fiber such as cotton:

- absorbent
- wrinkles
- durable
- can be laundered frequently

Clothing selection—lines, colors, and textures appropriate for certain body types such as the tall and slender shape:

- contrasting belt
- western yolk
- warm and bright colors
- bulky fabrics

Housing—architectural characteristics typical of a certain style such as Dutch Colonial:

- gambrel roof
- dormer windows

- story-and-a-half construction
- clapboard or shingle siding

Interior design—characteristics of a certain period of furniture such as Chippendale:

- mahogany
- cabriole leg
- pierced and carved splat back
- Chinese influence

Four of a kind—three to four players

The object: to make as many books as possible. Each book is to consist of four cards having pictures of foods that represent good sources of the same nutrient or foods from the same Basic Four food group. Wild cards can represent any food in a group or any nutrient designated by the player holding that card.

Directions:

1. Deal each person seven cards. Form a discard pile by turning one card face up. Place the remaining cards face down in the center of the table.
2. When individual players take turns, they may draw two cards from the pile that is face down or pick up the entire discard pile. The discard pile may be picked up only if the top card can be used to form a book. After completing a move, the player must put one card face up on the discard pile.
3. Place each book on the table as it is made. A book can be made and placed on the table only during a player's turn, not during anyone else's turn.
4. The game is ended when a player has no playing cards left, after having discarded. Play is also ended when there are no cards on the pile from which to draw and when the discard pile cannot be picked up by anybody. The player who has the greatest number of books wins the game.

Fishing for food—two or more players

The object: to get cards that make a nutritious meal including foods from each of the Basic Four food groups. The first person to do this wins.

Directions:

1. Scatter cards face down on the table.
2. Each player draws any five cards from those on the table. The remaining cards are left face down.
3. During each player's turn, one card is drawn and one card is discarded face down with the others.
4. Play continues until there is a winner.

Nutrition points—two or more players

The object: to identify correctly the food group, the number of servings required daily, and the function of the foods appearing on the cards.

Directions:

1. Stack cards face down. Each person turns up a card from the pile.
2. Score in the following manner:
   a. One point for identifying the food group of the item pictured on the card
   b. Two points for stating the number of servings of the food required daily
   c. Three points for telling the function of the major nutrients in the food
   d. Minus the specified number of points for incorrect answers
3. When the players have gone through the entire deck, the person having the greatest number of points is the winner.

Trading game—three or more players

The object: to collect cards that are all in the same food group.

Directions:

1. Deal the entire deck of cards to the players.
2. Players trade cards in any direction across the table by holding the card or cards face down and calling out the number of cards they want to trade. A player trades with a person who wants to exchange a like number of cards.
3. The first person who collects nine cards in any one of the Basic Four food groups receives ten points. At the end of the game, two points are deducted for any card displaying foods with empty calories. The first person to reach 100 points is the winner.

Truth or bluff—three or more players

The object: to get rid of all the cards in one's hand.

Directions:

1. The entire deck of cards is dealt.
2. In turn, each player places one to four cards face down on the table and states what the cards are. For example, the student can say, "These two cards are in the meat group." This may or may not be true.
3. The player on the left can either accept the statement or challenge it. If the statement is accepted, play proceeds to the next person. The discarded cards remain on the table. When the play is challenged, the cards must be shown. If the truth was told, the challenging player must take the cards laid down by the preceding player plus all the cards in the discard pile. If the cards were misrepresented, the player who tried to bluff must take these cards and the discard pile.
4. The first player without any cards wins the game.

Nutrition solitaire—one person

The object: to place 16 cards representing foods that are good sources of protein and vitamins A and C in a square. The square should have vitamin A-rich foods across the top, vitamin C foods at the bottom, and protein foods on the sides. The four cards in the center can represent any nutrients. Designated nutrients can be changed for different games.

Directions:

1. Place all of the cards face down on the table. Turn up one card at a time and place it where it should be, according to the designated rules.
2. The player automatically loses if a card is turned up and its line is filled. For example, if a card picturing an orange is turned up, but the line for vitamin C is filled, the player loses.
3. In order to find places for more cards and to complete the square, the player can remove from the square and discard any pair of cards in the same food group. For example, the player may take away two in the meat group, or two in the fruit and vegetable group, and so forth.
4. The game is won if the player gets the proper layout of cards. The game is lost when the player turns up a card and its designated line is full and when the deck of cards has been played through once.

ZINGO

This is an action-oriented game that can be used to review terms used in most home economics content areas. Zingo can be adapted for use in naming pieces of clothing construction and kitchen equipment; identifying clothing construction terms, nutrients, and furniture styles; and defining cooking terms. A card is needed for every student. Each card should consist of 16 different words or terms. Not all cards will have the same terms. For those cards that do have the same variation of terms, the placement of words must be different. Small squares of construction paper can be used as covers for responses.

A series of questions corresponding to the words or terms on the cards is needed. Some samples are: (1) What is the spool called that holds the bottom thread while you are machine sewing? (2) What is the diagram called that shows you how to place your pattern pieces on the fabric? (3) What do you use to find out how many inches (cm) there are around your hips, waist, and bust?

Directions: This game is a variation of bingo. When a question is read, the word or term that correctly answers it should be covered with a paper square. Players have "Zingoed" when they have covered a vertical, diagonal, or horizontal line on the game sheet. Four corners do not count.

There is one best answer for each question. The accuracy of the winner's answers should be checked. If there is an incorrect choice, the questioning continues until another Zingo winner is found. It is the teacher's responsibility to make this game a valuable learning experience by explaining why a choice may have been incorrect and by giving additional examples to illustrate correct responses.

ZINGO			
Tracing wheel	Pins	Guide sheet	Measuring tape
Thimble	Iron	Gauge	Scissors
Pattern	Bobbin	Shears	Carbon paper
Needles	Sleeve board	Layout	Pressing cloth

Some variations of Zingo include:

Cooking terms

Fillet	Julienne	Parboil	Core
Cream	Knead	Poach	Broil
Dredge	Marinate	Simmer	Baste
Fold	Pare	Sauté	Braise

Kitchen equipment

Colander	Corer	Pastry cutter	Egg poacher
Whisk beater	Ricer	Liquid drainer	Pastry brush
Meat tenderizer	Grapefruit spoon	Tongs	Pizza cutter
Egg separator	Egg slicer	Melon scoop	Skewer

Communication terms

Body language	Gestures	Poise	Attention
Conversation	Listening	Respect	Timing
Eye contact	Grooming	Posture	Introductions
Facial expression	Grammar	Smile	Rambling

HOME ECONOMICS TIC-TAC-TOE

Tic-tac-toe is a simple game to set up and play in class. The grid for the game can be drawn on the chalkboard or on a poster board. If poster board is used, cardboard "X's" and "O's" can serve as markers for the squares. The teacher or a class member can serve as the questioner and scorekeeper.

The class can decide upon an equitable means of selecting the team that goes first. The questioner then asks the first member of this team a question. Team members are not allowed to consult each other about answers. When students answer questions correctly, they place their team's mark on the grid. Team members may consult about where to place the marker. Whether or not the student answers the question correctly, the next turn goes to the other team. When a question is missed by one team, a student on the next team gets an opportunity to answer the same question. Turns for answering questions are rotated among team members.

A score of 5 points is given to each team for every marker it has on the grid. A bonus of 10 points is awarded to the team that goes tic-tac-toe. The team with the greatest number of points wins the game.

HIDDEN-CLUES PUZZLE

Hidden clues is a word game that can be used in a variety of ways. Teachers, as well as the students, can develop hidden-clues puzzles very easily. First, an important concept consisting of approximately five to twelve letters is chosen. Then words are selected that are related to the major concept. Each of these supporting words or subconcepts must contain at least one of the letters in the mystery word. Letters in the related words need to be scrambled. Finally, in the letter blanks supplied for each of the related words, circle the letter used to make the surprise answer. The following is an example of one puzzle.

Directions: Unscramble each of the following groups of letters to form two words related to consumer economics.

EHKCC	O ___ ___ ___ ___
TENITRES	___ ___ ___ ___ O ___ ___ ___
TPYNAME	___ ___ ___ ___ O ___ ___
TBDE	O ___ ___ ___
PPNRLICEI	___ ___ O ___ ___ ___ ___ ___ ___
OTEN	___ ___ O ___
RYLAAS	___ ___ ___ ___ O ___
ONAL	___ ___ O ___
TSOC	___ ___ ___ O
IFCNANE	___ O ___ ___ ___ ___ ___
NOYEM	___ ___ O ___ ___
RCGEHA	___ ___ ___ ___ O ___

Now arrange the circled letters to discover the mystery answer. These two words are important to every consumer. ("Credit rating" is the mystery answer.)

Answers

check	salary
interest	loan
payment	cost
debt	finance
principle	money
note	charge

After the puzzle is solved, the relationship of each of the words to the mystery answer should be discussed. It would be an added challenge to have students formulate a generalization using some of the hidden-clue words.

GO FORTH

Go Forth is a board game involving skill and chance. The object of the game is to answer correctly as many questions as possible. It can be played by two or more players and one questioner-scorekeeper.

The materials needed for the game are:

1. Board—The playing board should be approximately 9 inches by 14 inches or larger. Poster board or cardboard provides a firm backing. A board rendition similar to the diagram at the end of this chapter can be made. Sketches and phrases should be keyed to the specific subject.
2. Number cards—Colored construction paper is suitable for all of the cards used in the game. Numbers are to be written on cards that measure approximately 1½ inches square. Four cards numbered 1, 2, and 3, and one card numbered 4 are needed.
3. Stars—Stars are drawn on 1-inch-square cards. Approximately 50 cards are needed.
4. Dots—Dots are drawn on 1-inch-square cards. Approximately 50 cards are needed.
5. Question cards—Questions to be asked during the game should be typed or written on one side of cards about 2 inches by 3 inches or on small-size index cards. Write on the cards content questions and the number of spaces that a player can advance for giving a correct answer. Label one-third of the cards in the deck with 1, one-third with 2, and one-third with 3. The numbers may or may not relate to the difficulty level of the questions.
6. Markers–Disks or other objects are needed to serve as markers for players' board positions.

Directions: Before beginning play, shuffle the number and the question cards separately and place them on the board in the appropriate spaces. Appoint a questioner-scorekeeper to read the questions that are drawn by the players. The cards are not to be seen by the players.

1. Draw a number card and advance the number of spaces indicated.
2. Select a question card and hand it to the questioner-scorekeeper to be read aloud. If the question is answered correctly, draw a star. If the question is answered incorrectly, draw a dot.
3. Continue to draw question cards, taking turns.
4. If players land on a crossover, they have a choice of continuing on the same path or taking a shortcut.

5. When players land on a "count your dots" square, they should count the number of dots received for incorrect answers. If the count is five or more, they need to go back to the starting position and begin again. If players have ten or more dots when they arrive at the finish, they must begin again.
6. The game ends when the first player crosses the finish line. The player with the largest number of stars wins the game.

CROSSWORD PUZZLES

Crossword puzzles can be excellent devices for student self-evaluation and for reviewing key concepts of previously covered subject matter.

To construct a crossword puzzle, use a grid with intersecting lines forming small cells measuring about ½ square inch. Graph paper may be used if the squares are large enough.

Choose a concept for the puzzle topic that is broad enough in scope to have many words associated with it. Then list as many words as possible related to this topic. Ideas can be obtained by using a book index or thumbing through the pages of a text or reference book.

Select one of the longer words to be inserted either horizontally or vertically near the center of the grid. Each letter should be entered in a separate cell. Add other words that can interlock and cross one another. Be sure one word does not end at another word without a space between them. As each is used, check it off the master list of words.

Number the vertical and horizontal words as they appear in the puzzle. Begin at the upper left-hand corner of the puzzle and move horizontally on each line to the right. Write the sequential number, 1, 2, 3, 4, and so forth, in the cell that has the first letter of a word. Number the words in sequence regardless of whether they are vertical or horizontal. In other words, the numbers 1, 2, and 5 may designate horizontal words, and numbers 2, 3, and 4 may be for vertical words. Sometimes a square contains a letter that begins both a horizontal and a vertical word. In this case, the same number is used for both words.

Instead of completely filling in the unused blank spaces, which is very time-consuming and tedious, you might place an X in each unused blank. Paper-clip the puzzle to your ditto master in four corners and in one or two other places to keep it from slipping while transferring the puzzle to the master.

List the horizontal and vertical words separately and in numerical order. Write definitions, questions, or fill-in-the-blank statements appropriate for each of the words used in the crossword puzzle. These should be clearly worded and consistent in format. If the completion format is used, place the blanks at or near the ends of the sentences. See page 69 for more information about writing fill-in-the-blank items.

Students who are especially adept in language arts or particularly enjoy working crossword puzzles may like to make some to share with the class. This can also be done in small groups. The discussion that relates to making the puzzles could serve to reinforce subject-matter concepts. A Scrabble board can be used to form the word patterns.

Consumer Crossword

1 C		2 F						3 B	U	Y		4 V	E	5 T
6 R	A	T	I	N	G			A			7 P			V
E		C				8 I		N			E		9 C	
D						N		K		10 U	N	I	O	N
11 I	N	T	E	R	E	S	T				A		N	
T						T					L		T	
	12 D	O	W	N	P	A	Y	M	E	N	T		R	
13 B						L					Y		A	
U		14 R	E	15 V	O	L	V	I	N	G			C	
D		I		A		M					16 N	O	T	E
17 G	A	S		18 L	I	E	N		19 T		E			
E		K		U		N		20 S	A	L	E			
T			21 D	E	B	T			X		22 D	E	E	D

Down

1. When people use future income to meet present needs and wants, they are using ______.
2. The abbreviation for the government agency that is responsible for protecting consumers against false advertising is ______.
3. An institution with low rates of interest on loans is a (an) ______.
5. It is important to check the warranty when buying a (an) ______.
7. Late payments for a loan may have a (an) ______ charge imposed.

8. A sum of money owed and paid at specific intervals is a (an)______ .
9. A written agreement between two or more parties is a (an)______ .
13. It is necessary to plan for finance charges when making a (an)______ .
14. A person with a proven ability to pay is considered a good credit______ .
15. If money is borrowed, it should be used for something that has______ .
16. In using credit, it is essential to be able to tell a want from a (an)______ .
19. In figuring the cost of a purchase, it may be necessary to compute the sales ______ .

Across

3. It is wise to compare interest costs before deciding to______ .
4. A person may be able to finance a home at a low rate of interest if he or she is a (an) ______ .
6. An evaluation of one's ability to pay is based on one's credit______ .
10. An organization in which members pool their money and from which they can borrow is called a credit______ .
11. The rental fee paid for the use of money is______ .
12. The cost of credit is affected by the size of the______ ______ .
14. A credit plan involving minimum-sized monthly payments with interest figured on the unpaid balance is called a (an)______ charge account.
16. A written paper indicating an amount of money owed is called a (an)______ .
17. When traveling by car it may be helpful to use credit to buy______ .
18. A legal charge placed on personal property until an outstanding sum of money is paid is a (an)______ .
20. At the end of a selling season, many items are placed on______ .
21. Money owed to someone is a (an)______ .
22. A written document showing ownership of real estate property is a (an)______ .

Answers

DOWN

1. credit
2. FTC
3. bank
5. TV
7. penalty
8. installment
9. contract
13. budget
14. risk
15. value
16. need
19. tax

ACROSS

3. buy
4. vet
6. rating
10. union
11. interest
12. down payment
14. revolving
16. note
17. gas
18. lien
20. sale
21. debt
22. deed

START
YOU'RE IN CHARGE OF THE HOUSE
YOU CLEANED THE CLOSET GO FORWARD 4 SPACES
THINK HARDER
YOUR CHOICE
GOOD LUCK
HANG IN THERE!
GO BACK 3 SPACES
HAVE A SEAT
SMILE!
Take a deep breath!
YOU LEFT SPILLED WATER ON THE FLOOR
YOUR TURN AGAIN SOON
KEEP GOING

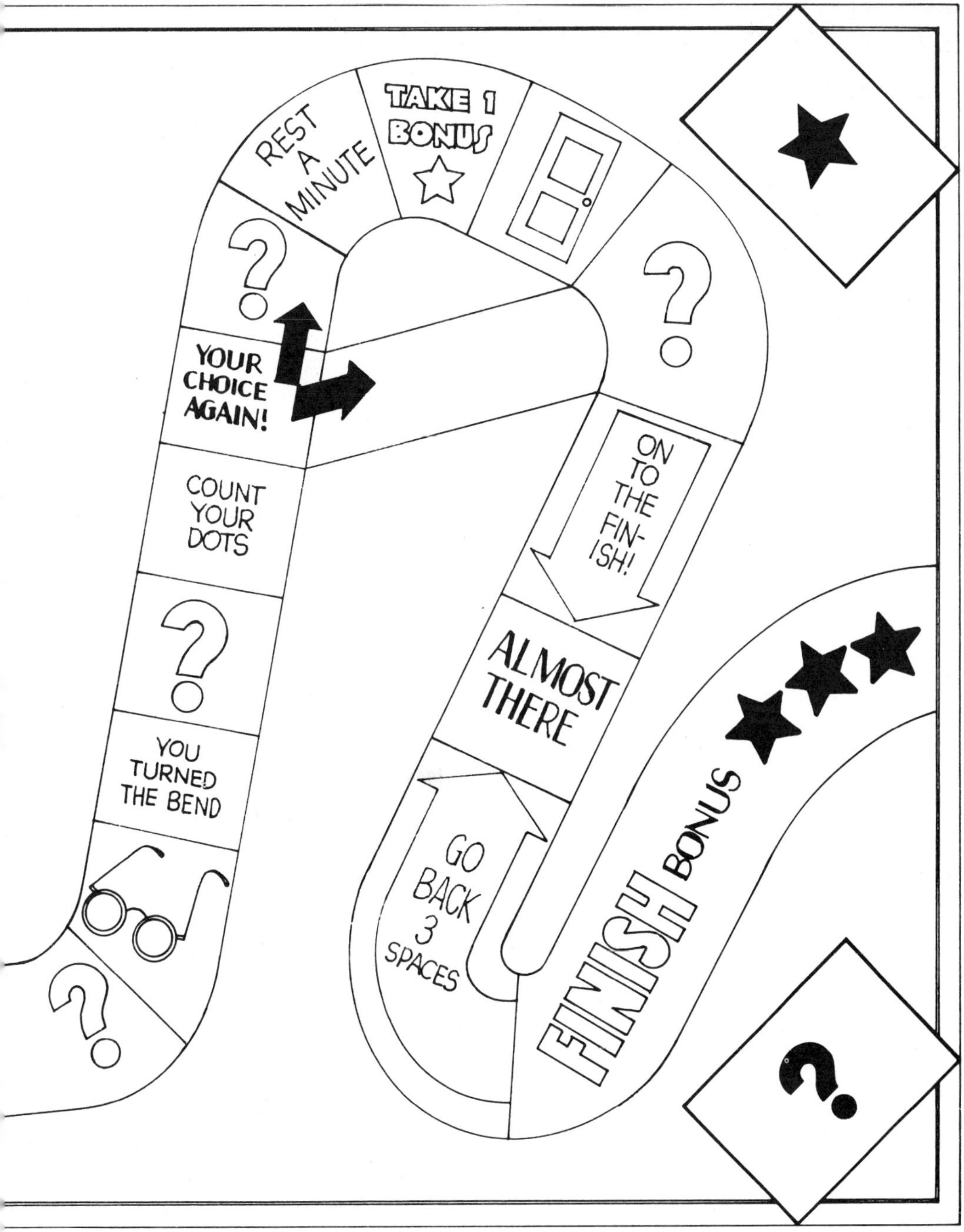
REST A MINUTE
TAKE 1 BONUS
YOUR CHOICE AGAIN!
COUNT YOUR DOTS
YOU TURNED THE BEND
ON TO THE FIN- ISH!
ALMOST THERE
GO BACK 3 SPACES
FINISH
BONUS

DEMONSTRATIONS 13

Demonstrations can be very helpful in providing maximum opportunities to learn. They can be used to show procedures, to explain new techniques, to establish standards for individual and group work, and to illustrate methods when funds or time are limited. However, it is frequently better not to give a demonstration than to give one that is poorly executed. If there isn't time to give a really well-planned demonstration, there is probably another way of presenting the material, such as through a film, filmstrip, or film loop.

The purposes or objectives of the demonstration should be absolutely clear to the person preparing and giving it as well as to the students viewing it. Many behavioral objectives for demonstrations will be in the psychomotor domain since the students are usually expected to repeat the procedure viewed or to adapt it to a similar situation. Students may apply the knowledge gained through the demonstration in a laboratory experience, at home, or in on-the-job training.

FIVE ESSENTIALS IN PLANNING GOOD DEMONSTRATIONS

First, outline the material to be covered and determine the way in which it is to be presented. A concise outline should include an introduction, the major concepts to be covered, and a summary of the main points. It is wise to review the outline and to be thoroughly familiar with its contents. Practicing the introduction will help you begin smoothly and with confidence.

Second, develop a sequential plan. A time schedule is helpful; in many cases, such as with food preparation, it is essential. Allow sufficient time for questions and discussion. List all the items needed for the demonstration and check to see that they are all available before starting. Students can often help with the pre-preparation or presentation of the demonstration. However, student participation also needs to be planned.

Third, determine the steps that can be done ahead of time or eliminated from the actual demonstration. Pre-preparation of materials and premeasurement of ingredients can help make a demonstration run smoothly and efficiently. Student interest will be lost if too much time is spent on repetitious and time-consuming tasks. However, care must be taken that none of the essential steps is omitted. A happy balance is reached when enough of the actual procedure is shown so that the viewers understand what is happening, but it is not so time-consuming that they become bored.

When there is insufficient time in food demonstrations to prepare and completely cook a product, a finished or partially finished product may be made in advance. Through such a procedure, all the preparatory steps can be viewed and the finished product can be sampled in a limited amount of time.

Fourth, select the best equipment for the demonstration and practice using it. Be sure that the equipment needed for the demonstration is in good working order and is positioned conveniently for working and viewing. Equipment should be placed close enough to the central work area so that you do not distract students by walking back and forth; yet the arrangement of equipment should not obstruct their view. A stationary or portable overhead mirror may help students see the entire procedure, particularly if the group is large.

Fifth, plan to display the finished product. If food is to be sampled, have utensils out and make provision for a clean counter or tabletop for serving. If the demonstration is such that the product demonstrated can be hung on a bulletin board or displayed on a table or tray, make these arrangements ahead of time. The display may be very simple, but it should be effective. The impact of the demonstration is lost if the end product does not sell itself.

DEMONSTRATION TECHNIQUES

1. Be prepared, so that the action will begin quickly. Opening remarks should be brief and to the point.
2. Maintain good body posture and avoid leaning on work areas. Using proper work heights contributes to good posture and lessens fatigue, an especially important consideration if the demonstration is repeated during several class periods.
3. Work at a pace that allows the students to follow the details of each step of the demonstration.
4. Practice techniques ahead of time so that manipulation becomes almost automatic.
5. Use both hands whenever possible but try to avoid crossing your hands and arms.

6. Work in full view of the students. They may become inattentive if they are too far away to see clearly or if equipment or materials obstruct their line of vision.
7. Keep the work surface neat and well organized throughout the demonstration. When the work surface is cluttered with equipment or other items, attention is diverted from the demonstration.
8. If the process or technique being shown is repetitive and time-consuming (for example, shaping nails during a manicure), plan to do enough so that the technique is understood but do not spend time completing the entire operation. Either have the demonstrated work partially done beforehand, with enough left unfinished so that it can be adequately shown and completed, or do only part of the work from the beginning and have a sample completed to show as the finished product. To save time and to be more comfortable, thread needles for hand sewing ahead of time.
9. If the nature of the demonstration is such that it should be viewed closely (for example, clothing construction techniques), provide sufficient space and a seating arrangement so that everyone will be able to see easily. If the group is too large to permit everyone to see simultaneously, demonstrate to part of the class at a time. To avoid discipline problems, make provision for the other students to be occupied constructively.
10. Items should be passed around after the demonstration. If items are passed during the demonstration, the students' attention will be diverted so that continuity and interest are lost.
11. References or resources may be provided for student use if demonstrations are complex or detailed, if students need more help, or if students are absent at the time of the original demonstration. Some possibilities include: printed illustrations and directions, step-by-step bulletin boards and posters that can be used over again, duplicated sheets with detailed directions or diagrams, and folders with samples and directions that students can use individually or in small groups. Students can also be referred to filmstrips, loops, and programmed instructional materials after the demonstration has been completed. However, if additional materials are available after every demonstration, students may come to expect and rely on them. Therefore, it may be neither necessary nor advisable to have illustrative samples after those demonstrations in which the concepts presented are relatively easy to understand.
12. Use every possible opportunity to set a good example and to illustrate proper procedures and safe practices, even though you will not actually call attention to all of them in the course of any one demonstration.

Specific Techniques To Use In Food Demonstrations

Getting ready to demonstrate

1. Cover supply trays, assembled food products, and previously prepared displays. This will create interest and an element of surprise.

2. Dress as students are expected to dress during laboratory lessons. This may include wearing an apron and a head scarf or brushing and fastening the hair so that it is away from the face. A teacher may want to wear a uniform or lab coat while demonstrating, to create a professional and authoritative image. Clothing should be simple without long ties or sleeves that could dip in the food or be dangerous near equipment. Jewelry should be kept to a minimum or removed.
3. Wash hands well before beginning and call attention to the fact that this is being done.
4. When possible, use low-cost foods that are high in nutritive value. This will not only stretch the department's budget but also show students how to cut costs. You will also have an opportunity to incorporate some subject matter relating to nutrition.

Preparing and mixing foods

1. When preparing food in a mixing bowl, leave the bowl on the table for the mixing process. A damp cloth placed under the bowl eliminates slipping and minimizes noise. Using a clear mixing bowl allows students to see the contents. When necessary, the bowl may be lifted and tilted to provide a better view.
2. Give food on a spoon a firm shake in the palm of the hand so that the material falls into the bowl. This is preferable to hitting a spoon or beater on the side of a bowl.
3. When pouring a mixture from a bowl, be careful that fingers do not come in contact with the food. Use a flexible scraper to remove the mixture quickly and easily.
4. Place a damp cloth or pastry cloth under a cutting board to prevent slipping. When working with flour, put in a container the extra flour that will be used on the board or cloth.
5. When fresh eggs are to be used, have extras on hand in case they are needed. Because an egg may be spoiled and because eggs are not always separated without getting some yolk in the white, break or separate only one at a time into a cup or small dish. Then transfer each egg to the bowl or mixture to which it is to be added.
6. When spreading a mixture on bread, leave the bread on a board and use an assembly-line technique.
7. Clean greens in advance and store them in plastic bags or clean, wet dish towels to save time during the actual demonstration.
8. Turn meats with tongs or two forks to minimize splattering.
9. Clean up spilled food immediately. Do not put food that has been spilled on the working surface back in the bowl you are using.

Being efficient and organized

1. Put ingredients and equipment needed for the recipe in the order of use.
2. Put trays in numbered order so they can be located easily. As an aid, use cards

that list the supplies to be placed on each tray. Protect cards and recipes by placing a sheet of clear plastic over them.

3. Remove a used tray from the table before a clean one is put in its place.
4. After each piece of equipment is used, place it back on the tray, not on the counter or tabletop. This makes cleaning up more efficient.
5. Place the wastebasket next to the table, not under it, so you will not have to duck to find it.
6. Line the wastebasket with a bag or newspaper to make cleaning up easier.
7. Complete the demonstration with a clean, cleared work surface. This may serve as the display area.

Using equipment and appliances

1. Put canisters, measuring equipment, rolling pins, and other items to the side when not in use. If these are placed in front, the students' view will be obstructed.
2. After a small appliance has been used, remove it from the demonstration area.
3. When an electric mixer is used, remove the used beaters to a tray before the bowl is moved.
4. Have a spoon holder or saucer on the range for used utensils.
5. When lifting a lid from a hot pan, turn it away from the body and place it upside down on the working surface.
6. Turn pot handles away from the front of the range.
7. Stand to the side of the range when opening the oven door.
8. Use potholders to pull out oven racks or to remove hot food from the oven. Leave potholders at the range but not near the burners or heating elements. Do not use paper towels or dish towels as potholders.
9. Use pans whose sizes are appropriate to burners and units.
10. Turn off the burner or unit when the cooking process has been completed. Students may be shown how to use the heat retained in electric units for cooking and warming foods.

COMMENTARY AND REMARKS DURING DEMONSTRATIONS

1. It is not necessary to talk every minute during a demonstration, but extremely long pauses may make it difficult to hold the attention of the group. When it is unnecessary to describe the process being demonstrated, use the time to add depth to the subject matter at hand. Present supplementary material or ask thought-provoking questions.
2. Use impersonal pronouns and articles such as "this," "a," or "the." This eliminates the need to use the possessive. It can be awkward to refer to "your greasy bottom" or "our liver."

3. Avoid saying "The next thing I'm going to do is . . ." Use impersonal terminology such as "The second step is . . ." It is unnecessary and distracting to announce every movement you will make.
4. Complete a sentence or thought before turning to something else.
5. Stop talking when moving from one place to another, when turning away from the group, or when handling noisy equipment or materials.
6. A good time to summarize what has been shown is when the product is being prepared for display.

INVOLVING STUDENTS IN DEMONSTRATIONS

1. Encourage students to ask questions and tell about personal experiences related to the topic being demonstrated. Ask them to give reasons for using different procedures, for variations and substitutions, and for alternative methods.
2. If it is a food demonstration, make sure that students have the opportunity to sample the product. It can be frustrating to watch food being prepared for an entire class period only to have the bell ring and the food whisked away. Capitalize on the motivation built into the fact that teenagers like to eat!
3. Let students take turns being assistants. Teenagers seem to enjoy cleaning up and washing dishes when they are away from home! Serving and passing food can be a meaningful learning activity for students with limited social experience. For example, they can be prompted to serve a guest, if one is present, first.
4. Organize advanced classes so that students give demonstrations individually, in pairs, or in small groups. Establish criteria for evaluating these demonstrations, which can be an integral part of almost any subject-matter area being studied. Students can demonstrate such varied procedures as preparing formula and feeding an infant; using, cleaning, and caring for large and small appliances; making accessories and decorative items for the home; and repairing furnishings and equipment.
5. Encourage students to show the class the procedures and techniques used for home experience projects. These demonstrations could be brief and presented during class-sharing sessions.

LABORATORY EXPERIENCES 14

Laboratory experiences can provide excellent opportunities for student participation in planning and carrying out learning activities, applying principles, and practicing desired behavior. To be truly educational, laboratory experiences must be based on concepts that have been covered in class. Basically, there are three general types of laboratories: productive, experimental, and observational.

PRODUCTIVE LABORATORIES

Planning

In productive laboratories, the emphasis is on developing psychomotor skills and gaining experience in managing resources. Although the final product may be important, the processes used to produce it are equally important.

Laboratory experiences require careful preplanning and scheduling. Tasks need to be coordinated so that precious class time is not wasted, so that all students have jobs that are challenging and meaningful, and so that situations are as realistic as possible. For these reasons, it is usually more effective to prepare and serve complete meals in food laboratory lessons than it is to make only one food product. After all, how many times in everyday life are there four or five people to make one salad, one pie, or one vegetable dish? If a student's sole contribution during an entire class period is to separate an egg, this person is likely to feel very frustrated and look upon home economics as a waste of time. If the meal-project approach is used, there may be fewer laboratory sessions because of the expense involved, but each student will have a more realistic and meaningful experience.

Students should be given some choice in deciding what foods to prepare within a meal pattern. The pattern is established so that certain identified principles of cooking are involved and specific nutrients are included. When students learn about nutrients in the foods they prepare and eat, the study will be more meaningful than when nutrition is studied as a separate unit. Instead of studying about calcium, thiamine, and vitamin A in a nutrition unit preceding food preparation, these nutrients can be covered in a meal pattern that includes milk-rich food, quick bread, and green salad. The importance of calcium can be reemphasized, and protein and vitamin C can be studied when preparing foods within a meal pattern of: a fruit salad, a meat-extender dish, and a milk-rich dessert.

Appropriate principles, such as those used in milk cookery, are studied and then applied through laboratory experiences. When using the meal-pattern approach in food and nutrition laboratories, it may take a week to complete the appropriate learning activities. If a one-unit kitchen group in a home economics class is divided into subgroups consisting of two or three students, the schedule might be like this:

MONDAY

Group A Plan own menu in quantity to serve the large-unit kitchen group, select recipes, make out market order, develop work schedules.

Group B Follow same procedure as Group A with own menu.

TUESDAY

Group A Pre-prepare as much food as possible for serving the next day (Wednesday).

Group B Pre-prepare as much food as possible for serving on Thursday.

WEDNESDAY

Group A Complete final preparation. Serve meal to entire unit kitchen group. Clean up with help of Group B.

Group B Work on assignment relating to meal pattern for the week or evaluate management skills and preparation techniques used by Group A. Enjoy meal. Help Group A clean up.

THURSDAY

Group A Work on assignment relating to meal pattern or evaluate management skills and preparation techniques used by Group B. Enjoy meal. Help Group B clean up.

Group B Complete final preparation. Serve meal to entire unit kitchen group. Clean up with help of Group A.

FRIDAY

Group A Evaluate laboratory experience and complete related assignments.

Group B Follow same procedure as Group A.

Of course, if funds will not permit serving all students on both days, the meal can be planned for only the two or three students. However, bear in mind that planning and serving meals for four or five is, for most students, more like their present home situations. It is also possible to serve only one subgroup in a given week and to serve both subgroups another week to vary the quantities in which students prepare foods.

A work schedule should be developed that designates the tasks to be performed by each student and the time at which each should begin. Asking students to make time schedules that are unrealistic can greatly diminish student enthusiasm for home economics. The following example provides enough detail to show the teacher that each student has specific tasks to perform, that the sequence is logical, and the approximate time allowed for each step is appropriate.

MEAL PATTERN: fruit salad, meat-extender dish, milk-rich dessert

MENU

Citrus Mold
Individual Hamburger Pizzas
Custard
Milk

TUESDAY—PRE-PREPARATION DAY

Student A

1:00—Comb hair, put on apron, wash hands.
1:03—Cook hamburger meat.
1:10—Prepare other ingredients for pizza sauce.
1:15—Cook sauce, stirring occasionally.
1:18—Prepare eggs and sugar for custard.
1:25—Pour scalded milk over eggs and sugar; stir custard mixture.
1:38—Begin to clean up.
1:53—Check out.

Student B

1:00—Comb hair, put on apron, wash hands.
1:03—Prepare gelatin using ice cubes.
1:13—Scald milk for custard.
1:18—Prepare orange and grapefruit slices.
1:30—Add fruit to gelatin mixture.
1:35—Clean lettuce and store.
1:43—Pour custard into serving dish; refrigerate.
1:45—Help with cleanup.
1:53—Check out.

WEDNESDAY—SERVING DAY

Student A

1:00—Comb hair, put on apron, wash hands.
1:03—Roll hamburger buns flat.
1:08—Pour pizza sauce on buns, bake at 350° for 10 minutes.
1:11—Set table.
1:16—Pour milk.
1:18—Serve meal.
1:38—Begin to clear table.
1:40—Wash dishes.
1:53—Check out.

Student B

1:00—Comb hair, put on apron, wash hands.
1:03—Warm pizza sauce.
1:06—Unmold gelatin salad.
1:10—Place salad on lettuce leaves, refrigerate; help set table.
1:16—Put custard in dishes.
1:18—Serve meal.
1:38—Begin to clear table.
1:40—Dry dishes.
1:53—Check out.

It is often helpful to have a poster, indicating a general time schedule, to which students can refer. After observing this chart based on a 55-minute class period, it should be obvious to students that they have to use every minute to their best advantage.

If the teacher will allot 2 or 3 minutes for a check-out at the end of a foods laboratory session, many problems that are associated with leaving a disorderly laboratory can be avoided. At the designated check-out time, students should be in their kitchen units with drawers and cupboard doors open. Then the teacher can observe three or four items, varying the items checked for each laboratory session, to see that they are clean and in the proper place. Only after this quick check are the students in that kitchen group dismissed to go to their next class. This procedure ensures that the facilities are left in order for the next group using them.

While students in one group are preparing their menu, the others can be engaged in worthwhile activities. These might include reading about, and answering questions pertinent to, foods and nutrients emphasized in the meal pattern for that week; planning menus for a day to accompany the one being served; and observing and evaluating the students who are working in the laboratory at that time. Students in one subgroup may evaluate those in another subgroup by completing checklists or rating scales relating to laboratory work habits or by conducting time and motion studies. For example, the students who are not serving on a particular day could draw or be given a scaled sketch of their group's kitchen. On this, they could trace the movements of the other group members who were serving that day. Lines drawn in different colors might show the pattern made by each of the working students. Later the movements can be analyzed by pointing out unnecessarily repeated movements or by explaining what could have been done differently to conserve time and energy.

Evaluation

Whether students are evaluating themselves or other students, the methods used should be changed frequently. After students have used the same rating device several times, they tend to lose interest in it, which affects the quality of their evaluations.

Evaluating a foods laboratory experience

See pages 79–81 for a checklist and rating scale that could be used to evaluate food and nutrition laboratory lessons. The following, with open-ended questions, suggests another format. These instruments can be used by individual students, students working in groups, or the teacher. On evaluation forms used during consecutive laboratory lessons, you can emphasize different concepts such as nutrition, cost of the menu, and meal service. Appropriate questions can be developed for other concepts, as well.

MENU

1. What factors contributed to a pleasing menu?
2. How could the menu have been improved?

WORK SCHEDULE

1. In what ways was the work schedule helpful?
2. What time-saving principles were used by members of the group?
3. How could the work schedule have been improved?

MARKET ORDER

1. In what ways was the market order well planned?
2. How could the market order have been improved?

PRINCIPLES OF COOKING

1. What principles of cooking were practiced because of the choice of menu?
2. What new principles were learned by the group during this laboratory session?

TABLE SETTING

1. What were the good points about the table setting?
2. What points could have been improved?

CLEANUP

1. In what ways was the cleanup managed efficiently?
2. In what ways could the cleanup have been managed better?

PERSONAL WORKING RELATIONSHIPS

1. In what ways did members of the group work well together?
2. How could the work load have been distributed more fairly?
3. How could personal relationships be improved among group members?

Evaluating a clothing laboratory experience

In all types of productive laboratories, students will be most highly motivated if they have some opportunity for selecting their projects. Some teachers may not feel that they can handle the situation in a clothing construction laboratory if all the students are using different patterns, but students can be offered choices among alternatives. A number of patterns appropriate for different ability levels and figure types can be designated as those from which students may make their selections. It is unjustifiable to cover concepts relating to line, design, and color and then to expect everyone in a class to make identical garments.

It may be easier for a teacher to evaluate specific features while a garment is being constructed than to judge many completed projects all at one time. By using periodic evaluations, students are helped to see the strengths and weaknesses of their work as it progresses and to make improvements as they continue. There is also value in having students judge their work as it progresses and compare and discuss their evaluations with the teacher.

The following checklist would be appropriate for use with beginning students.

STAYSTITCHING: Rate the quality of your staystitching by placing a check mark in the appropriate column. Total the points assigned and put this number in the space provided. The highest possible number of points is 30.

Desirable qualities	Comments	5 Excellent	4 Very Good	3 Good	2 Fair	1 Poor
1/2 inch from seam allowance						
Even distance from cut edge						
Stitched in proper direction						
10–12 stitches per inch						
Proper machine tension						
Same color thread as garment						

TOTAL POINTS ____________

It is recognized that a simple evaluation device like this implies that all the qualities listed are of equal importance. This may not necessarily be true. However, if comments are given, this shortcoming can be minimized.

See below and p. 166 for the chart and instructions for evaluating work on facings. The facings checklist would be appropriate for more advanced students.

FACINGS: Rate the quality of your facings by placing a check mark in the appropriate column. Total the points assigned and put this number in the space assigned. The highest possible number of points is 50.

By using a series of checklists like these, points can be accumulated to help determine a final grade. Provision must be made for adjusting the total point value when all the identified clothing construction techniques are not included in all students' projects.

Desirable qualities	Comments	5 Excellent	4 Very Good	3 Good	2 Fair	1 Poor
Intersecting seams pressed open and flat						
Seams graded with wider seam allowance toward right side of garment						
Seams clipped or notched as needed						
Understitching straight and 1/8 inch from seam allowance						
Understitching through facing and both seam allowances						
Clean finishing done without tucks						
Facings pressed flat						
Hand-tacking inconspicuous						
Facing cannot be seen from right side of garment						

TOTAL POINTS ____________

EXPERIMENTAL LABORATORIES

Problems researched through experimental laboratory sessions often dictate that scientific methods be used. Using experimental methodology helps give home economics status in the eyes of those who think of it only as "stitchin' 'n eatin'." Preferably, students will experiment to seek answers to questions rather than to prove facts already clear to them. The learning experiences suggested here can be developed using scientific and experimental methods.

Students should realize that experimental methodology requires a control for each experiment. If a comparison is to be meaningful, it must be a comparison of the effects different procedures have on samples of the same test object. For example, to check the effect chlorine bleach has on nylon fabric as compared with nonchlorine bleach, three samples of the fabric must be tested: one with each bleach and, for the control, one with no bleach.

Food and Nutrition

- Conduct experiments to determine the effects of various cooking temperatures and food-preparation techniques on different food products. For example, ascertain the smoking point of fats such as margarine, vegetable oil, shortening, and animal fat. Use these findings to develop guidelines for frying foods such as eggs, potatoes, and chicken. Prepare piecrusts using a variety of techniques and different fats. Compare the results for taste, appearance, and cost. Hard-boil and hard-cook eggs to determine if there are differences in flavor, texture, and color. Vary the baking temperature and the amount of beating for the same cake or muffin batter and note differences in shape, texture, and color. Vary the temperature and method of cooking small samples of tender and less tender cuts of meat. Draw generalizations from these experiments.
- Weigh three differently priced varieties of ground beef so as to make three exactly equal portions of each, or nine meat patties in all. Cook one sample of each variety to the same degree of doneness by frying; then cook one of each by broiling, and then by charcoal broiling. Weigh each portion after cooking to determine the amount of fat lost. Compare and contrast for flavor and appearance. Draw conclusions from this experiment. Using the same method of preparation, quality, and quantity of ground beef, salt the patties before, during, and after cooking. Report on what you learned by doing these experiments.
- Follow each of these procedures: Gently spoon sifted flour into a cup and pack flour into a cup without sifting, tapping frequently. Sift each of these and remeasure. Determine procedures to be followed when measuring flour. Predict what might happen when preparing baked products if these procedures are not followed.
- Use standardized tables of substitutions to interchange several food items in a recipe. Evaluate products made for possible variations in quality and nutritive value. Explain why each of the foods listed in a table of substitutions can be exchanged for the other. Determine if all substitutions are reciprocal.
- Experiment with different spices and flavorings on a variety of food products to find out which have a high degree of acceptance. After preparing foods using different condiments in varying amounts, ask a panel of judges to rate the products on a continuum. Use these ratings to develop special dishes designated as "Some of ______ High School's Favorite Recipes."

Clothing and Textiles

- Use a variety of cleaning agents, common household products, and methods to remove different types of spots and stains, such as those caused by fruit juices, coffee, chocolate, grease, lipstick, blood, and ink on a variety of fabrics. Utilize the findings of the experiments by removing common spots and stains on different types of fabrics.

- Experiment with a variety of fabrics made from different fibers and with various finishes to ascertain the effects of several laundering techniques. Before beginning, outline the size of each fabric sample on a piece of paper, indicating the lengthwise and crosswise grain. Wash in hot, warm, and cold water for different time periods to note if there is shrinkage and, if so, how much. Press fabric swatches at several temperature settings to note effects on different fibers and finishes. Keeping the fabric, type of soil, and water temperature the same, experiment using cold-water detergents, soaps, bleaches, presoaks, and enzyme-spray products to compare results and cost. Establish guidelines for washing family laundry.
- Dry fabrics of varying fiber content and with different finishes, using a clothes dryer set for several time and temperature readings. Remove some fabrics immediately after the cycle is finished and leave others to cool in the dryer. Hang items such as knit shirts, underwear, and washable slacks on a clothesline, using a variety of techniques. Determine which methods minimized puckering, stretching, and the amount of pressing needed. Make a list of suggestions for machine- and line-drying clothes.
- Conduct weathering experiments with fabrics of different fiber content. Hang some swatches indoors where they get a lot of sun and leave others outdoors. Note changes in color, strength, and the degree of disintegration after established periods of time. Make generalizations about fibers that are most and least suitable for curtains, draperies, and outdoor areas.

Consumer Education

- Compare a variety of commercial products designated for cleaning ovens, washing windows, polishing furniture, cleaning and waxing floors, and shampooing carpets. Consider the results, time and energy required to do the job, and cost involved. Compare and contrast commercial products designed for one purpose with common all-purpose household products, such as ammonia, for cleaning ovens and windows. Block off the floor in the home economics laboratory into several equal sections that receive about the same amount of traffic. Try various types of cleaners and floor waxes on each portion. Compare and contrast the sections of the floor one, two, and three weeks later. Make a generalization about the cost of household products in relation to their effectiveness.
- Use several varieties of household cleaning-equipment items such as different types of vacuum cleaners, mops, and rug shampooers. Determine the variety of tasks for which each can be used. Compare and contrast the items for efficiency, cost, care required, and features such as warranties and local facilities for repairing or replacing parts.
- Compare and contrast baked products such as cakes, muffins, and pies made from scratch with those made by using convenience foods. Consider flavor,

texture, appearance, cost, ease of preparation, time involved, and freshness after varying lengths of time. Suggest situations in which it would seem advisable to buy a specific food product already completely prepared, to use a mix, or to make the product from scratch. List the advantages and disadvantages of using convenience foods.

Management

- Store different types of foods in the refrigerator and freezer using various products for wrapping, such as plastic bags closed with metal twisters, foil, waxed paper, and heat seals, as well as different types of containers. Leave some products (such as carrots) uncovered in the refrigerator and (ice cream) uncovered in the freezer. After specified periods of time, compare the products for flavor, texture, and freshness. Experiment with freezing eggs, tomatoes, and potatoes in different forms. Establish guidelines for storing and freezing different food items.
- Practice making a bed until the most efficient system is determined. Demonstrate to others how to make the bed this way. Then have time trials or relay races to see how fast a bed can be made while meeting standards of performance established previously.
- Use these two procedures to clean rooms that get about the same amount and type of use:
  1. Clean the ceiling, walls, and draperies first; dust the furniture next; vacuum the floor last.
  2. Vacuum the floor first; dust the furniture next; clean the ceiling, walls, and draperies last.

  Check the rooms three days later. Establish an efficient procedure for cleaning rooms.

Evaluation

The most educationally valuable part of any laboratory experience should be the evaluation. It is during this time that generalizations are formulated and conclusions are drawn about the work done. Questions are posed, such as "Why did this happen (or not happen)?" Without evaluation, the laboratory activity tends to become an end in itself, if not just busywork. If students follow instructions and carry out an experiment without making generalizations about what they have done, they are unlikely to acquire the understanding originally intended.

OBSERVATIONAL LABORATORIES

In observational laboratories, the teacher must furnish guidance so that students have a clear understanding of what they should be noting. The student views situations and phenomena so that certain concepts will become clearer. Usually students are expected to draw conclusions and to make judgments about what they have observed. Although learning experiences of an observational nature are most often associated with child development, they are actually relevant in studying all areas of home economics.

Food and Nutrition

- Have a "treasure hunt" to point out unsafe practices that have been planted in a roped-off laboratory kitchen or drawn in a sketch. Use items such as these:
  1. Potholder near a burner
  2. Pot handle turned toward the front of the range
  3. Coffee pot cord extending over the edge of the range
  4. Unlabeled bottles containing poisonous chemicals stored under the sink
  5. Knives left on the counter top

  Develop a set of guidelines for kitchen safety.
- Observe mold as it develops and grows. Leave vegetables, fruit, or meat in the refrigerator for extended periods of time. Moisten bread, place it in a closed container, and leave it in a warm and humid place for several days. Using the findings from the experiment, make a list of suggestions for storing these foods.
- View a display showing the different forms in which milk is available commercially and the various types of cheeses. Have a tasting party. Compare costs and nutritive values. Suggest ways in which each of the forms of milk and cheese can be served and used in cooking.

Consumer Education

- Observe eggs, both in the shell and as raw eggs displayed on a small plate, in the grades and sizes that are available locally. Note differences. Also view various grades of meat, poultry, and canned fruit or vegetable products. Determine factors that would affect the selection and use of each of the grades by comparing appearance, texture, flavor, and cost.
- Visit a grocery store to observe the location and placement of specialty and novelty items that are unlikely to be on a shopping list. Note the position of staple foods, dairy products, and nonfood items. Discuss the techniques used that may influence a consumer to buy more than was planned. Discuss factors that influence the choices a person will make when grocery shopping.

Management

- Observe demonstrations by classmates or guest speakers in which they exhibit efficiency and skill in performing specialized tasks such as decorating cakes, setting in sleeves, or dovetailing kitchen chores. Notice techniques used to save time and energy.
- Watch classmates make the same single dishes or simple meals in a U-shaped, L-shaped, and one-wall kitchen (or whatever layouts are represented in the home economics department). Trace the steps of the cooks on scaled floor plans of the kitchens. Measure the total length of the lines drawn. Determine in which types

of kitchen the cook walked most and least. Discuss whether that necessarily makes this the best type of kitchen. Why, or why not? Other than the shape of the kitchen, what influenced how much the cook walked? What conclusions can you draw from this time-and-motion study?

- Use the layout of a local grocery, with the fixed location of various types of products, to trace in colored pencil or with string the probable route followed by a homemaker using a disorganized and jumbled shopping list. Make a grocery list, including the same items, that fits the arrangement of this store. In other words, list the products to be bought so the homemaker can begin at one end of the store and go up and down each aisle once, without backtracking. Measure the distances covered by shoppers using the different procedures. Decide which part of the store should be visited last, just before checking out, and why.

Child Development

- View children's TV programs. Develop a checklist for judging programs for children of various ages. Rate some programs using the checklist. Make a list of suggestions for improving the programs and send it to the appropriate networks.
- View a display of children's clothes that illustrates features such as these:
  1. Expansibility–clothes that grow with children
  2. Self-help items–clothing that enables children to help dress and undress themselves
  3. Special features–mittens or feet that are part of sleepwear or outerwear

  These clothing items may be borrowed from a store or brought to class by students. Discuss the desirable and undesirable features of each garment from different standpoints:
  1. Ease of putting on and taking off the garment
  2. Self-help features
  3. Comfort
  4. Washability and ease of care
  5. Durability
  6. Safety
- Relate scenes observed in a laboratory at school, or in a child-care facility, in which children seemed to illustrate social and emotional maturity or immaturity for their presumed ages. Tell whether adults, involved in the situations where immature behavior was displayed, seemed to handle them well or poorly.
- Observe preschool-age children, other than one's own brothers or sisters, in any three of the following situations:
  1. At play
  2. At mealtime
  3. Being dressed or undressed
  4. On a shopping trip or other outing
  5. Going to bed for a nap or for the night

  Observe the children on a playground or in nursery school, Sunday school, the neighborhood, a store, or their homes. Use the same child for all three observations or use different children. In the observation report answer questions such as these:

1. How old were the children? If you do not know for sure, how old do you think they were? What were they doing that helped you judge their ages?
2. How did the children react in these situations? Why did they react these ways?
3. What provisions were made to let the children do things for themselves? Did they? Why, or why not?

- Visit child-care facilities and observe the children, teachers, toys, equipment, furnishings, and kitchen facilities. Note the precautions taken to maintain the children's health and to promote their safety. Evaluate the child-care facilities visited, by answering questions such as those in the following checklist. However, fill out the checklist after leaving, not while visiting, the child-care center.

Features to look for in a child-care facility

Answer the following questions with a yes or no and be prepared to justify your answers.

1. Is the child-care facility licensed?
2. Is there adequate space indoors to move about freely while skipping, running, and dancing?
3. Is there adequate space indoors to build with blocks, to play house apart from the group, and to paint without being jostled?
4. Is there adequate space outdoors for running, climbing, and tricycle riding?
5. Is the outdoor equipment suitable for the developmental levels of the children attending the facility?
6. Is there some place outdoors for playing quietly if children choose to do this?
7. Are the toys and equipment sturdy, clean, and safe?
8. Are there blocks, balls, dolls, housekeeping toys, dress-up clothes, large- and small-wheel toys and puzzles easy enough for young children to do?
9. Are there easels, paint, clay or dough, crayons, scissors, and plenty of paper for many uses?
10. Are there games and toys that help children learn about shapes and sizes?
11. Are there tables and chairs that are the right size for working comfortably with both feet on the floor?
12. Does the program seem to meet the needs of growing children?
13. Are there quiet times for rest, stories, conversation, and refreshments?
14. Are there free play periods when children can choose what they want to do?
15. Is there time for the children to make things for themselves and to grow in creativity and independence?
16. Are the work periods of short duration so the children do not lose interest?
17. Do the teachers seem to show interest in the children as individuals?
18. Do the teachers seem to be constantly alert to the safety of the children?
19. Are the children supervised constantly?
20. Do the children seem happy?

By going over questions like these before visiting child-care centers, students have been given some guidance toward making their observations meaningful experiences. It is recognized that many other points could be included in such a checklist. These questions are suitable for students with very limited experience in child development and serve to help them become aware of only a few of the features to consider in selecting a child-care facility. Furthermore, these are questions that one should be able to answer by observation only, without having to distract the facility employees by asking them to furnish additional information. Students can be encouraged to add their own questions to a checklist like this one.

In observational laboratory lessons, students are not physically involved, as they are in productive and experimental laboratories. However, with appropriate guidance and direction in observation, students should be just as involved intellectually, and should be learning just as much, as in other types of activities.

TEACHER GUIDANCE

Laboratory lessons require careful planning by both the teacher and students if the activity period is to run smoothly and available time is to be used to the best advantage. If the lessons preceding laboratory work have provided students with essential background material, most students should be able to work with a reasonable degree of independence and cooperation. However, students do not need to know everything about a subject before participating in a laboratory experience. In fact, if too much time is spent on meal planning, table setting, and kitchen management before the first foods laboratory lesson, the teacher may have failed to capitalize on the inherent motivation students have for this type of activity. The best procedure seems to be to guide students into selecting comparatively simple activities at first, so they can have a sense of achievement, and to provide just enough background in the subject beforehand to enable them to carry out the planned activities successfully. Related concepts can be covered in greater depth as the unit progresses and can be interspersed between subsequent laboratory lessons.

Students who ask for help loudly and repeatedly tend to monopolize the teacher's attention. If, however, the instructor makes the effort, there are procedures that can be used so that all those who need individual guidance are likely to get it. In some classrooms, students write their names on the chalkboard as they need assistance. The teacher helps them in the order in which their names appear on the list. Another system that can be used is to have a set of numbered cards the students may pick up in order. The teacher gives guidance to pupils who have requested it by calling out their respective card numbers in sequence order.

The problem of students becoming overdependent upon the teacher can be a very real one. Sometimes, rather than answer students' questions directly during a laboratory lesson, the skillful teacher can ask questions of the students instead, until the correct responses become apparent to them. Students can be guided to ask, "Is this what I do next?" rather than "What do I do next?" The first question suggests that the student has given the problem some thought and has tried to arrive at a suitable solution. The latter question suggests that the student has come to expect the teacher to do most of the thinking and problem solving.

During the laboratory period the teacher should supervise all the groups, making sure that guidance is not limited to only a few. This gives the teacher an opportunity to observe the managerial processes used and the interpersonal relationships among students.

MANAGING LABORATORIES

The teacher who is secure and has the students' respect will not hesitate to pitch in and help clean up the lab. If students realize that the lab is really theirs and not the teacher's, they are likely to take pride in it and cooperate in keeping it orderly.

Cleanup charts can be used so that duties are rotated every few days or once a week. The following might be suitable for an all-purpose laboratory. Students can suggest the jobs that need to be done because these will vary from one situation to another.

MANAGEMENT MATRIX

Duties	Weeks						
	9-1	9-8	9-15	9-22	9-29	10-6	10-13
Check roll	1	8	15	6	13	4	11
Straighten supply cabinets	2	9	16	7	14	5	12
Dust	3	10	1	8	15	6	13
Put chairs and tables in order	4	11	2	9	16	7	14
Sweep floor	5	12	3	10	1	8	15
Water plants	6	13	4	11	2	9	16
	7	14	5	12	3	10	1

STUDENTS

1. Booker	9. Angelina
2. Jim	10. Beth
3. José	11. Camilla
4. Jill	12. Eileen
5. John	13. Rachel
6. Marty	14. Jeff
7. Lisa	15. Eva
8. Ann	16. Sandy

At the end of a unit or the term, devise a system that will ensure that all students have some responsibility in the final cleanup. For example, when classes have concluded their work in the food and nutrition laboratory, make a list of all the jobs that must be done in order to "close up shop." Include as many tasks as there are students in all the classes that have been using the lab. Then duplicate the list and cut one copy into strips. Each student draws a slip from a bag or box. On the master sheet, a copy of the list that has not been cut into strips, write students' names next to the jobs for which they are responsible. By doing this, you can check later to see how well each student has performed the assigned task. Those who have done poorly can be asked to do their jobs again, and those who have done well can be complimented and thanked.

DISADVANTAGES

Laboratory work may present problems for the novice teacher who does not yet realize how much longer it takes teenagers to complete a project than it does adults, or how much longer it takes a group to perform some tasks than it does a person working alone. If a class is large, there may not be room or sufficient equipment for everyone to work at once, and the teacher may not be able to provide continuous guidance. If the teacher does not supervise adequately, the students may not practice the skills they are supposed to be mastering. Furthermore, the freedom and informality in a laboratory situation may lead to excessive talking and wasting time if students are not highly motivated and if planning and organizing have been haphazard.

Unfortunately, laboratory experiences often result in low-level projects that are neither challenging nor motivating. Making an apron usually has much less appeal to a teenager than making an item of clothing that is popular at the time and will be worn where peers of both sexes congregate. Similarly, making muffins, biscuits, and other quick breads year after year is not very challenging or stimulating.

Laboratory lessons are expensive, not only in a financial sense but also in terms of time, material, equipment, and facilities. When laboratory sessions become everyday routine, little learning takes place in spite of the practical experience gained and the entertainment value inherent in them. When teachers rely on too many laboratory lessons, they fail to provide the variety and stimulating environment that challenge students and foster creative activity.

ADVANTAGES

Laboratory lessons provide an excellent opportunity for students to have input into the teaching-learning process by direct participation in planning, organizing, and carrying out individual and group projects. Students are encouraged to be creative and resourceful and to manage their resources advantageously. They are also provided with opportunities to generalize and to apply generalizations in new situations.

Laboratory lessons can furnish favorable circumstances in which students may practice desired behaviors under supervision and with guidance. Students work with concrete problems rather than with abstractions. In addition, laboratory experiences may help clarify concepts for those who have difficulty with verbalizations. For many, the greatest advantage of laboratory work may be the experience of working and learning to get along well with others in a democratic situation.

HOME EXPERIENCES 15

Home economics experiences outside the classroom began with what were called home projects. Today these activities are not limited to students' homes. Many meaningful learning opportunities exist in the community and may be available in the student's place of employment. They may be called extended out-of-class experiences, outreach activities, coordinated experiences, extended learnings, or individualized extended experiences (IEE). The term *home experiences* is used in this chapter to include all of these.

No matter where home experience projects are conducted, they should make significant contributions toward the students' growth and provide realistic opportunities for reinforcing and applying home economics subject matter. Home experiences can capitalize on individual students' interests. Ideally, projects are selected, planned, and evaluated by the student with support and guidance from the school and home. Some schools or school districts require home experience projects; others handle them on an informal basis. The teacher who is new to a school system will want to check to find out if there is an established policy in regard to this.

IMPLEMENTING A HOME EXPERIENCE PROGRAM

As with any activity, home experiences stand little chance of being completed successfully if they are viewed by students as an assignment imposed by the teacher. Teachers who present out-of-school learning experiences in an enthusiastic manner, who have ideas related to each unit of study, and who are knowledgeable about their students' backgrounds will be better able to guide students toward a satisfactory selection of their home experiences and achievement in meeting their goals.

When classes first meet, many teachers have their students complete personal data sheets. By doing this, teachers have access to information that is useful in counseling students. The data sheets can include items related to personal and family background: family members currently living at home, family interests, individual interests, activities and responsibilities at home and away from home, and personal goals for the next few years. Unless a teacher is very familiar with school policies and community attitudes, he or she should ask an administrator to check over the proposed personal data sheet before it is given to students to complete. This may minimize the chance of having items on it that could be offensive to some groups in the local area.

There are a variety of ways to stimulate students' thoughts about possible home experiences. The teacher might suggest a few interesting ideas initially and then through a discussion solicit additional student ideas. Another way to obtain suggestions from a group is to conduct a brainstorming session that would provide a variety of ideas to be refined or clarified later. The teacher might promote a problem-solving situation in which some information is given about a hypothetical student's plight in identifying a home experience. Students can then be led to ask significant questions and offer possible solutions for the problem. An additional idea would be to invite students and/or graduates who have successfully completed home experiences to share their observations in planning, implementing, and evaluating projects. It is important that graduates include some of the problems they faced. If former students are not available to share their experiences with others in person, an audiotape correlated with slides of various projects could be used to create interest. Pictures illustrating a variety of home experiences that were completed during previous school terms could be used to make a thought-provoking bulletin board. Include the name of the student who did the project.

An explanation of the home experience program should be provided for the students' families before individual class members become involved in extensive planning. This may serve to foster closer cooperation between the home and the school. An open house in the home economics department can be held to interpret the program. Telephone conversations, home visits, or letters written by either the teacher or students may serve the same purpose. See pages 178 and 179.

Planning the home experience is one of the most crucial elements of the activity. Carelessly made plans often produce poor results and can affect a student's attitude toward the other aspects of a program. It is essential that students understand the importance of the planning stage. The plans do not have to be elaborate, but they should include the objectives, the proposed steps to be taken, the resources available, the approximate costs, and provisions for record keeping and evaluation. A simple home experience report form providing for the planning and evaluation phases follows. It simplifies paperwork for the student and the teacher if the statements relating to planning appear on one side of the page and the evaluation statements are produced on the reverse side. See page 180 for an example of a simplified home experience report form.

POSSIBLE LETTER TO EXPLAIN HOME EXPERIENCE AND HOME-VISITATION PROGRAMS

Since it may be some time before I can meet you personally, I hope that this letter will help you better understand the home economics program at (name of school). The work this (term or year) in (name of course) will include these topics:

(Major concepts to be covered)

____

____

____

____

Every student is expected to complete an extended home experience project as one of the requirements for (name of course). Since this project usually takes a considerable amount of time, may involve other family members, and may involve spending some money, it is hoped that you will discuss plans for the project at home. It is important that you approve the proposed project and support the plans made to carry it out.

The home experience project should involve more than practicing some skill learned at school. The project should involve setting a goal, planning ways to reach this goal, and judging how well and to what extent this goal has been reached. If I can help in planning the home experience project, please call me at (telephone number), and I will return your call. Perhaps I can visit you in your home or where you work to discuss this project.

Making home visits is an important part of the home economics program. This year I hope to visit the homes of many of my students. If this is not possible, we may make plans to meet some other way. Perhaps a home visit will be helpful in the future to discuss the home experience project as it progresses or to judge its value when it is completed.

Sincerely yours,

(NAME)

PRELIMINARY PLAN FOR HOME EXPERIENCE PROJECT

Your name ______________________________ Class________ Period________

Home economics course I have completed: ______________________________

Home experiences I completed in each course: ______________________________

____

Home economics course(s) I am enrolled in now: ______________________________

1. Brief description of this home experience project: ______________________________

____

2. Date I plan to finish project: ______________________________

3. Goals and objectives (What I want to learn):

4. What I plan to do to accomplish these goals and objectives:

5. Information or knowledge I will need:

Knowledge needed	Source(s)

6. I will evaluate this project by:

REPORT OF HOME EXPERIENCE PROJECT

Name________

Date ________

For my project I plan to:

I have chosen this project because I hope to accomplish the following:

I plan to carry out my project by doing the following:

Family member comments:

Teacher comments:

(reverse side)

These are the things that I actually accomplished by doing this project:

These are the *new* things I learned by doing this project:

The following is a report of my work (How many times it was done, how many were made, how much money was spent, how long it took, etc.):

This is how I could have improved my project:

Family member comments:

Teacher comments:

SELECTING HOME EXPERIENCE PROJECTS

The projects selected by students should be realistic ones related to their needs and interests and to those of their families. Caution should be exercised when a student wants to make another shirt just like the one completed in class or when a student selects a project that is not related to material that has been or will be covered in class. The advantages and disadvantages of working on a project when the subject matter will not be presented in school should be discussed with the student. The additional time needed to obtain sufficient background information in order to proceed with the project needs to be considered. If students choose such projects, it may be necessary for them to plan independent study in order to gain competence in the areas selected.

There is also the problem of how and by what criteria to evaluate a home experience when the student has not studied the subject matter in school. If a student makes a garment before a unit in clothing construction has been covered in class, and has not straightened the fabric nor understitched the facings, it may very well be that the student had no way of knowing that these steps should have been taken. If, on the other hand, clothing construction had been covered, the teacher would recognize that the student should have known these techniques. However, it may also be that making a particular garment meets an immediate and pressing need for the student. Each teacher will have to decide whether the home experience for a given term must relate to the subject matter covered during that time. Perhaps this could be the general guideline with exceptions made on an individual basis only after a student-teacher conference.

Suggestions for Home Experiences

The following are ideas for home experiences that might stimulate students' thoughts about their own projects:

Family relations

- Plan and carry out a family fun activity without telling that you are doing it for a school project. Try to make the activity a pleasant surprise. Note reaction of family members. Determine how such activities can contribute to family stability.
- Review books, magazine articles, movies, and TV series that focus on family life. Make recommendations to other students for reading and viewing.
- Develop strategies to include your grandmother or grandfather in family activities that help them take an active part in family life.

Home management and consumer education

- Plan a week's menus for the family, staying within the money allotted. Buy the groceries, keep a record of the costs, and assume responsibility for preparing most of the meals.
- Discuss and plan with the family ways you can help to reduce family expenses. Follow the plan and evaluate its effectiveness.
- Analyze the morning rush at home. Identify trouble spots. Develop a plan with

family members that will relieve some of the pressure. Follow the plan and determine its usefulness.

Food and nutrition

- Plan a diet and activity routine to gain or lose weight or correct a complexion problem. Follow the routine for a period of time long enough to evidence a change.
- Check your diet for a week to determine if a sufficient quantity of all food groups is being obtained. Plan and follow a diet including the suggested amounts of the Basic Four food groups.
- Identify areas in the food budget that present problems to your family. Investigate ways in which these expenses can be reduced. Recommend food products that will provide comparable or improved nutritional quality in the diet at reduced costs.

Housing and home furnishings

- Organize a plant clinic and sale. Arrange to have an expert present a program on plant selection and care. Include a question-and-answer period.
- Identify storage problems in your home. Investigate good storage facilities in homes of your neighborhood and look through magazines and catalogs for other suggestions. Modify and implement these ideas in order to improve your home storage areas.
- Clean, straighten out, and efficiently organize items in the garage, closets, cupboards, and other appropriate areas of the home. Apply the principles of storage. Take before-and-after pictures.

Child development

- Interview parents about the satisfactions and problems encountered in rearing children. Identify things you can do now that will help prepare you to assume responsibilities related to children in the future.
- Read stories, play quiet games, and appropriately entertain children in a hospital over a period of time. If this is not feasible, it may be possible to instigate a children's story hour at a community library. Choose appropriate books and practice reading the selections aloud beforehand. Make up simple finger exercises and hand motions for the children to follow with selected poems and readings.
- Investigate ways in which working mothers provide for care of their children, manage responsibilities at home, and continue full-time employment. Determine the implications your findings might have for you in the future.

Clothing and textiles

- Identify current fashion trends and examine well-made garments that are fashionable. Determine ways you can update your present wardrobe to incorporate some of these trends. Carry out your plans.
- Assist someone in selecting or adapting a wardrobe to meet the specific clothing needs of a growing child, a person with arthritis, or someone who needs

protective clothing because of exposure to extreme weather conditions.

- Develop and distribute a questionnaire, or interview other students, to determine attitudes toward and acceptance or rejection of new fashions, fabrics, and consumer products. Summarize your findings and report them to the class. (This type of simplified research project often appeals to academically oriented students and lends itself to any area of home economics. Students may take surveys to ascertain attitudes toward divorce, alternate and changing lifestyles, or child-rearing practices.)

CHECKING PROGRESS ON HOME EXPERIENCE PROJECTS

Many teachers find it advantageous to have their students submit progress reports relating to their home experience projects. Progress can be checked in a number of ways, depending upon the nature of the projects. Students can bring reports to class, illustrated with pictures of work done. Or the work can be seen during a home visit. There are many advantages to using time contracts with home experiences. Teachers may make brief notes to themselves indicating how much each student had planned to accomplish by a certain date. The teacher can then write out one or two personalized questions, to be given to each student on a specified day: Has anticipated progress been made? If not, why not?

Home visits afford an excellent opportunity to discuss proposed home experiences with students and parents, to check progress, and to view the projects personally. In fact, evaluating some home experiences fairly almost necessitates seeing them, and sometimes this can only be done by visiting the student's home.

See page 184 for an example of a checklist that could be used for a student progress report. By reading over student self-reports, teachers should be able to detect those students who may need encouragement, help, or both.

EVALUATING HOME EXPERIENCE PROJECTS

Asking students to submit progress reports minimizes the likelihood that students will misrepresent home experiences. It is always a ticklish subject to handle when the teacher strongly suspects that certain students have had someone else do all, or almost all, of the work. The sensitive teacher will not confront these students bluntly, thereby possibly damaging forever a chance for rapport with them and perhaps with others as well. Instead, the teacher may ask carefully selected questions about how and in what sequence certain parts were done. Students may even be asked to repeat some of these pertinent steps in the teacher's presence. If these are not done adequately or questions cannot be answered accurately, the teacher can make a remark such as, "It seems that you did not really learn very much from doing this home experience project. Therefore, it would be to your advantage to do another or to repeat parts of this one."

Record keeping and evaluation will vary, depending on the type of project selected. A diary may be an appropriate means of recording and assessing growth toward improved interpersonal relations. If specific products are to be made, a checklist of desirable characteristics or qualities would be helpful. When a project involves other people's satisfactions and pleasures, then letters or testimonials will offer evidence of growth or quality. Students can suggest other appropriate evaluation measures that are suitable for their own individual home experiences.

It is important for the teacher to remember that emphasis should be upon the quality of the project itself and what the student learned by doing it, rather than upon a fancy and impressive notebook that may be submitted as evidence of work done. Sometimes it is difficult not to be influenced by an exceptionally well-written report, but the scope and depth of the project must be considered carefully. The real purpose of the home experience program, to meet individual and family needs, must be kept in mind when making evaluations.

Procedures regarding grades for home experiences differ. Sometimes an A, A−, B+, or the like is assigned and averaged into an overall term or unit grade. In other situations, only a system of P (for passing) versus F (for failing), or S (for satisfactory), versus U (for unsatisfactory), is used, with the understanding that a passing or satisfactory home experience must be completed in order to earn credit for the designated period of time.

See page 185 for an example of a final home experience project report form. This could be completed by the teacher as well as by the students.

GUIDE TO SELECTING AND SELF-EVALUATING A HOME EXPERIENCE PROJECT

This is a guide for you and your teacher to use to help in planning and discussing each step in your home experience project. This is to be checked by both of you during your conferences:

At the time the home experience project is selected (I).
When plans are being made (II).
As the home experience project is being carried on (III).
To sum up what you have gained from the home experience project (IV).

	YES	NO
I The *selection* of my project		
a. Is the experience based on one of my personal or home needs?	______	______
b. Am I really interested in it?	______	______
c. Does it provide real opportunities for me to learn to manage?	______	______
d. Have I had sufficient experience at home or school to carry it out successfully?	______	______
e. Can I carry it out with the cooperation of my family?	______	______

	YES	NO
II My *plan* for my project		
a. Have I clearly stated on the home experience record the things I want to learn?	______	______
b. Have I clearly and definitely *written down* each step, telling how I am to carry out my plan?	______	______
c. Have I considered the help I may need and have I included it in my plan?	______	______
d. Does my plan take into consideration the management of time and money and the cooperation of my family?	______	______
III *Carrying out* my plan		
a. Am I following my plan, making necessary changes?	______	______
b. When I meet a difficulty, am I using good judgement in overcoming it?	______	______
c. Am I keeping a careful record to show a complete picture of my work?	______	______

	YES	NO
IV *Summing up* my results		
a. Did I really do what I planned to do?	______	______
b. Was I interested in my project until it was completed?	______	______
c. Was my plan a helpful guide?	______	______
d. Have I a feeling of pride and satisfaction in my project?	______	______

HOME EXPERIENCE PROJECT EVALUATION

Rate each characteristic below by placing in the blank to the left the number corresponding to the words that best describe your home experience project. Numbers that indicate in-between ratings may also be used. Briefly explain or justify your rating on the reverse side.

SCALE:

Excellent		Very Good		Adequate		Fair		Poor	
10	9	8	7	6	5	4	3	2	1

(Total possible points = 70)

______ 1. *Selection of project*

Met personal and/or family needs.
Involved new learning experiences or development.
Involved assuming responsibility.

______ 2. *Goals or objectives*

Were challenging but realistic.
Were planned with or had approval of family.
Were stated clearly.

______ 3. *Planning*

Organized steps in logical order.
Made realistic time schedule.
Anticipated resources needed.

______ 4. *Management*

Used resources efficiently.
Asked for help when it was needed or referred to written materials.
Maintained established time schedule.

______ 5. *Progress reports* (oral or written)

Handed in or given at scheduled time.
Kept records accurately.
Showed appropriate progress.

______ 6. *Quality of completed project*

Met established goals or objectives.
Could identify what was learned from the project.
Could write or verbalize the value of the project.

______ 7. *Evaluation of project*

Could point out strengths and weaknesses of project.
Made appropriate suggestions for improvement.
Was realistic in making judgment about the quality of the project.

______ TOTAL

TAPPING COMMUNITY RESOURCES 16

A variety of community resources is available to all teachers. The quality and quantity of these vary from community to community. Numerous benefits can be derived from identifying and tapping local resources. Channels of communication can be established between people in the community and students and teachers in the home economics program. Local residents and agencies often become sources of support for your program. Involvement in the community can provide subject matter with realistic learning situations and practical applications that would not otherwise be available. Students often become more motivated and involved in course work when they have contact with people and places outside the classroom.

PLANNING FOR RESOURCE PEOPLE AND FIELD TRIPS

There are several guidelines to keep in mind when inviting resource people into the classroom or when planning field trips with students.

1. As long-range plans for classes are being made, begin to identify resource people and field trips that can become integral parts of the learning activities. Valuable suggestions may be obtained from students, co-workers and other school personnel, newspaper items, and the advertising pages of the telephone directory.
2. Contact resource people well in advance of the time you would like to have them work with the students. The initial contact may be made through a personal visit, telephone call, or letter. After agreement has been

reached about an appropriate date, time, and place, a letter of confirmation including this information should be sent. It is equally important to specify exactly what material is to be covered. Many resource people find it helpful to know the general background of the class and the extent of preparation in the subject matter that students will have before the guest's contact with the group. Resource people may suggest or ask that students view a specific film or filmstrip; read a selected story, case study, or article; or be introduced to specific information before they come to speak. This ensures that the students and the speaker have a mutual frame of reference. There may be opportunities for individual students or student committees to assume some of the responsibility for identifying community resources and contacting appropriate personnel. This not only helps the teacher, but also provides the students with valuable experience.

3. Field trips outside the school usually involve detailed planning to obtain permission from school administrators and parents and to arrange transportation. For field trips that are longer than one class period, there may be additional planning involved to determine the cost of the trip, set departure and arrival times, obtain additional chaperons, and make provisions for meals, if necessary.
4. Students should be adequately prepared for guest speakers and field trips. Students can discuss what they hope to learn and formulate some questions they would like to have answered by speakers or during field trips. Having each student write one or two questions to be asked usually increases participation during question-and-answer periods, but it might also result in questions that sound rehearsed. At any rate, it is advisable to encourage students to ask questions about points they do not understand rather than to allow them to rely on you to keep a discussion going.
5. Students may need to be reminded that their behavior, when a guest comes to class or they go on a field trip, reflects on the entire school. Encourage students to be courteous and helpful to visitors. On trips away from school, it may be wise to remind students not to make negative comments about what is observed while on the site and not to sit down in a furniture store or in a private home unless invited to do so.
6. When a resource person has finished talking to the group or it is time to conclude a field trip, some words of thanks from both the teacher and the students are appropriate. It may be advisable to remind students beforehand to stop and informally thank a speaker for having come or a host for having let you visit. In fact, you can use all such occasions to help students learn socially acceptable behavior.
7. After a speaker or field trip, a thank-you note is appropriate. It is helpful and can be effective if a student or a student committee assumes this task. You may want to read over student-written thank-you notes before they are put in final form and mailed.
8. When resource people come to the classroom, there are several things that can be done to help make the visits pleasant and profitable:
   a. The school office should know when guests are expected. If at all possible, assign someone to meet guests at the office.

b. When speakers are introduced, sharing a little of the persons' background with the class can help guests establish rapport with the students.

c. People invited to the classroom are not always accustomed to public speaking and may direct their voices to the teacher rather than the students. Consequently, if you sit near the back of the room, speakers are more likely to project so everyone can hear. You also have more control over student behavior from this position in the room.

9. Occasionally a guest speaker does not come as scheduled, or plans for a field trip have to be canceled at the last minute. Therefore, it is advisable to have alternate plans ready for the class period. Sometimes a lesson planned for two or three days in the future can be used.

Although it may be very desirable to have a resource person come to class or to take a field trip, circumstances and scheduling may prohibit it. There are alternatives that can be considered. If a resource person can speak to only one class, an audiotape or videotape could be made and played for other classes. The tape could become part of a library to be used as an additional resource or for individualizing instruction. A person who is unable to visit the school might be able to speak to a small group of students or the teacher at his or her residence or place of business. In this case, the interview could be taped on a cassette recorder. If a field trip cannot be scheduled for an entire class, it may be possible for a group of students or the teacher to go outside of school hours and take pictures for slides. The slides and information about the trip can be organized into an interesting classroom presentation.

RESOURCE PEOPLE

A variety of people in diverse professions and occupations can make contributions to home economics programs. Some to consider are: handicapped persons, the parents of handicapped people, first-generation immigrants or people of different ethnic background, interior designers, builders, architects, real estate and insurance representatives, credit bureau employees, merchandising personnnel, religious leaders, social workers, counselors, and lawyers. In addition to providing expertise in specific areas, many of the people mentioned can serve as effective resources in career education. The responsibilities, opportunities for advancement or specialization, and satisfactions and limitations of their positions can be explored.

Beauticians and cosmetologists might be invited to class if they avoid a commercial approach. Doctors are excellent resource people; however, their schedules frequently rule out speaking engagements. A nurse, whose schedule may be less demanding than that of a doctor, could also provide an authoritative and professional viewpoint. Retired people often have more flexible schedules than those who are employed full-time; consequently, it may be easier to arrange meeting times with them. Inviting older citizens to serve as resource people can help to minimize the so-called generation gap and at the same time provide older citizens with the satisfaction of making a valuable contribution to the community.

A change in format from the customary lecture and question-answer period can add to a presentation considerably and provide a stimulating frame of reference for discussion. Students might act out a hypothetical counseling situation with the resource person. Other topics that could be used are problems related to dating, engagement, and marriage; personal financial crises; unexpected or unwanted pregnancies; or child abuse.

A panel discussion can be an excellent way of involving a number of resource people in one classroom presentation. A panel of people of different ages and responsibilities might discuss how they manage their time, money, energy, and other resources. A panel of parents might discuss the responsibilities of child rearing or special problems in caring for children.

FIELD TRIPS

Field trip opportunities are available in most communities. Trips to places of business, museums, institutions, private residences, recreational facilities, and state and federal offices offer interesting educational possibilities. Many manufacturing plants, research organizations, clothing retailers, department stores, and furniture and appliance stores welcome visits by students. Such field trips can promote a better understanding of merchants' and manufacturers' roles in the business world and in the local community.

Various local facilities for the care of young children and the elderly could be toured. Retirement and nursing homes, as well as public and private child-care centers, are interesting and informative places to visit. Some of the following might be observed or noted: special provisions for caring for a specific age group, the type and diversity of activities offered, the approximate cost, and the concern shown by personnel.

Concern about community problems can provide a basis for a variety of field trips. Inadequate playground facilities, community centers that have deteriorated, or poor methods of refuse disposal could serve as focal points for involving young people. One possible result of such field trips is that students may be motivated to analyze existing problems, collect additional information, and propose—and possibly become involved in—satisfactory solutions.

Comparative shopping trips can be enjoyable and informative. Depending on the specific products, features, and services being investigated, students can be divided into investigating teams. Each team could be responsible for going to a different type of retail establishment and checking the same or comparable items for particular features. For example, in comparison shopping for a particular appliance, the following points could be identified: brand name, special features, directions given for use, warranty, certification or endorsement by various organizations, cost, and finance charges if purchased on credit. When students return to class, each team can report its findings. Thus, a considerable amount of information can be shared. Students could decide which would be the best buy for a variety of given situations. They could also be asked to defend their choices.

Making full use of community resources offers you a variety of ways to reinforce and expand the content of your course and to motivate students and help them grow.

REINFORCING BASIC SKILLS 17

A great deal of publicity has been given to the disappointing results of student performance on national, regional, state, and city academic competency tests. Widespread reports have circulated about the inability of high school graduates to write an intelligible letter, fill out an application form correctly, and make correct change. These limitations and other concerns such as the increasing cost of education have been partly responsible for the movement back to basics. Basic skills are those in language, reading, science, and math. Although home economics teachers are not specifically charged with the responsibility of teaching English or math, all professionals in an educational setting need to work together to reinforce basic skills.

If teachers do not take time to reinforce basic language, reading, science, and math skills, the result may be that students will not learn all the home economics subject matter. Also, by not emphasizing both subject matter and basic skills, the implication for students could be that English, math, and science have no application in other courses or in the real world.

Home economics teachers can work with other teachers to reinforce subject matter from course to course, planning to teach certain concepts simultaneously. Many researchers have pointed out that students learn more and are more highly motivated when the subject matter is relevant to their lives and to their personal goals. There are a number of concepts that can be taught simultaneously in home economics and English and math. Using credit in making consumer purchases can be correlated with computing interest in math classes. Math problems can be worked in cooperative education classes dealing with subject matter such as commercial food preparation, interior design, and clothing-care services, to reinforce computation skills emphasized in a math class. Students can write letters of application, complete job-application forms, and write summary reports at work when business correspondence is taught in an English class.

MATH SKILLS

In many content areas of home economics, it is important that students do some basic math computation to solve problems and to assimilate subject matter. Converting standard measurements to metrics, managing money, understanding paycheck statements, figuring income tax, computing the cost of credit, making price comparisons, and purchasing fabric and making alterations in clothing construction are but a few of the areas where some basic knowledge of math is needed.

Many stories are told of students who have an aversion to math. Nevertheless, math is frequently used in everyday life. You can help students see how knowing basic math procedures can facilitate reaching some goals that may be important to them, such as using credit to make a consumer purchase. Work a sample problem on the chalkboard and then have students individually compute a similar problem. Put math problems related to specific subject matter on flash cards. Have students use a pocket computer to determine unit prices, to figure the cost of credit, or to tally grocery costs.

SCIENCE SKILLS

There are many opportunities to show how science principles relate to many aspects of everyday life. For example, it is possible to demonstrate the relationship between physical well-being and an adequate diet, as shown in animal feeding experiments. Demonstrate the principles behind different methods of food preservation; after different time intervals, compare the quality of the preserved food with food products that have not been preserved. Demonstrations can be done to illustrate the nutritive composition of some food such as the oil in peanut butter and the starch in potatoes. Illustrate different chemical reactions in food preparation when various food substances are combined, such as the production of carbon dioxide when baking powder and water and baking soda and an acid are mixed, and the reaction of easily oxidized cut fruit when treated and not treated with an acid. Conduct experiments to identify various textile fibers by using burning and acetone tests. Test flame-retardant properties of different fabrics; compare the effect of correct and incorrect laundry procedures used on fabrics to which flame-retardant chemicals have been added by the manufacturer. Demonstrate how water conditioners work in hard water.

WRITING SKILLS

Evaluating written assignments can be time-consuming and tedious work. However, writing does provide students with the opportunity to organize their thoughts in a logical manner and receive constructive criticism.

In addition to the traditional subject-matter reports and term papers, there are many other opportunities for students to do written assignments. Some of these include: summarizing a reading assignment, evaluating a lab or project, writing job-application letters, developing written directions, composing book reviews for childrens' books or books of interest to one's peers, and writing letters to congressional representatives, to the editors of newspapers and magazines, and to manufacturers and service organizations.

Some points to keep in mind when formulating written assignments follow:

- Select topics of interest to students, ones that are highly motivating and have evident relevance to their lives.
- Have students submit an initial assignment to be critiqued but not graded at the beginning of the term.
- Review with students grammar and spelling errors frequently made in written assignments.
- Have a speaker whom students respect stress the importance of written communication skills in everyday life.
- Have resources available, such as a dictionary and a thesaurus, and teach students to use them.
- Give clear directions that provide structure for the assignment.

READING SKILLS

Numerous research studies have indicated that student comprehension of reading material is not solely the interaction of the student and the text but the interaction among the student, the text, and the teacher. Teacher intervention makes a difference in students' reading comprehension. Reading assignments can present problems for students with inadequate reading skills and a lack of familiarity with the subject matter.

Teachers can take several different approaches to provide some short-term solutions for reading problems:

- Spend time helping students become acquainted with the reading resource materials that will be used in the classroom. For example, when using a textbook it is important for students to understand the layout, index, table of contents, headings, questions, chapter summaries, footnotes, and purposes of italicized words.
- Use materials as they were written, but make adjustments in the instructional strategies used. For example, familiarize students with vocabulary and content by giving pre-instruction. Provide advance organizers that are summary statements of chapter content to help facilitate comprehension and recall. Define key words and use them in a context sentence. Suggest that students focus on the title and the first sentence of each paragraph since these give direction to the content that follows.
- Develop a list of questions to be answered or discussed later. These can be given before students begin reading, at the end of each paragraph or section, or at the end of the entire reading selection. Questions can be formulated to require higher

levels of thinking rather than the recall of isolated pieces of information. For example, for assigned reading on the types of maturity, students might list the types simply by copying the subtitles or headings. On the other hand, if students were asked to give examples of the various types of maturity, other than those provided, comprehension of the subject matter would be required.

- Write directions and develop your own reading materials at appropriate reading levels. Short sentences and short words help reduce the reading level. Unfamiliar words can be used if they are defined in the written text.

EVALUATING READING MATERIALS

Well-chosen reading materials can spark student interest, and they can even serve as a form of encouragement to students to pursue some subjects in greater depth. Therefore, judging the appropriateness of written resource materials is an area of concern to many teachers. Resource materials may include textbooks, paperbacks, magazines, and newspapers. Some points to consider when selecting written materials follow.

Cover

The cover of a book or magazine is the first of its features to be noticed. The cover can do much to attract a teenager's interest and establish a positive attitude toward reading, by stimulating curiosity about what is inside. A colorful cover that is not dated is an asset. The cover may convey a contemporary approach that has appeal to teenage readers or it may dissuade them from wanting to investigate further.

Illustrations

Illustrations may be used to arouse interest or to teach, but they should be as timeless as possible. This means that styles in hair, clothing, and furnishings must not make the book appear to be old-fashioned in the adolescent's eyes. Pictures showing hemline lengths or fads of any kind should be kept to a minimum. Occasional cartoons, line drawings, and diagrams add variety and interest and tend to minimize the problem of becoming dated.

Illustrations should achieve a balance between females and males and minority-group members so that all readers feel that the book is relevant to and concerned with them. Illustrations also have to appeal to the particular age group by whom the textbook will be used. In addition, a variety of lifestyles, family structures, and economic situations should be portrayed. If pictures depict only middle-class conditions, some students may feel alienated.

Illustrations without captions or descriptive explanations lose much of their educational value. Pictures, sketches, and diagrams should also be placed as close as possible to the related subject matter in the text. Although color illustrations increase the cost considerably, they have much motivational value. It is more effective to have a number of colored pictures distributed throughout material than to have the same number of colored pictures confined to only a few sections. Illustrations should be sufficient in number to break the visual monotony of the printed material but not so numerous that they make it difficult to follow the continuity. It is possible to have so many illustrations that they become a distraction rather than an asset, and they can take up space needed for adequate coverage of the subject.

Subject Matter

The subject matter covered in books and other reference materials must be compatible with the conceptual framework and behavioral objectives established for the course or courses in which the materials will be used. In addition, the amount of material devoted to various topics needs to be well balanced in relation to the phases to be covered in class. Analyzing the table of contents, if available, should provide insight into whether the reference work is compatible with the course of study.

The subject should be applicable to the geographic area in which it will be used. Material with special appeal to students living in one area of the country will have limited appeal to students living in another region. Illustrations, too, must be chosen so that students in a variety of geographic situations can relate to them.

Of course, the subject matter as well as the illustrations, should be up-to-date. The presentation must be reliable and authoritative without causing students to feel they are being talked down to or lectured. A reference work that seems to say, "This is the only way to do it," will have little appeal and acceptance. More than one point of view should be expressed on controversial issues, and both the advantages and disadvantages of the alternatives explored. Moralizing and value judgments have no place in reference material if it is to be well received by the majority of young people today. Material must be appropriate for the age group that will use it, and must make provision for individual differences among students. As with graphic illustrations, verbal illustrations such as problems, examples, and case studies should be balanced as to race, ethnicity, and gender.

Format and Organization

A two-column page is usually easier to read than one wide column. The type should be large and clear enough to be read easily. The durability of material used in the book's construction, and its thickness and shape, must also be considered. For example, books that are very thick may have a negative psychological effect on students.

Of value to teachers and students are resources that suggest learning experiences. They provide ideas for teachers and encourage students to delve further into those areas in which they have special needs or interests. Projects to be carried out at school, in the home, and in the community may be suggested. Case studies, teaching aids, and thought-provoking questions for discussion may be proposed. The learning experiences suggested should appeal to students at various achievement levels and should help the teacher individualize instruction.

Examining the authorship, copyright date, and publisher's data can furnish valuable information. If a resource is a revision, it is advisable to determine the extent of revision by noting changes in the table of contents, illustrations, format, and several selected pages.

Evaluating Reading Level

The reading level should be appropriate for the students using the materials. Written materials that are too far above or too far below students' reading levels can be a "turn-off" to students. Generally, short words and sentences are indicative of lower reading levels, whereas long words and long, more complicated sentence structures are found in materials with a higher reading level.

There are a number of tests available that can assist you in estimating the reading level of written material. The Flesch, Fry, Dale-Chall, Danielson-Brian, and Farr-Jenkins-Paterson tests provide fairly accurate assessments of reading level. They have the disadvantage of being somewhat tedious to compute.

A rough estimate of grade level can be obtained quickly by using word length and sentence length as indicators.*

- Compute the average number of words per sentence in a sample of 100 words.
- Count the number of words having three or more syllables. Do not count the following: proper names; combinations of short, easy words such as *bookkeeper*; and verb forms which are three syllables because of *-ed* or *-es* endings, such as *created* and *trespasses*.
- Add the two figures and multiply by $\frac{4}{10}$ (0.4).

  For example, if there are 3 difficult words (three or more syllables) in the 100-word sample, and the average sentence contains 13 words, the computation is $3 + 13 = 16 \times 0.4 = 6.4$ grade reading level.

USING A VARIETY OF READING MATERIALS

In addition to textbooks, there are a variety of other types of reading materials available for use in the classroom, such as magazines, paperbacks, and newspapers. One obvious advantage of using different types of written resource materials is that the variety may serve to promote additional interest in the subject matter. When interest is developed, the teacher is more likely to be able to reinforce the basic skills. For example, students can read several people's opinions about solving the energy problem or curbing inflation, write a summary of the conflicting viewpoints, and take a stand on which approach would seem to be in the best interests of consumers. Some suggested activities using paperbacks, periodicals, and newspapers follow.

Paperbacks and Periodicals

Paperbacks are comparatively inexpensive and often up-to-date, and they may have special appeal to the students because they are currently popular. Paperback

*Robert Gunning, *The Technique of Clear Writing*, McGraw-Hill Book Company, New York, 1968.

books dealing with consumerism, interpersonal relationships, and laymen's psychological theory are well suited for use in home economics classes. Because of the relative ease with which paperbacks can be obtained, students can read from many sources and share information, thus enriching their experiences. The wide variety of paperbacks available also enables students at various maturity levels and from different cultural and socioeconomic backgrounds to satisfy their diverse needs and interests.

Magazines also focus on a number of issues relevant to home economics and can be used effectively in the classroom. The recency of material in current magazines makes them especially appealing. Articles in them can be shared and discussed; stories can be put on audiotape and left unfinished, allowing students to supply the endings and to compare their conclusions with those of the authors; and pictures can be used by students in making notebooks, mobiles, collages, posters, bulletin boards, and a myriad of visuals of other kinds. Students who regularly receive certain magazines in their homes can assume responsibility for bringing to the attention of the class articles related to topics discussed in class.

One caution in using paperbacks and magazines is that information—especially in some fields like nutrition and popular psychology—may be unreliable. Stress with students the importance of *evaluating* sources. Develop a short checklist in class that would aid such evaluation. Sample criteria might be: "What are the author's credentials?" "How recent is the information?" "Where does it come from?" "Is the article balanced or one-sided?"

Newspapers

Using newspapers in the classroom helps students see the relevance of education. After all, reading newspapers is one of the basic ways to learn about the problems of the world. Although newspapers cannot substitute for textbooks, they are an excellent supplement. Using newspapers in teaching can promote critical thinking. Students can compare articles covering the same issues and situations and look for discrepancies.

The examples that follow illustrate just a few of the ways in which the different components of a newspaper can be used in teaching home economics. Many of these learning experiences could be coordinated with assignments and projects in other subjects.

News stories

- Supply headlines for articles, from which the titles have been cut, relating to consumer affairs, family relationships, and child abuse. Compare and discuss the merits of different students' suggested headlines.
- Read newspaper articles to become better informed about local, state, and national efforts to solve problems relating to energy conservation, pollution, ecology, use of resources, food surpluses and scarcities, inflation, unemployment, and other pressing issues. Discuss the responsibilities of citizens to question or support legislation and programs pertaining to these problems.

- Collect articles telling about home accidents. Suggest ways by which these mishaps might have been avoided.
- Hold a press conference in which you pretend to have just discovered another nutrient, developed a new synthetic fiber, or invented a revolutionary household appliance. Write news stories describing how this new product will change consumer practices and affect personal and family living.

Advertisements

- Analyze advertisements to differentiate between those that have a primarily emotional appeal and those that provide factual data. Determine what the emotional advertisements are suggesting to the consumer. Underline or circle information that both appeals to the emotions and provides meaningful consumer information.
- Discuss the psychological effects of various phrases such as: for three days only; only two to a customer; must be sold immediately; last chance to buy; stock up while they last; limited number available; hurry, they're going fast. Give examples of other phrases used in advertisements that are designed to persuade the consumer to act quickly. Distinguish between "for sale" and "on sale."
- Compare food ads and plan menus for a week, utilizing as many specials as practical. Determine why grocery stores sometimes sell items below cost; advertise coupon specials; and promote features such as trading stamps, hours open for business, and bonus gifts that are not directly related to buying food. Discuss the values of advertising to the consumer and to the seller.

Classifieds

- Analyze want ads in a newspaper over a period of time to determine the types of employment for which there are the greatest and least demands locally. Analyze the reasons for these findings.
- Select a job being advertised in the want ads of a local newspaper and write a letter applying for that position.
- Analyze your own employment potential by writing an advertisement to appear in a situations-wanted column. Determine how personal assets relate to different types of employment that might be sought.
- Spread out the classified sections of several newspapers on tables. Have a scavenger hunt to locate all the jobs advertised relating to specific areas of home economics, such as child development, clothing and textiles, food and nutrition, home management, or any other areas being studied.

Columns and features

- Read letters appearing in personal-advice columns and formulate replies. Compare return letters with those written by the columnist. Discuss, in large or small

groups, letters appearing in newspapers in which advice is sought, and point out the possible effects of different courses of action that could be suggested.
- Analyze comic strips to determine values held by the author as reflected through various characters.
- Pretend to buy a few stocks and follow the market every day. Compute gains and losses at the end of a specified period. Analyze reasons why some stocks may have increased in value while others may have decreased.

Many of these learning experiences can be adapted for use in studying any home economics subject and simultaneously reinforcing basic skills. In a rapidly changing field, there is no excuse for using outdated reading material. Fortunately, home economics teachers have an abundant supply of up-to-date publications that students can use. However, your ability to use these materials effectively is as important as the quality of the publications themselves. Students need guidance in using textbooks, periodicals, and other written materials to ensure optimum learning.

PROFESSIONALISM AND PUBLIC RELATIONS 18

Professionals know the value of a good public relations program that effectively interprets their profession and activities to the public. Programs that maintain a positive image are likely to receive public support, thus assuring the future growth of home economics.

PROFESSIONALISM

Professional home economists are proud of the profession. However, professionalism is more than pride; it is a way of behaving. There are identifiable characteristics often associated with professional conduct, no matter what the field. Professional people strive to:

- render service and show concern for people.
- be loyal to colleagues.
- assume responsibility for personal behavior.
- seek and accept advice and criticism objectively.
- maintain a sense of humor.
- keep up-to-date on subject matter, resources, and local, national, and worldwide concerns.
- meet commitments and obligations fully and on time.
- maintain high work standards.
- get involved in the local community, professional organizations, and legislative matters.
- possess good communication and public relations skills.
- express ideas objectively, clearly, and concisely.
- wear clothing appropriate for the occasion.
- manage time effectively.
- establish a satisfactory balance between personal and professional lives.
- maintain good physical, mental, and emotional health.

These characteristics are not necessarily listed in priority order. It should be recognized that different characteristics will be more or less important and visible at various times in an individual's career. Nevertheless, taken as a whole, they represent the first step in establishing and promoting the image of home economics at every level.

PUBLIC RELATIONS

All organizations have a public relations program—planned or unplanned, good or poor. Public relations, or PR, is what you do to build the image of an organization. It involves informing the public about the activities and policies of the organization and working toward the creation of a favorable public opinion.

A carefully thought-out and well-organized PR program pays dividends in support and good will. All disciplines, programs, organizations, and agencies are in competition for recognition and funding. Contemporary home economics programs need to be explained. Home economics has as much relevance today as it had in the past, if not more. We are concerned about many of the contemporary issues facing society—strengthening personal and family relationships, providing opportunities for the growth of children, developing good nutritional habits and promoting healthy lifestyles, identifying resources and developing management skills, and providing information about consumer concerns and helping to shape consumer policy.

How do you go about improving and shaping your public image? There are many possible approaches, but the following are essential for a successful public information program:

1. *Identify Target Groups.* You have more than one public. The organizations and individuals to whom you are responsible and who have an impact on your existence and status are diversified and numerous. Some of the most obvious are:

School

Administrators
Counselors
Teachers
Students—home economics and non-home economics
Support personnel such as librarians, custodians, secretaries, teachers' aides

Community

Parents of both home economics and non-home economics students
Taxpayers
School board members
Elected officials
Business-community leaders and personnel

It is essential to assess the knowledge and attitudes of the people who fall into the above categories, as they probably have the greatest impact on your department. Beyond this, you need to decide who other target groups are.

2. *Evaluate your image.* What do your target audiences know about your program? What are their attitudes about home economics? Guessing the answers to these and other questions will not provide an accurate picture. Getting representative and objective information is an important first step. Informal information-seeking can simply involve talking to people about home economics and listening to their comments—positive, negative, and neutral. Developing and distributing a questionnaire is a more formal approach. By sending a questionnaire to parents, to determine which areas of home economics would be most helpful to their children, you are not only gathering needed information; you are also informing parents about the broad scope of the home economics program. Similar questionnaires can be distributed to students. Course evaluations during the term and at the end of a course can be helpful in determining what subject areas were most and least meaningful and relevant and what areas need to be improved. Questionnaires should be clear, simple, short, and well organized.
3. *Determine goals and implement PR strategies.* Planning and implementing procedures to increase the visibility of, and to upgrade the image of, home economics require thoughtful, detailed planning. The strategies you choose may vary, depending on the target group you are addressing. Establish realistic short- and long-range goals and set priorities. Be as specific as possible. For example, "to improve the image of home economics" can be worded more specifically by stating "to increase enrollment in home economics classes," if that is your goal.
4. *Identify and refine PR tools.* You already have training and experience in interpersonal communication. Brushing up on the use of some tools you have at your disposal may be all it takes to get your PR program going. The tools, like the strategies, may depend on your target. Some of these tools are discussed under the headings that follow.

Verbal Communication

In the course of a professional day, there are numerous opportunities for informal and formal contacts with students, school personnel, parents, and members of the community. During informal contacts, a smile, good eye contact, and a display of interest, respect, and concern will usually help set the right tone.

On more formal occasions, such as parent-and-student conferences and professional meetings, the same courtesies extended during informal contacts will continue to be appreciated. Be sure others know the purpose of the meeting before they arrive. A personal note or a phone call to parents before a conference and an agenda distributed ahead of time are helpful. Begin with a few general comments to establish rapport before addressing the major concerns. As much as possible, keep the tone of the discussion positive. Be prepared. Be familiar with relevant material and have any figures, facts, or samples of work available for documentation purposes. Keep your remarks concise. People's time is often limited, and telling every small detail may only confuse the issue. Be sure others have an opportunity to express their opinions and feelings honestly. Allow time for a summary of what has been discussed.

Newsletters

A home economics newsletter sent to parents and interested community members can be used to give an accurate account of the activities in your department, thus providing others with a broader viewpoint of home economics. Class and student activities and special projects and programs can be discussed. You might also include a calendar of future events. It is important that students be involved in as much of the writing and production work as possible, relieving you of the total responsibility and providing them with an opportunity to share their pride and enthusiasm about the program. Work done by students must be checked for accuracy, however.

Newspaper Articles and Other Media

Publicity is made; it does not come about spontaneously. Fires, disasters, and elections are usually going to be the number-one news items. The events that make up the everyday life of a community are equally important and worthy of public interest. It is the second category into which many home economics-related activities fall.

There is no guarantee that because you are doing something interesting, your story will receive publication, but some of the qualities that newsworthy items have include:

- *Timeliness*—People want to know what is happening *now*.
- *Proximity*—People read stories that are *near* to them, either geographically or in relevance.
- *Prominence*—The more prominent people are, the more valuable they are as news features.
- *Consequence*—People are interested in events that will affect their lives.
- *Human interest*—People like stories that arouse their curiosity or sympathy.

Television and radio

For local radio and television programs, contact the program director, and for radio and television news, talk to the news editor. If you have an item of sufficient interest, the news staff may be very receptive. Remember that the Federal Communications Commission (FCC) encourages radio and television stations to provide a certain percentage of free air time for public service announcements. Since you represent a nonprofit organization, your news story may qualify. You will want to find out the primary interests of the station and the person to notify about special events, deadlines, and other pertinent policies.

Press releases

For articles in a large daily newspaper, contact the city editor, and in a weekly or small-town paper, notify the editor. Don't underestimate the power of the press. It has been estimated that over 75 percent of the adult American population reads newspapers, and there are over 12,000 newspapers published in the United States.

A press release is the most commonly used method for presenting a news story. It consists of a statement of facts written in news style. When writing a press release, keep the following four basic guidelines in mind:

- It must be about something that has news value and is accurate.
- It should be written in the third person.
- It should be presented in an acceptable form. (See sample.)
- It should reach the editor early enough to be used in the edition for which it is intended. Generally, it should be on a daily editor's desk a week ahead of time. Most weekly editors print their newspapers one or two days before they are delivered. Therefore, delivering the release ten days ahead of the publication date is a good idea.

SAMPLE PRESS RELEASE

Home Economics Class ABC High School, Town, State	For additional information: Teacher's name Telephone number
(Place the above in upper left-hand corner.)	(Place the above in upper right-hand corner.)

3 inches

FOR IMMEDIATE RELEASE, or
FOR RELEASE AFTER 12 NOON, DATE

2 inches

Press release appears here.

##

(Sign off with the above mark.)

The lead paragraph of the news story should answer these questions: who? what? when? where? why? how? Although the lead does not have to be limited to the first paragraph, the first paragraph should contain the main thrust of the story. It provides a synopsis of the entire story for the reader. The second and subsequent paragraphs add secondary information.

Some additional guidelines to consider when preparing press releases follow:

- Use white paper and type or mimeograph, with double-spacing, on only one side of the paper.
- Try to limit your release to one page.

- Use short, tight sentences. State facts concisely.
- Do not editorialize. Use direct quotes instead of stating opinions.
- Avoid using unusual words.
- Read your local newspaper for style.
- Be sure your story has the "time" specified. A story relates something that happened today, or else is qualified by adding such expressions as "it was announced today that . . ." or "it was learned today that . . ."

Programs and Special Occasions

Make the most of special events and projects carried out by the department and the chapters of Future Homemakers of America (FHA) and Home Economics Related Occupations (HERO). A car wash, an open house, a bazaar, contests, awards, home economics awareness week, or a bake sale are often newsworthy events—especially if they have a slightly different slant. For example, if the proceeds from a car wash or bake sale are going to a charitable cause, it is more newsworthy than if the money is going into an organization's treasury. Home economics students helping to educate the public about child abuse is a topic more newsworthy than students giving a Halloween party for children in a local orphanage. The timelessness of the child-abuse topic allows it to be used as a news item during any slow news period, whereas a Halloween party is newsworthy only on Halloween itself.

Presenting a special program about what students have been learning in class, or a project in which FHA or HERO have been involved, is a way to establish additional contacts with parents and other community members. Establishing a home economics week or taking advantage of the opportunities available during an open house permit students to arrange eye-catching displays and give five- or ten-minute demonstrations on topics of possible interest to the public. Students interested in photography can take pictures, and students talented in writing can write press releases or articles for the school newspaper.

ADMINISTRATIVE CONTACTS

To assume that all school administrators are familiar with the home economics program is a mistake. Including administrators as an important target group in your public relations program is essential. When the administration sees home economics as a worthwhile contemporary program, students will be encouraged to enroll, school policies will be interpreted in your favor, and requests will more likely be granted.

There are many things you can do to increase your program's visibility in the eyes of the administration. Discuss some of your long- and short-range plans and solicit input from key administrators. List the outside speakers who will be meeting with your classes and check to see whether administrators would like to meet any of these people. Invite administrators to attend special class sessions and functions sponsored by your department. When your program receives publicity in the media, try to include administrators' names, comments, or pictures if it is possible and warranted. Keep in mind that although your department truly depends on the "small" things—your ongoing, everyday work—it is often the special events that establish positive recognition by the administration.

LEGISLATIVE CONTACTS

Many public policies have an enormous impact on individuals and families. Writing a letter, sending a telegram, or making a phone call to an elected representative are means by which you can participate in the political process. It is important to write, and to encourage students to write, to your member of Congress, mayor, or other elected official to whom you wish to express your opinion on a topic. Here are a few suggestions for writing an effective letter:

- Address the recipient correctly. For a U.S. representative, send it to: The Honorable (name), U.S. House of Representatives, Washington, D.C. 20515; or if a senator, The Honorable (name), U.S. Senate, Washington, D.C. 20510.
- Be specific. When writing about a particular bill, try to identify the bill by name and number. In the House, bills are listed H.R. (number) and in the Senate, S (number). If you do not know the number, then give a description.
- Write early so that it will do some good.
- Be brief, but take time to give your own views. Avoid sending form letters because they are not considered as seriously as personally written letters. If the particular topic you are writing about directly affects your life, state this. Whether you support or oppose legislation, give reasons for your position.
- Be polite. Name-calling and other similar approaches detract from the effectiveness of letters.
- Ask for assistance. Members of Congress are happy to answer questions and provide information. Some have newsletters you may receive.

ADVISORY COUNCILS

The advisory council becomes an important vehicle of communication by bringing ideas from the community to the home economics department and by interpreting the home economics program to the community. The advisory council serves only in an advisory capacity. It is not a policy-making board. The major tasks of the council are to assist in collecting and interpreting information for use in program planning and evaluation, to make recommendations and offer suggestions to school authorities and personnel, to help plan and evaluate the home economics program, and to help interpret the home economics program to the community. All vocational home economics teachers are required to work with an advisory council. Some advisory councils serve only one school, while others are organized to provide input to all the home economics programs in a town, city, or school district.

If you are responsible for establishing an advisory council, the following pointers should be helpful:

The composition of the council is directly related to its effectiveness. If it is to communicate advice and the opinions of the community accurately, it must be representative of the entire community, drawing members from families of different ethnic and socioeconomic groups and from families of differing composition. These might include intact families with children, single-parent families, families with females employed in the home, families with females employed outside the home, and single-homemaker families. However, if the advisory council is to provide effective interpretation of a program to a community, to obtain community support, and to promote home economics projects in the community, it also must include well-known, influential people. Once the desired composition of the council is determined, suggestions for membership can be solicited.

It is advisable to make some preliminary preparations so that the council can function effectively. It is a helpful first step to make arrangements for members to become acquainted with each other. The members of the advisory council need to know the purposes of the council—why it has been organized and what its role and limitations are. In addition, members need to have background information about the home economics program and the guidelines that have been used to plan the current program. With this preparation, the council members will be able to participate fully and meaningfully.

Meetings of the advisory council must be well planned. Members are busy people who want to feel their input is worthwhile. The meetings should deal with relevant topics about which the council is knowledgeable. Responsibility for planning the meeting, making the arrangements, and taking care of the follow-up may rest with you, with the chairperson of the advisory committee, or with another responsible individual. Regardless of who assumes responsibility for making the arrangements, keep the following tips in mind:

- Send an agenda and an invitation to meet to the members.
- Make arrangements to meet in a comfortable and convenient location. Facilities for serving refreshments can be determined.
- Make information that would assist the council in discussing a problem available in duplicate form, on charts, or on transparencies.
- Send a summary of the meeting proceedings to council members, along with a thank-you note.
- Follow up on suggestions made by the council. This may involve working with individual council members, talking to administrators, contacting other teachers, working on learning experiences and future plans for the department, and discussing ideas with students. It may not always be possible to take action on all suggestions made, but it is important that suggestions be explored. Either by way of a memo or a report during a future council meeting, you should report to members of the council the outcomes of their suggestions.

Home economics teachers have many additional means of communicating an accurate image of the profession. Some of these within the school include bulletin boards, display cases, library displays, and assemblies, open houses, and parent-teacher association meetings. Programs emphasizing a variety of aspects of home economics can be prepared for local business personnel, community organizations, and civic groups. Exhibits are appropriate for community centers, public buildings, and county and area fairs. The task of expanding and improving the image of home economics is the responsibility of each individual in the profession.

MANAGING A DEPARTMENT AND COPING WITH BUDGET CUTS 19

In the business world, management is stressed so that businesses can operate smoothly, maintain standards, and balance the budget. Good management practices are important in home economics classrooms for the same reasons. Effective management helps the teacher facilitate classwork and learning and run the department smoothly. This chapter focuses on two areas of management: functional management for effective teaching and administrative management dealing with records, reports, and finances.

FUNCTIONAL MANAGEMENT

In the home economics classroom, teachers have the opportunity to implement and illustrate many managerial processes. Students who have had an opportunity to work in an attractive department that is efficient and conducive to work will be able to see theory put into practice.

Establishing Good Relations Within the School

Home economics teachers have a responsibility to see that the students and department are not exploited, but many requests can be fulfilled while providing enriching experiences. Common requests are to furnish refreshments for faculty meetings, to make draperies for other areas of the school, to repair or launder athletic uniforms, to make robes for the choir or costumes for a play, and to perform a myriad of other tasks. The teacher will have to use good judgment in deciding when to grant or refuse a request. Certainly, the home economics department should not become a service center to the extent that important, planned learning activities have to be curtailed. However, many of the jobs requested by others can be carried out as valuable learning experiences for the home economics students involved.

Students can take turns serving refreshments at meetings and teas, and a small group of students can plan and set the table to facilitate quick service. Appropriate foods can be prepared earlier in the year during a class when procedures for freezing are taught. Students who complete their laboratory assignments faster than others can be meaningfully involved by working on special service projects. For example, students making costumes for a play may also have an opportunity to do some historical research or to apply knowledge of fabric characteristics or of clothing as an expression of identity. Assembly-line techniques of clothing construction can be used to produce many similar items, such as choir robes.

Organizing and Maintaining Laboratory Space

During the course of a day, many different students use the home economics department facilities. It is important that each group leave the equipment and other resources in good order and condition so that subsequent groups can proceed with their work as planned. It is helpful to post a list of procedures for using department facilities where it can easily be seen. In this way, home economics classes and other groups who use the facilities will know what is expected in the way of leaving the department in order.

Labeling cupboards, drawers, and shelves makes it easier to keep equipment in its proper place. Sometimes numbers or dots of different colors can be painted on items to designate the unit kitchens in which they belong. By using plain dinnerware of varying colors for different kitchens, the dishes can be combined for special occasions; afterward, they can easily be returned to their respective units.

Other suggestions that facilitate keeping the department orderly, attractive, and efficient follow:

1. Have duplicate cleaning supplies and equipment so that housekeeping tasks can be performed quickly.
2. Have a box or drawer that serves as a lost-and-found, and have students check there first for misplaced items.
3. Provide space near the door for students to leave clothing and books that will not be needed.
4. Conceal supplies and materials needed for future activities by using a decorative screen or one that can double as a bulletin board.
5. Put instructional materials in one designated place, once they have been used, so that students, assistants, or aides will know where to return them.
6. Plan lessons so that more than one class can use the equipment, materials, and supplies while they are out.
7. As much as possible, repair or replace worn items as necessary

Most schools require an annual inventory of equipment, utensils, and supplies on hand near the end of the academic year. Usually, forms for this purpose are provided for teachers to complete and turn in. They are kept on file in an administrative office. It is advisable to make duplicates and to keep at least one copy of the inventory in the home economics department. Students can help take inventory, and this activity can be related to on-the-job experiences and clarification of principles of storage and efficient management.

Preparing and Using Professional Files

One of the home economics teacher's most valuable resources should be the files. Materials in the departmental files when a teacher comes to a school, visual aids made with school supplies, and those items ordered in the name of the school are public property. They should be left in the department if a teacher changes positions. However, obsolete materials should be discarded. Materials that a teacher may buy with personal funds or make with personal supplies and those acquired in college classes belong to the individual teacher.

The files usually contain professional reports and records, lesson and unit plans, teacher-made and commercial teaching aids, newspaper and magazine articles, booklets, pictures, information sheets made available through the Extension Service, and any other materials that are helpful in classroom teaching and individualizing instruction. Whether the teacher is revising an established file or beginning a new one, the filing system should ensure quick location and easy replacement of materials.

Filing Systems

Select a filing system to which folders can be added logically without having to rearrange the established sequence. In an alphabetical arrangement, an extra folder can be slipped in place easily or the materials in one folder can be subdivided into additional categories. No two folders should have the same title. When a numerical system is used, folders are initially placed in alphabetical order and numbered accordingly. As additions or subdivisions are made, numbers are either added at the end of each section or decimal points or letters are added to the original designation, such as 12.1, 11.1, or 12A, 12B. A folder designated "miscellaneous" should either be put in sequence alphabetically or placed at the end of a section. When such a procedure is employed, there is less tendency to fill the folder than when it appears in front.

Labels

Labels of various colors can be used to designate broad areas included in the file, such as child development, clothing and textiles, and consumer education. The labels may be typed so that the general subject appears in red or in capital letters, or is underscored.

Coding

Coding an item facilitates its return to its proper folder. If all materials are coded in the same easy-to-see place, such as the upper right-hand corner of the page, filing can be done quickly. The coding may be placed on a small piece of the colored label used to designate that subject. If an alphabetical filing system has been selected, abbreviations such as CD, C & T, and CE may be used. (See the preceding section.) It is helpful to include on the file folder label any abbreviation used in coding. Subheadings may be written out or shortened in code, provided no other folder contains the same abbreviation. If a numerical system is used, coding is very simple, since 1.1, 1.2, and 1.3 would indicate the exact folder to which an item should be returned. Since coding is a time-consuming task, students may be able to help.

Cross referencing

Often an item can be filed logically in one of several folders. A leaflet entitled *Birthday Cakes for Tots* could be placed under child development, food and nutrition for special occasions, baking, or several other headings. Once a decision has been made about where to file a specific item, reference can be made to it in other folders. This cross reference can be recorded by writing on the folder itself, or on some durable material in it, "Also see . . . for. . . ." Name specifically the item to which reference is made so that time will not be wasted by examining an entire folder of materials.

Index

An index is to a file what a card catalog is to a library. The index should be double- or triple-spaced so additions can be made to it without retyping. It is advisable to indicate the color designating each area and any abbreviations used. The pages of the index can be preserved by putting them in sheets of plastic. Using an index is more efficient than looking through a drawer full of file folders; the index can save time for both teacher and student.

Using Student Assistants and Teacher's Aides

If a school does not have a system for utilizing student assistants, it may be possible to start such a program, perhaps through chapters of Future Homemakers of America or Future Teachers of America. In some schools, students are assigned as assistants to a specific teacher. They earn one-half unit of credit in office management or clerical practice and are assigned grades for their work. It is advantageous to have a student assistant who has skills in typing, filing, and operating business machines, as well as some background in home economics. There also are many advantages in selecting a student assistant who has previously been in the teacher's classes but who is not currently enrolled in one. This student will be familiar with the procedures used in the department, with the location of equipment and teaching materials, and with the subject matter. If the student is not in a home economics class while serving as a student assistant, the possibility of confidences being revealed to others is minimized. More work can be accomplished if the student assistant is available during the teacher's planning period than when the teacher is in class.

Teacher's aides are widely used in schools today. Usually they are chosen because they like working with people and have competencies that enable them to perform tasks that free teachers from routine work of a paraprofessional nature. Very often those teachers who are able to think of ways to use a teacher's aide are the ones who receive the most help.

The services of both student assistants and teacher's aides can be utilized in typing letters; reports; masters for duplicated copies of classwork, assignment sheets, and handouts; and materials for making transparencies. However, some school administrators request that neither teacher's assistants nor teacher's aides type or grade tests. Their services may be used in making media such as flannel boards, posters, bulletin boards, flip charts, and audio tapes. They can set up displays, prepare foods for the supply table, develop composite market orders, partially prepare materials for a demonstration, check students' lockers or tote trays, straighten supply cupboards, file materials, and help take inventories.

In schools where neither student assistants nor teacher's aides are available, there are other alternatives available to the teacher. Students may be able to prepare home economics materials in other classes, such as typing or art, or in school-related clubs. If students are permitted to perform certain tasks traditionally carried out by the teacher, they will help lighten the teacher's workload and at the same time gain valuable experience.

ADMINISTRATIVE MANAGEMENT

Organized reports and budgets, although not usually considered to be the most exciting and creative aspects of teaching, are essential to a well-run home economics department. Once a functional system is developed, it is usually easy to maintain.

Keeping Records and Preparing Reports

Accurate and detailed records provide information you can use to document the accomplishments and annual reports that affect the future status of the department. You can use the information to evaluate student progress and to manage the budget in a more objective manner. In addition, you are able to evaluate the curriculum and teaching strategies implemented during the year.

It is helpful to keep a file of newspaper clippings and pictures pertaining to activities of the home economics department. Date the articles, indicate the paper they were taken from, and record the names of people appearing in photographs. Students can be responsible for doing this and for writing brief reports summarizing special activities. The reports should identify the event being described and answer these questions—who, what, where, when, and why. A student, perhaps an FHA or HERO member, may be designated as the official department photographer. Snapshots of not more than five persons are most acceptable. At the end of the school year, articles and pictures can be used to provide evidence of departmental accomplishments.

It is advisable to keep a log in which conferences with students and contacts with parents are recorded. Each entry can be brief, including the date, the nature of the meeting, and the main points covered. It is also important to keep a record of the instructional units and the time devoted to each. When reports are due at the end of the school year and plans are made for the next year, this information will be readily available. For future reference, the following should also be on file:

1. The number of students enrolled in various home economics courses
2. Class roll and grade books
3. Plan books, including objectives and concepts covered in each course and the length of time devoted to each subject area
4. Records of activities, programs, and achievements relating to FHA and HERO
5. Number of home contacts made
6. Summary of types of out-of-school experiences completed and descriptions of examples of one or two
7. Descriptions of one or two new and innovative ideas incorporated into the home economics program that year
8. Copies of annual reports
9. Evaluation devices that can be revised for future use
10. Evaluations of films and the guide questions or follow-up activities used with them as well as with filmstrips, skits, and reading assignments
11. Expenditures made in previous years and during the present year
12. Needs for maintenance, repair, and replacement
13. Inventory records

The financial reimbursement received by a school and the reputations of both the school and a teacher may be affected by the accuracy of reports, particularly the annual report. Reports may be your only contact with the central office administrators; therefore, it is important that information be reported accurately, clearly, concisely, and on time.

Managing Finances

When preparing the budget for the department, it is necessary to allow for repairs and replacements. It is a good idea to keep notes of what is needed as the school year progresses, since you must be prepared to justify all expenditures that are planned.

Involving students in making up the budget helps them realize that the department is theirs as well as their teachers' and can be a valuable learning experience in money-management concepts. In working with the budget, it should become apparent to students that the expenditures per individual are greater in smaller classes than in larger ones. This fact can be related to the cost per person of preparing meals for one or two individuals as compared with preparing foods in larger quantities. When prices are charged for products made and services rendered by students in home economics classes, it is usually required that any profits go back into the program. With guidance, students can help decide how these funds will be reinvested.

During these inflationary days, there is a need to keep tight control over departmental expenses. Many teachers are operating on last year's budget while paying today's prices. The problem is compounded when trying to maintain a quality program and increase student enrollment in home economics classes. Thinking of different ways to do things more economically is likely to be a top priority. Some of the following suggestions may be helpful:

- Investigate whether repairs on equipment can be made free of charge by others in school, such as industrial arts classes or the custodial staff.
- Visit local businesses such as department stores, florists, fabric stores, and other specialty shops to request material such as fabric remnants and swatches, wallpaper books, rug and upholstery samples, flowers, and ribbons that can be used as teaching aids.
- Save trading stamps to obtain equipment, furnishings, and accessories needed in the department.
- Duplicate handouts and student worksheets so both sides of a sheet of paper are used, if the material is readable.
- Use free filmstrips and films rather than give a demonstration to show food-preparation principles and techniques for expensive lessons in an area such as meat cookery.
- Arrange for food demonstrations to be given by home economists from utility companies and by personnel from bakeries, specialty food stores, and catering services.
- Try to secure donations of food or other materials from local businesses.
- Encourage students to think of and use less expensive substitutes for ingredients in recipes, such as generic brands instead of nationally advertised brands, crunchy cereals in place of nuts, and canned cheese soup for cheddar cheese sauce.
- Shop for "specials" in stores if you have the time and if you are not restricted to purchasing supplies from a designated store.
- Use cents-off coupons when shopping.
- Identify stores that give school discounts.
- Obtain certain foods needed in quantity, such as dried milk, through the school cafeteria.
- Buy lower-priced seasonal foods in quantity if storage facilities are available.
- Grow herbs that can be used in cooking and as garnishes, and that also make the department attractive. Use garbage such as avocado seeds and the tops of pineapples to grow decorative plants.

Sometimes students ask if they can collect money to buy expensive food items or bring extra foods to use in meal preparation. Teachers should realize that some students may feel uncomfortable because they are unable to contribute, but they would be reluctant to say so. Check the school policy to determine whether student contributions of this nature are allowed.

Taking advantage of opportunities to implement good management practices in operating a classroom and department pays dividends in the long run. Once you have invested the time needed to establish good management practices, you have more time to devote to other professional activities.

MOTIVATION AND CLASSROOM CONTROL 20

Motivation and classroom control go hand in hand. Students who are motivated and interested in their work are unlikely to present major behavior problems. Providing purposeful and stimulating learning activities that will interest students is a challenge that must be met in order to achieve an environment conducive to learning.

MOTIVATION

Dealing with students' attitudes toward school and their interpretations of subject matter may necessitate learning about the lifestyles of students in the class, as well as their views of the environment. Sometimes it is appropriate to indicate situations when the subject matter is likely to be especially valuable. A teacher might begin a lesson with "You will be able to use this information when . . ." or "You will need to know this if . . ." or "It will help you at work to know . . ."

Teachers need to realize that they teach through their verbal behavior and their actions. Anything teachers say or do may significantly change a student's self-concept, feelings, and attitudes, either for better or worse. Undoubtedly, you can recall an instance in which something a teacher said had an enormous impact on your self-concept. Remember that a positive self-concept is one of the prime factors in motivation and achievement.

Self-Concept

Teachers are not likely to motivate students by saying "I like you." Teachers have to establish an atmosphere of mutual trust and respect that makes each student feel worthy. Teachers do not get the respect of students by demanding it. Esteem and honor must be earned. One way to start is to take time to listen to what students have to say and to use their ideas and suggestions whenever possible. Teachers who are receptive to students' feelings show this with remarks made in a positive manner. If a student seems to disagree with a statement another has just made, you might say, "John does not seem to see it that way. How do you feel about it, John?" Wise teachers also bear in mind attitudes previously expressed and show this recollection by making a comment such as: "Yesterday Marie expressed the opinion that . . ." Motivating students and building their self-confidence is partially dependent upon consistently listening to what they have to say.

Self-concept is also related to the students' realistic selection of objectives. When students are given a choice of problems to work on and are told that these are ranked in order of difficulty, low achievers typically select either the easiest or the most difficult. They choose from among the simpler items because of their lack of self-esteem or, conversely, from the more difficult because they reason that nobody else in the class can handle the problem, either. The incentive and rewards for achieving at such a high level may be so great for these students that they become unrealistic about the situation. Average or above-average achievers are likely to select problems of medium difficulty.

When students of average or above-average ability are unsuccessful with their problems, they generally select easier and less challenging ones the next time they are offered a choice. In other words, failure in one situation affects one's self-concept and the goals one sets for oneself. The old saying "Nothing breeds success like success" has wide implications for teachers. It is their responsibility to help students choose projects and assignments from which they can gain a sense of challenge, achievement, satisfaction, and success. Of course, it is also necessary to give students enough guidance and help to enable them to accomplish their tasks reasonably well in relation to their backgrounds, previous experience, skills, and overall abilities.

Teachers' Behaviors That Affect Student Motivation

It is important to realize that students, like teachers, behave in terms of what seems to be true. Teaching and learning are accomplished not necessarily according to what the facts are, but according to how they are perceived. A sense of acceptance or rejection can be communicated to students by their teacher's posture, gestures, and demeanor. The teacher who frequently stands with arms folded may inadvertently be conveying the message, "Don't approach me. I'm unapproachable." Similarly, the teacher who is always sitting behind the desk rather than occasionally getting physically close to the students may be communicating, "I really don't care about you," or "I am the authority in this room." Slouching and slumping may reflect indifference and boredom, whether real or imagined. On the other hand, maintaining good eye contact, smiling, and giving students your full attention may communicate to students, "I think you are important."

Some factors that tend to lessen motivation in the classroom are overemphasis on the acquisition of knowledge and on memorization of facts; disapproval of curiosity; a great deal of negative criticism; rejection of suggestions for additional or alternative activities; overreliance on the lecture method of teaching, or on textbooks; and highly authoritative approaches to maintaining discipline. The teacher who asks, "Why did you do it *that* way?" is more likely to suppress a desire to learn than one who asks, following an unsuccessful student effort, "What do you suppose happened?" Other kinds of remarks teachers sometimes make that adversely affect motivation are:

"This is how *you* do it *in* my class."

"I tried it once. It won't work."

"You know you should not have done it like that."

Unfortunately, many experiences in school stifle students' enthusiasm for learning because of expectations of conformity—disapproval of breaking the traditional mold.

Teacher behavior that is inconsistent, distant, cold, and rejecting is far less likely to enhance self-concept, motivation, and learning than behavior that is warm and accepting and consistent. Self-confidence and self-respect are strong motivating forces. The teacher who realizes this will take every possible opportunity to help students feel wanted, worthwhile, and positive toward themselves. It is important to acknowledge that *all* students have the same need for recognition, attention, and achievement.

Comments on Students' Work

Writing comments on students' papers is well worth the effort. In fact, a personal comment usually has much more motivational value than the grade assigned to the work. A written remark, such as "I am disappointed because this is not up to the standard I have come to expect from you; I'm sure that you'll do your usual quality of work on the next assignment," should certainly encourage the student to do better. A teacher's sincere pride in a student's paper can be reflected by writing something like "I am very pleased with the way your work continues to improve. Keep it up!"

It is recognized that it takes a great deal of time to write remarks appropriate for each student, but personal comments usually have very positive effects on student achievement. A research study was conducted in which a large number of students' papers with grades ranging from A to F were divided equally into the following three groups: those on which only a grade was written; those on which a stereotyped comment such as "Keep up the good work," "Needs improvement," or "You can do better" was written; and those that contained statements showing personal and professional concern for the individual student. On the next assignment, the students who had been given only a grade the first time made the least progress; the students who had received personal comments made the most improvement. In fact, those students in the latter group who had done failing work on the first assignment made the greatest improvement of all the students in the study.*

When evaluating students' work, it is advisable to both begin and end with positive comments and to intersperse negative remarks between the favorable ones. Negative criticisms are more likely to be accepted and acted upon if they are preceded by positive ones. Finishing with a positive comment leaves the student with a better feeling than ending the evaluation on an unfavorable note. It is almost always possible to find something good to say about any project.

Extrinsic Versus Intrinsic Motivation

Extrinsic rewards are those that are not directly related to an achievement itself. Though they result from the achievement, they are really something extra. Examples include: giving a student $5 for every grade of A earned; promising new clothes if grades are raised in a certain subject; or making a down payment on a car if the student stays in school until graduation. In the classroom, students may be given food to eat if they work on their assignments quietly all period, or they may be promised a party if they finish their clothing construction projects on time. They are being motivated by external forces.

Intrinsic motivation comes from *within* the individual. It means wanting to do well for its own sake, and it brings a sense of self-satisfaction and self-fulfillment.

Many parents and educators shudder at the thought of motivating students extrinsically because the rewards have to cease at some time and, in life, people are not necessarily compensated for all their accomplishments. However, there is always the possibility that extrinsic motivation may evolve into intrinsic motivation. This is likely to happen if, in working for an extrinsic reward, the student also gains a sense of personal achievement and if the reward is as closely related to the accomplishment as possible.

CLASSROOM CONTROL

There are no hard-and-fast rules for establishing classroom control. The reason is that there are differences from one area of the country to another, from one school to another, and from one class to another. Effective solutions depend on the types of learners, teachers' personalities and abilities, the curriculum, and the unique interaction of all of these.

Problem students usually represent only a small proportion of the student population. However, for inexperienced teachers, one or two difficult students can seem like a classroom full of problems. Think positively. The majority of students are conscientious and hard-working.

It is not easy to teach in all schools, and not all classes are easy to teach. In some schools, the motivation to learn is high, and the environment in classrooms is relaxed and informal. In schools where the student population is more difficult

*E. B. Page, "Teacher Comments and Student Performance," *Journal of Educational Psychology*, XLIX, 1958, pp. 173–181.

to handle, teachers have to work harder to get and maintain students' attention.

If you are a new teacher in a school or if there is an administrative change in a school where you have been teaching, it is best to find out the school policies on discipline. Determine what type of support you can expect from administrators. Of course, that is a resource you would use only when you had tried everything else.

Getting off to a good start

The importance of "setting the right tone" in your classes at the beginning of school cannot be overestimated. During the first few days, students size up you, the class, and the situation. They test you to determine the limits you place on various forms of behavior and whether they will like or dislike the class. In other words, students decide how cooperative they intend to be.

Be in class before the students arrive if at all possible. It is an especially good practice to stand in the doorway at the beginning and the end of class and talk to students. Students need to know they are important and welcome.

Give students something definite and interesting to do the first day of class so they learn at least one new piece of information before they leave the room. Don't worry about how much material you cover the first week or two of class as long as there is an atmosphere conducive to learning. As you begin to develop rapport with students, involve them in helping you select the subject matter to be covered to ensure that it is helpful to them and meets their needs.

The first five minutes of class is very important in establishing class control for the remainder of the period. Begin class only after you have students' attention. Although you may have to wait a few minutes before beginning, there is little point in starting and then having to repeat what was said earlier.

There is no substitute for being organized when teaching. Disorganization—unscheduled time, poorly planned activities, and a lack of congruence in the subject matter—inevitably leads to confusion, lack of student interest, and potential behavior problems.

Interacting with students

As you go about the daily business of working with students both in and out of the classroom, be friendly, warm, and pleasant without becoming a part of their social group. Students want teachers they respect, not buddies.

When there is a disagreement between you and a student, avoid arguing with the student in front of the class. A confrontation serves no useful purpose and only disrupts the class activity. There are usually no winners in a confrontation. When a student does need extra help in establishing personal control and learning the limits of permissible behavior, try to talk quietly to the student at the end of the period or during a free period. Tell the student what behavior you expect. Be positive; focus on the desirable consequences of cooperating rather than on what will happen if behavior is unacceptable.

When it is necessary to correct students for misbehavior, each situation has to be evaluated on its own merits. However, it is important to be consistent in the way problem behavior is handled. Listen to a student's explanation carefully, patiently, and sympathetically. There is doubtful effectiveness in severe discipline, in punishing a class for the misbehavior of one student, or in making the offending student write "I will not . . ." 100 times. Lowering a student's grade for inappropriate behavior is also poor practice. The problem is not the student's achievement but the student's behavior. By lowering a grade, you are associating punishment with learning.

If you are sure a particular student is responsible for an act of inappropriate behavior, avoid forced confessions and apologies which only serve to encourage a student to lie. In many instances, you already know the facts. Tell the student you are aware of what was done, and that you do not want to see it repeated.

The longer you wait to to assert control in a classroom, the more difficult it will be to establish it. Students sense which teachers will enforce control and which will not. Nevertheless, it is important to keep a sense of perspective and not challenge the perpetrator of every minor offense. You may be the only one annoyed, and sometimes situations become magnified out of all proportion. Be *certain* a student made an offensive comment or misbehaved before you take action that might cause a confrontation in class or put you on the defensive with the students. Decide when to go along with a joke. It is important to maintain your sense of humor; you will need it at times.

People sometimes associate control with rules and policies. However, it is important to establish only the rules and policies you intend to enforce. When a multitude of rules are in effect and you try to enforce all of them, you spend a great deal of your time doing so. On the other hand, rules that are not enforced serve to encourage students to challenge other rules.

Be cautious about giving students passes to leave the room. Generally, it is best not to give students passes to leave the room at the beginning of the period. You might say, "You had a chance between classes. Class is beginning now." If students ask for passes to leave the room in the middle of a period, tell them to wait a few minutes. Probably they won't ask again because you have made it clear you do not approve of their missing part of the class. When students request permission to leave the room near the end of the period, tell them to wait until the class is over.

If a class tends to create disciplinary problems, keep your eyes on the students until you establish pleasant yet firm control. It is inadvisable to turn your back on an unruly class, even to write on the chalkboard. Make a list of students who are inattentive in class. Work to get them involved. It may also be helpful in especially difficult situations to change a disruptive student's seat to one near you. By having control over each individual in class, you have control over the entire class.

Cheating

Students' reasons for cheating are varied, and it is not always easy to decide how to handle such problems. It is impossible to prevent cheating from occurring altogether, but there are measures that can be taken to minimize the problem.

When students respect a teacher and perceive that they are treated equitably, and when rapport is developed between students and the teacher, students are less likely to cheat than when any of the opposite conditions exist. Teachers are responsible for creating an environment that makes it difficult for students to cheat when taking a test. For example, the period during which a test is being given is not an appropriate time for teachers to concentrate on work at their desks to the extent that they are oblivious to students' actions. On the other hand, the teacher who walks around the room and peers over students' shoulders throughout a test period can be very annoying and distracting.

Especially in crowded classrooms, be sure that there is ample space around individual students. This will make it less easy for them to look at others' test papers. If it is difficult to provide sufficient space around students or if cheating is a problem, you may want to develop two different test formats by arranging the same questions in different order. Giving a test on short notice or springing a test may cause students to resent the teacher's actions and make it easier for them to rationalize their cheating by telling themselves it is justifiable.

When cheating is suspected, the teacher must act carefully. Accusing a student of dishonest behavior, in the absence of concrete evidence, will put you in an untenable position and may have a detrimental effect on the student's future actions. The situation can often be handled subtly. For example, a teacher might take the two identical papers of students who sit next to each other and write across them, as if on one sheet: "My, but it is unusual that your two papers are exactly alike." Nothing further may be required. It can be predicted that these particular students will be grateful that an issue was not made of the situation, and they are not likely to repeat the behavior in that teacher's class.

When public accusations and confrontations occur, both parties may emerge blemished regardless of who is right or wrong. Often relationships are strained for too long afterward. Even if a student has cheated, it is important that the incident not affect the student-teacher relationship the next day. The incident is over. Harboring resentment and suspicion is not conducive to a positive relationship.

If several members of a class are involved in cheating, never penalize the entire class for actions of a few by giving another test the next day or making an extra assignment. The infraction is not the responsibility of the entire class. In addition, evaluation and academic work should not be associated with punishment.

All teachers have classroom-control or cheating problems at some time during their careers. It is important not to dwell on the bad days and situations that you might have handled poorly. Instead, think of all the students who do not create problems and of all the good days and good lessons you have had.

ETHNIC AND SEX-ROLE STEREO-TYPING 21

The aim of legislation in the areas of civil rights and sex equality is to encourage people to reappraise their basic assumptions and practices regarding different ethnic groups and the roles of males and females. It is natural for people to have some biases and stereotyped ideas about others. But when these are carried to extremes, the life experiences of individuals who have these prejudices are severely limited. Some forms of bias and some stereotyped ideas are blatantly obvious, and some are subtle. Most are the result of long-standing traditions.

THE MULTIETHNIC CLASSROOM

Generally, the longer families are a part of the mainstream of American life, the more they acquire the characteristics of the so-called "typical family" and the less likely they are to identify with, and be identified by, the specific characteristics of their origins. When people are not characterized as coming from society's mainstream or when they are new members of that mainstream, they are often treated as being different. Unfortunately, being different frequently carries the false connotation of being inferior.

Because of the increasing mobility of our society today, teachers often find themselves working with students from different ethnic backgrounds. If this is a new experience or one that has not been satisfactorily resolved, there are some guidelines that may be helpful in promoting positive relationships with people from other ethnic groups.

Communicating with Members of Ethnic Groups

Teachers who can communicate successfully with students from all ethnic and socioeconomic groups are often characterized as being self-accepting individuals, aware of both their strengths and their weaknesses. When people can accept themselves, they are likely to be able to accept others who are different. Nothing can replace a sincere interest in all students—a belief that all of them have worth and the potential for success in their own individual ways.

Calling each student by his or her name or by the name the student prefers, and pronouncing each name correctly, are aids to communication. When names from other ethnic or cultural groups are difficult to pronounce, it may be helpful to write the names phonetically (for your own use) or to get students' voices on a recorder as they give their names and tell a little about themselves and their interests.

In talking to students, it is important to be careful about using unintended "put-downs." These are often meant to "break the ice" or to be merely friendly remarks. However, they may not be interpreted that way by the people hearing them. Some comments may be considered racist; others may be regarded as patronizing—too solicitous or artificial. Examples of remarks that can easily "turn off" other people are:

"You people are such good athletes (cooks, entertainers, and so on)."

"My friend Juan is a Mexican-American."

"I know what it's like to be discriminated against, too."

"The people on your side of town ought to go together."

"Do you know Mary Wu in San Francisco?" (The mistaken assumption is that all people in an ethnic group know one another.)

These well-intended remarks and similar ones can inhibit communication.

If you are accused of prejudice by a member of another ethnic group, avoid appearing defensive by denying the accusation. Since you probably are not sure of exactly what the student is referring to, try to get more information. For example, you might ask, "What have I done that seems prejudiced?" Or, "I am not aware I have been. When did you see me do or say something that appears to be prejudiced? Please point it out to me." This approach will encourage dialogue. If the student has specifics to point out, you will have learned something new about the way others perceive your actions. On the other hand, the student may have no concrete evidence of prejudicial actions on your part but may simply make the remark to see how you will react.

If members of an ethnic group segregate themselves by sitting together all the time, avoid making an issue of it. It is likely that the students are apprehensive about mixing with others. Plan some activities in which students have to move around and mix with each other. When people get to know others on a one-to-one basis, the unknown becomes less threatening.

EXPECTATIONS AND ACTIONS REGARDING SEX ROLES

Students often have a very limited perspective of what life will be like five, ten, fifteen, or more years in the future. Teachers have a responsibility to help students explore the many options open to them.

The world of tomorrow is today. Lifestyles are changing, and people are gradually becoming more objective about current-day realities. For example, it is obsolete to view the husband as the primary wage earner and the wife as a wage earner only in times of crises, such as divorce or widowhood. The options of pursuing a lifelong career, marrying later, having a small family or not having children at all, having two incomes, remaining single, and deciding on single parenthood are being considered and taken by more and more women and men today. The traditional roles should not be discarded. They are alternatives for people. However, the advantages and disadvantages of the traditional roles and the new emerging roles for both males and females need to be explored objectively to enable students to make rational choices.

It is self-defeating to educate for changing role patterns if traditional sex-role expectations are perpetuated in the classroom. The following checklist should help you think about your professional practices with respect to sex stereotyping and sex bias.

SEX STEREOTYPING CHECKLIST

- Do you avoid using such biased language as *the doctor . . . he; mankind; the lady lawyer; mothering; John Smith and Mrs. Alex Brown; Amanda, a pretty brunette, and José, a skilled mechanic*? Instead, do you use bias-free language, such as *doctors . . . they; humankind; the lawyer . . . she; parenting; John Smith and Sara Brown; Amanda, an excellent athlete, and José, a skillful mechanic*?
- When you discuss career choices, do you provide nontraditional examples, such as administrative-level positions for females and clerical or nursing positions for males?
- In a class of males and females, do only male students pass out books and operate film projectors? Do only female students water plants and take notes to the office?
- If students were writing letters to business people, would you have them begin their letters *Dear Sir*?
- Do you encourage females to be more concerned about their grooming than males?
- Would you be as concerned about a senior female student as you would about a senior male student who was unable to make career plans?
- If a student made the statement that follows, would you ask the student to examine it? "Mothers pick up their children at day-care centers."
- Do you expect the males in class to be more boisterous than the females?
- Do you provide a variety of traditional and nontraditional role models of both sexes for your students?
- Do you have the same work standards for males and females?

- Do you recruit both males and females for your classes?
- Do you evaluate your teaching materials and curriculum for sex stereotyping and sex bias?
- If you have sex-stereotyped materials, do you find positive ways of teaching from them?
- Do you work with youth groups to ensure that teenagers, themselves, do not discriminate against members of either sex?
- If members of the administration or faculty make remarks that are sex-biased, do you draw their attention to this? Do you explain why such remarks are harmful?

Developing Sensitivity Through Class Activities

A variety of learning activities can be used to help students think through the effect sex-role stereotyping has had on their lives and the impact more equitable roles will have in the future. The following suggestions may help you generate other ideas:

- Give students a fact sheet on women's participation in the work force. For example "Nine out of ten females will work outside the home at some time in their lives. Include figures which show that about 42 million women are in the labor force; they constitute roughly 50 percent of all workers. A majority of women work out of economic necessity. About 60 percent of all women workers are single, widowed, divorced, or separated, or have husbands earning less than $7,000 per year. In all areas, women earn less than men." Using these figures, discuss the implications of women's increasing participation in the work force as it relates to educational preparation. Predict changes that will occur in interpersonal relations and the family structure.
- Divide the class in half. Have half the students prepare a list of gift items for a man and the other half, gift items for a woman. List the items on the board. Discuss any obvious stereotypes involved. Are perfume and beauty items emphasized for women, reinforcing concerns about physical attractiveness? Is sports equipment mentioned for men, reinforcing the image of athletic prowess?
- Duplicate and distribute or write on the board a list of ways in which teachers treat or react to male and female students stereotypically. For example, teachers often ask girls to put up bulletin boards and boys to repair equipment. Other examples might include: girls don't like math or science; boys have more difficulty learning to read; boys are disruptive and present behavioral problems; girls prefer home economics and boys prefer industrial arts; girls have no mechanical aptitude. Students can add to this list. Discuss the impact these behaviors and assumptions have on young people.
- Use role play to focus on role conflicts. For example, role-play a husband telephoning his wife. A VIP is in town and wants to take them out to dinner tonight. The husband feels that this meeting is a prelude to an important promotion for him. The wife has been asked by her boss to represent their department at an important company social function taking place at the same

time. She feels it is essential to her career that she attend the meeting. Encourage the students to think of and act out other role-conflict situations.

Some additional references on sex-role stereotyping that you may find helpful include:

- Educational Challeneges, Inc. *Today's Changing Roles: An Approach to Non-Sexist Teaching.* Washington, D.C.: The National Foundation for The Improvement of Education, 1974.
- Grant, Anne. *Removing the Mask: a Workbook for Teachers Concerned about Sex-Role Stereotyping.* New York, New York: New York City Board of Education, 1978.
- Sadker, Myra and David Sadker. *Beyond Pictures and Pronouns: Sexism in Teacher Education Textbooks.* Washington, D.C.: United States Department of Health, Education and Welfare, Office of Education.
- Sprung, Barbara, ed. *Perspectives on Non-Sexist Early Childhood Education.* New York, New York: Teachers College Press, 1978.
- Stacey, J. and Bernard J. Daniels, eds. *And Jill Came Tumbling After.* New York, New York: Dell, 1974.
- *TABS: Aids for Ending Sexism in School.* A quarterly journal of aids. 744 Carroll Street, Brooklyn, N.Y. 11215.

Although the school is not totally responsible for the problems created by ethnic and sex-role stereotyping, it is one of the major socializing agencies in our society and must assume some responsibility. Professional educators shape the milieu in which adolescents may or may not be free to develop to their full potential, without restrictions based on their sex or ethnic backgrounds. Teachers also have the responsibility to help students learn to accept and deal with a wide range of human differences. Teachers' values, perceptions, and attitudes are continually reflected in the curriculum planning and classroom interaction that influence learning and individual development.

INDIVIDUALIZING INSTRUCTION 22

Because the home economics profession serves all segments of the population, many of whom have special needs, providing opportunities for personalizing instruction is especially important. Certainly, some core material may be essential for all learners, but beyond that, chances to pursue special interests will help students maximize their learning.

During individualized instruction, students assume responsibility for their learning. Students select, plan, carry out, and evaluate their own learning experiences. There are many variations of individualized instruction. In some situations, the entire program is individualized, whereas in others, a lesson or even a unit of study may be individualized. The amount of responsibility students assume may be somewhat limited or fairly extensive, but choice and responsibility are key components. Throughout the process of individualized instruction, teachers are still active in the teaching-learning process, but their roles are primarily those of catalyst and resource person.

CAUTIONS RELATING TO INDIVIDUALIZING INSTRUCTION

There are certain problems involved in individualizing instruction. Developing materials in this area is time-consuming. There are some published materials available, but these are limited in number. However, if good individualized instruction materials are developed, they will be ready when needed the next time. Many classroom facilities do not lend themselves easily to individualizing instruction. In these cases, the teacher's and students' ingenuity can overcome structural limitations. Because students are working on a variety of projects in different areas of the room, the general appearance may lack the orderliness usually associated with traditional schoolrooms and the uniformity characteristic of large-group instruction. However, if teachers believe in the benefits of self-directed learning, they will become accustomed to and welcome this type of activity.

INITIATING INDIVIDUALIZED INSTRUCTION

Some suggestions that may help in the organization and management of individualized instruction follow:

1. Introductions should set the tone or mood for the work to be done. Students are turned on or turned off to new ideas depending on the enthusiasm shown and the positive approach used by the teacher. One or two class periods may be required to prepare students for the increased self-direction in their studies. They need to understand the meaning of self-directed learning, the purposes of the particular area or unit of study, the options available to them, the evaluation process, and the other necessary mechanics that enable the program to function smoothly. If this is the first time individualized instruction is implemented in the classroom, the teacher will want to encourage pupils to participate as fully as possible and will have to be prepared to evaluate the effectiveness of this instructional approach as compared with others.
2. As students' exposure to self-directed learning experiences increases during the course of a year, they will become more involved in planning their own learning programs. They probably will be unable to do this in the beginning because most students lack experience in directing their own classroom activities.

   It is difficult for people to make decisions when they are unaware of the alternatives available to them. At first, students can be given a limited number of choices. "Which would you rather do? A, B, C, or D?" This is better than simply asking, "What do you want to do?" The alternatives offer the student a starting point from which to exercise self-direction. Even if students do not like any of the choices offered, the alternatives will generally suggest other possibilities.

   When students progress to the point where they are ready to develop their own learning programs or conduct their own experiments and investigations, they can submit an outline of the proposed program to the teacher. This outline should include a justification of the choice of the particular project, the behavioral objectives to be met, the procedures to be used, the resources to be investigated, the type of progress reports to be submitted, and the type of final evaluation to be utilized. At first, students may need considerable guidance in formulating their plans, particularly in stating their objectives.
3. The traditional classroom can be transformed into a center for individualizing learning if the students and teachers collaborate and brainstorm ideas. Portable screens, movable chalkboards, and filing cabinets can be used as room dividers in order to establish small study and work areas. Desks, tables, and counter

tops can be made into carrels for quiet work by using simple cardboard partitions to divide space into individual study and work areas. Individual unit kitchens, living areas, or large closets with adequate ventilation can serve as meeting areas for small groups or as resource centers for materials needed for study.

A bulletin board can act as a clearinghouse for weekly class activities. For example, when a film and a field trip are possible activity choices, the teacher needs to know if there is enough student interest to justify scheduling them. Sign-up sheets with captions such as *Movie of the Week* and *Forthcoming Field Trips* could be used to determine possible student participation.

Self-contained learning centers can provide exciting experiences for students regardless of where the areas are located. These centers should be furnished with the materials and equipment students need in order to engage in a specific activity. Teachers can make activity cards for each area, so that students working at the center know some of the things they can do there. In food and nutrition, clothing and textiles, and other content areas, an information card will tell students what materials are needed to perform an activity. A series of questions, to record the students' observations and test their achievement, should also be on cards or paper. Answers to the factual questions can be printed on the back of the cards so that students receive immediate feedback if the teacher is not available at that moment. Another possibility is to use reporting forms on which the students write responses. By using these, teachers have assurance that students are actively responding to the learning activities.

4. Directions and materials should be as self-explanatory as possible. They should minimize the number of times students have to ask what something means or where an article is located. Such inquiries can be very disruptive when teachers have only a limited amount of time in which to guide and help students. They also make it hard for teachers to function effectively as counselors during the class period.

5. The role of teachers involved in individualizing instruction is a difficult one to define because it is continually changing. In the beginning, teachers must have goals clearly in mind and must prestructure the materials and the setting to meet these goals. Teachers who provide opportunities for students to become involved in self-directed learning typically collect and use everything they can think of for learning experiences. Teaching files and mobile equipment suddenly become very important. It is difficult to know what will be helpful to every student. It is easier to allow students to make those decisions. Teachers can use students to help select activities and materials. Students will ignore those that they find uninteresting and unhelpful. The material in that category can then be removed from circulation.

Teachers should circulate among the students to offer assistance and check student progress. By suggesting new directions to take, references to use, and projects to develop, they may encourage students to expand their exploration. Teachers will want to check students' comprehension of what they are studying and also identify learning difficulties and offer individual and small-group instruction. At this time it is also helpful to recommend appropriate follow-up activities that could serve as reinforcement for new learning. When teachers are free from the task of controlling students, they can then act effectively as resource people and tutors.

6. Keeping records of students' plans and work is an integral part of the organization involved in individualizing instruction. Each student should have a folder in which to keep written materials, samples of work, and evaluations. It is easy for folders to become disorganized and messy if little pieces of paper that describe activities are continually added, so avoid this. It may be wise to develop a one- or two-page checklist that itemizes specific available activities and that has blank lines for students to use in listing other learning experiences in which they have been involved. Students may be requested to date each activity or to indicate the length of time spent on each. Teachers can use students' records to determine growth, to diagnose areas of difficulty, and to help students plan additional or alternative activities.

   Teachers may want to add comments and words of encouragement to the students' records. Phrases such as "improvement over last week," "organization shown," or "leadership evidenced" act as positive reinforcement for students.

   Although it involves additional work, teachers may want to keep a personal log of student progress. This can be done by listing the students' names in a column down the left side of a sheet of paper. Activities are abbreviated and written horizontally across the top of the page. Lines are then drawn to form columns and key items are checked off when students complete them.

7. Evaluation should be an integral part of individualizing instruction and may take many forms. Students can list their accomplishments, use a checklist indicating the proficiency they believe they have achieved, take a written posttest, give a demonstration, have a conference with the teacher, or select or devise an evaluative instrument that they believe is meaningful. Evaluation should be kept in the students' folders.

8. As students become self-directed learners, they will also become self-starters when they enter the classroom. A sign-up sheet may be used to encourage students to begin work. At the end of a class period students can sign up for activities they plan to do the next day. Students may change their minds, but the sheet can serve as a reminder for those who forget.

   If students seem to have difficulty beginning work in class, the teacher may make suggestions based on their previous activities. As students become more self-directed in their learning, they will be doing more long-range planning, and their inability to initiate their own activities will be minimized.

CONTRACT TEACHING

Contract teaching has gained academic recognition in recent years. At one time, many teachers did not like it because it emphasized the quantity of work students did rather than quality *and* quantity. For contract teaching to be successful, certain criteria, standards, or behavioral objectives must be established and met in order to judge whether the student has earned a grade of A, B, C, or D. For example, reading six books emphasizing family relationships or making five garments may not be as educationally advantageous as reading three books or making two garments. The caliber and length of the books and what the student gains from reading them may be more valid criteria for judging achievement than the number of works read. If a student meets established standards of quality for a few clothing construction techniques, that may be a greater accomplishment than making four or five very simple garments from the same or similar patterns.

The contract for reading books on the subject could be coordinated with reading assignments for an English class. In order to earn the agreed-upon number of points for such a long-term contract, students would have to read a certain number of books listed according to a point scale based on the difficulty of the books. Thus, students would have to read only two books from the three-point list to accumulate six points but would have to read three books from the two-point list or six books from the one-point list to earn the same number of contract points. Other arithmetical combinations are possible, such as reading two books from the two-point list and two from the one-point list to accumulate the required score for an A. Under the contract system, students make decisions about what and how much work to do. In this example, students who read at a lower level of achievement than most others in the class can compensate for this by reading a greater number of books that are easier to comprehend. Students would know when making the contract that they would receive a certain grade if their summary, annotation, evaluation, or other evidence of reading comprehension met specified standards.

In an advanced clothing construction unit or course, students may contract for an A by agreeing to do ten to twelve of the following at specified standards of quality:

1. Bound buttonholes
2. Machine-made buttonholes
3. Set-in sleeves
4. Matched plaid or print
5. Collar
6. Cuffs
7. Hidden zipper or hand-picked zipper
8. Waistband
9. Self-covered belt
10. Armhole and neck facing in one
11. Flat-felled or French seams
12. Pocket set in seam
13. Welt pocket
14. Lining
15. Gusset

Of course, there are other clothing construction techniques that can be listed. These may be incorporated in as few as two garments or in as many as students have the time, money, and skill to make. A scale for determining grades may be established that is similar to this one:

GRADE	NUMBER OF CONSTRUCTION FEATURES
A	10–12
B	7–9
C	6–8
D	5–7

If students chose to make bound buttonholes for one of the contract points, they might be evaluated according to the following criteria:

BOUND BUTTONHOLES

1. On grain
2. Appropriate size for button
3. Proper distance from edge of facing for size of button
4. Equal distance apart
5. Appropriate number and size for garment
6. Lips appropriate width for length
7. Lips equal size and even
8. Facing finished securely on wrong side
9. Durable
10. Pressed flat without shine

Points such as these, and those relating to other clothing construction techniques, could be incorporated into a checklist, scorecard, or rating scale. (See page 164.) Perhaps the teacher and students together could decide, before any evaluation actually takes place, exactly what will constitute a satisfactory performance on any given task for earning points toward meeting the contract.

Sometimes a designated number of learning activities completed satisfactorily during a given unit or period of time can be used as the basis for designing a contract. In a time contract, students designate a date by which certain parts of a project will be completed. Time contracts are especially suitable for long-term assignments such as those in home experiences or clothing construction. By making time schedules, students are required to think through the necessary steps in a sequential order. Sometimes teachers specify that students cannot earn a higher grade than that originally contracted for. It would seem that this is a decision that the entire class, including the teacher, should make together when the contract system is first introduced and explained. However, it should be kept in mind that imposed grade limitations may stifle and limit student growth potential. It is logical that, if students fail to complete the number of points contracted for or if their work is below standard, the grade will be lowered. Obviously, variations of contract systems are limited only by teachers' and students' imaginations, resourcefulness, and ingenuity.

PROGRAMMED INSTRUCTION

Programmed instruction is one means of individualizing learning that is particularly appealing to students who enjoy reading and working alone. It is best used with factual material such as textiles or nutrition. These four characteristics are the essentials of programmed instruction:

1. Logical, ordered sequence of subject matter that builds in small steps
2. Items requiring student response by filling in a blank or selecting the best answer from a list of choices
3. Reinforcement through immediate presentation of the right answer
4. High degree of probable success

Programmed instruction consists of sequentially ordered items, questions, or statements to which students are asked to make responses before proceeding. The subject matter is presented in such small units that usually only one or two sentences are given before a question is asked. Lead-ins and prompts are built into the text so that it should be easy for students to recognize or recall the information requested. As soon as students make a response, their answers can be checked. Success is acknowledged immediately. Sometimes authors also write in words of encouragement such as "Good work, go on to the next page" or "You're doing fine, keep going."

Periodic summaries can be built into programmed instruction to increase its effectiveness. When students have not answered questions in one of these summaries correctly, they may be asked to go back over the section in which the concept was covered. Conversely, when students have answered lead questions correctly, they may be directed to skip certain parts. This skipping or repeating is called *branching*.

A major disadvantage of programmed instruction is that only a limited number of home economics programs are available commercially and they are time-consuming for teachers to write themselves. They usually have to be used and revised several times before they are perfected. Other disadvantages are that few senses are involved in this type of learning, there is little interaction among students or with the teacher, and the method in itself offers little variety during the class period. However, programmed instruction has the advantage of allowing students to move at their own pace so that fewer bright students are bored. Once good programs are developed, they can be used again and again. Utilizing them during class times gives teachers some freedom to plan and do other things.

INDEPENDENT LEARNING PACKAGES

A well-constructed independent learning package relates to a broad concept that is divided into manageable components or subconcepts. Each subconcept serves as one section of the learning package. For example, the major concept may be entitled "The Developing Child," with three separate yet related sections covering physical, psychological, and social growth.

Each section is similar in format. It should include the behavioral objectives for that particular section, the directions, the learning activities, and some means by which the students evaluate their progress.

The directions indicate how the students are to proceed. Generally, they are required to choose one or more of the activities listed. The required activities provide the background material needed in order to gain some knowledge relating to the concept. After completing the required activities, students can select from a variety of optional ones. The choices should be attractive to students, depending on their interests, intellectual skills, and individual style of learning. For instance, some students learn most effectively by reading or by listening; others require the visual stimulation of pictures, and still others need to become involved through psychomotor activities. Although the choices should be varied, they must be equivalent in their learning potential for meeting the designated behavioral objectives. Ideally, the alternative activity choices serve to reinforce the learning.

Self-evaluation is an integral part of a well-designed learning package. Students evaluate their achievements when they complete each component. Depending on the nature of the concept being studied, students may answer specific questions, solve problems, distinguish between pictures or objects, use a checklist, or employ some other summarizing device. An answer key is included so students can check their work. It is more interesting for students if the self-evaluation devices or reinforcement techniques used throughout a package are varied. When they are satisfied with the results of the self-evaluation, students progress to the next section. If students do poorly on the self-evaluation, they may be directed to review the material previously presented and to do some of the reinforcement activities that were not initially chosen.

Upon successfully completing the independent learning package, students may be motivated to do additional work or research in a particular area related to the subject matter studied. Therefore, a number of diverse enrichment activities may be suggested at the end of the learning package. It should be stressed that these activities are not required, but that they are available for interested students.

Accompanying the students' section of the independent learning package is a separate teachers' section. This includes a statement regarding the type of students for whom the independent package was designed and the approximate level of learning. Specific directions are also included that provide teachers with a list of all materials needed to implement the package. This should include a complete bibliographical citation for periodicals, books, films, filmstrips, and games.

Pre- and posttests, as well as the answer keys, should be included in the teachers' section. The more knowledgeable students can be directed to bypass a particular package and proceed to another activity. Students who do poorly on the pretest may be directed to complete part or all of the requirements contained in the package. The posttest may be the same as the pretest or it may be a comparable evaluation. Both the pre- and posttests should provide a valid measurement of the students' attainment of the behavioral objectives. That is, they should contain a representative sample of the expected learning at the appropriate cognitive, affective, or psychomotor levels of learning.

SPECIFIC AUDIENCES 23

As the role of home economics is continually evaluated and redefined, new programs take shape and broader audiences are reached. Today, home economists find themselves working with people in diverse age groups, people coming from a variety of backgrounds, and people having a broad spectrum of goals. Among these students are adult learners, low-income learners, and intellectually gifted learners. Although each of these groups share some like characteristics, each is also distinct and special.

ADULT LEARNERS

Learning is considered a lifelong process that occurs in both formal and informal settings. A look around reveals that learners include people from all segments of society—and all age groups.

The reasons for the ever-increasing interest and participation in adult education are as varied as the learners themselves. Common motives for going back to school are to keep up with new information in a changing society, to learn better ways to cope and survive in that society, to use leisure time to better advantage, and to prepare for career changes.

Adult education programs are housed almost everywhere. Some of the varied organizations that provide opportunities for adult education are public schools, community and four-year colleges, libraries, museums, correspondence organizations, radio and television stations, professional societies, business and industry, labor unions, penal institutions, government agencies, community organizations, religious groups, volunteer social and welfare agencies, and special-interest groups.

As a discipline, home economics has a great deal to offer adult students. Home economists are trained to deliver up-to-date information in many subject-matter areas as well as to help people assess their personal and career status and prepare for the world of work.

Although there are many commonalities among adults and younger learners, there are some important differences that teachers should recognize and use to advantage. As a group, adults are very heterogeneous. The older people get, the more different they become as a result of their greater insight and experience. Adults are also likely to know what is and isn't going to work. Adults have a longer attention span than younger learners, are more highly motivated, and have immediate goals. Adult learners are also more likely to strive for perfection, because they know from experience that mistakes can be costly. They are more concerned about what they learned *today* and how well their work measures up. Adults may also be more concerned about failure, because they have been out of the educational setting for a while and may have had previous school failures.

The following guidelines can help teachers to promote a beneficial environment:

- Create an informal atmosphere. A highly structured environment may be too reminiscent of secondary education. Arrange the physical setting so that all can see and hear one another.
- State your desire for *all* members of the group to participate in the activities and discussion. Keep a close watch for nonverbal clues of confusion or lack of interest.
- Keep the group's remarks focused on the main topic.
- Avoid talking down to the group or being condescending in your manner.
- Provide continual reinforcement in a variety of ways in order to counter any feelings of inadequacy.
- Present new ideas in an appealing way. Long-established habits and attitudes may prevent people from being open to new ideas and suggestions.
- Consider the pressure adults may feel in trying to balance school, work and family responsibilities in a schedule limited by time.
- Be prepared to help adults operate effectively in the educational system. They may be unfamiliar with school procedures or with the services available to them. They may need to brush up on study skills.
- Emphasize your role as a facilitator rather than as a disseminator of information. A facilitator helps learners identify resources in order to achieve specific outcomes.

Older Adult Learners

The increasing life-span of the average American and the expressed needs of older people to be active in all facets of life have caused society to take a look at the older person and the aging process. Many previously held assumptions and myths about older people are being reexamined in the light of new research evidence. For example, it was previously believed that intelligence increased up to early adulthood, maintained a plateau for about ten years, and began a decline during the fourth decade of life. According to recent data, this is not true. Using various measures of cognitive functioning, researchers have found that several dimensions of intelligence either remained the same or increased with age.

As you work with senior adults, it is important to be aware of physiological changes that are a normal part of the aging process and to make accommodations for them. Some of these physical limitations, together with suggestions for minimizing them, follow:

- Eyesight weakens. Provide good illumination. Use large type on handouts and visuals. Arrange materials so they can be seen clearly and easily. Post materials high enough so people with bifocals can read them easily.
- Hearing declines. Speak slowly and distinctly. Use visual media frequently. Try to eliminate outside and inside noises that interfere with hearing. For the benefit of others, repeat questions asked by students. Check with people at the rear of the group to be sure they can hear easily.
- Motor abilities diminish. Strength available for pulling and gripping is limited. Physical repair after an injury also takes more time. Teach work-simplification techniques. Conduct time-and-motion studies and experiment with various household products and types of equipment.
- Speed and reaction time decline. Avoid rushing. Schedule meetings at accessible locations. Assign a realistic amount of work within a given period. Avoid keeping people overtime.

Displaced Homemakers

Displaced homemakers are people in middle age who have functioned in the traditional role of homemaker but who now, through divorce, death, or loss of family have been removed from previous positions that generally afforded greater security than these persons now have. Almost all displaced homemakers are female. They face many problems as they work toward rebuilding their lives. It is often difficult for them to find employment because they are older and because they usually have very limited work experience outside the home, or none at all. They are not eligible for unemployment insurance because they have not been salaried employees. Most are too young to qualify for social security.

There are an increasing number of programs designed to assist displaced homemakers, but more help is needed. Vocational educators are beginning to work with displaced homemakers and offer a variety of services. Very often home economists are members of a team that provides occupational training and support services. Some displaced homemakers may find that vocational training is unnecessary. With proper counseling, skills learned in doing homemaking and volunteer work can be identified. These skills can help qualify displaced homemakers for a variety of positions. Support services take the form of assistance in the following: assessing personal and job-related assets and limitations, building self-esteem, planning life experiences, developing assertiveness, learning appropriate techniques for employment interviews, writing résumés, searching for a job, and managing resources—money, time, and energy.

LOW-INCOME STUDENTS

The proportion of students from low-income families varies from school to school. Poverty gives rise to disappointments and frustrations that can affect the outlook and behavior of students. Some of these characteristics are discussed below. However, it is important to remember that poverty does not necessarily mean that home conditions are undesirable. The first step in establishing a relationship with individual students is to give the family the benefit of the doubt. Do not assume that the parents are irresponsible, that conditions are immoral, or that there is constant quarreling. The home may be loving and supportive, and thus may be an ally of the teacher in helping the student.

Low-income students are not all the same, then, but many do share some common characteristics. Low-income students often lack motivation, need immediate gratification, learn better by concrete rather than abstract examples, have poor self-concepts, have fatalistic and/or antagonistic attitudes, have short attention spans, are deficient in language and reading skills, and are alienated by educational programs. You can provide immediate recognition of student achievement by using progress charts to indicate when individual students have completed each step in the process of reaching a goal. You can feature a "student of the month" on the bulletin board; suggest a news story about activities in the department, using students' names in the article; and hand back examination papers and other submitted work as soon as possible.

It is always important to consider the students' circumstances, but do not allow students to use their circumstances as excuses for not doing work. Avoid giving false, unearned, and misleading praise because students will either assume they are working up to par or recognize that you are being insincere. Give praise when it has been earned and point out how improvement can be made. Students definitely need encouragement but encourage discreetly. Many students are embarrassed if they receive excessive praise in front of their peers.

If there is a family problem, avoid interfering. If a situation is serious and seems intolerable for a student, report this to the proper authority. It would be wise to check with school administrators first to see what recommendations they would make.

Show a genuine interest in students' plans for the future. Help students to be realistic and avoid fostering impossible dreams, but help them to assess concretely *what they can do* to attain their goals. It may be possible to put the student in touch with someone who would serve as a role model.

Many work-study programs for low-income youth have reported some success in keeping such students in school. Some students stay in cooperative-education school programs only because of their jobs and the salaries they earn. They understand that dropping out of school or being absent from classes too often means they will lose their jobs. Some continue in cooperative programs because they have learned that many unskilled jobs are unexciting. They realize that by learning some skills their chance of getting a good job is much better. It is important that their classes in school help them develop skills for the world of work and skills for survival.

INTELLECTUALLY GIFTED STUDENTS

Intellectually gifted students have superior ability to deal with facts, abstract ideas, and relationships. It is reported that many gifted students do not enroll in home economics classes because they are told or they surmise that classes have a very narrow scope and are not challenging. If the broad scope of the home economics program and the opportunity for in-depth study are emphasized and publicized, there is a good possibility that more gifted students will be attracted.

- Expand the curriculum to provide more depth and breadth. Avoid repetition of, and drill in, material already learned. If students become interested in a particular topic, encourage them to do in-depth reading in that area and/or have them talk to people with expertise in it. In order to offer more breadth, provide students with opportunities to investigate topics related to the main concept or allow them to delve into other areas of interest.
- Provide enough detail so that gifted learners understand a phenomenon. Intellectually gifted students often desire more details than other class members want or need at the moment. Referring gifted learners to references that supply more depth, or indicating that you will discuss the concepts in more detail later may be appropriate approaches.
- Give gifted students opportunities to use their extensive vocabularies in writing, in giving reports, and in participating in classroom discussions. Other students must expand their vocabularies and can do so if definitions of difficult words are provided. On the other hand, the gifted need to know how to say things in simple terms and be sensitive to the feeling of those around them.
- Encourage gifted learners to use their broad fund of information. Their keen memories and their ability to retain and relate information can be helpful in providing interest and depth of content for a class. Care must be taken that the gifted student does not seem to be a "know it all" and thus become alienated from other class members.
- In a class of students having different abilities, some means of individualizing instruction can be used to allow gifted learners to move at their own pace. Permitting students to plan their own individualized learning programs with your assistance and approval will provide opportunities to explore special areas of interest. It may also be possible for your students to do a joint project with students in another class such as physics, chemistry, English, or a foreign language.
- Structure learning experiences so that gifted students discover information for themselves rather than through facts and figures given by you. Encourage them to use the same processes and procedures used by experts in the field. In this way, students learn how to find facts and discover how facts fit together. You might encourage gifted students to carry out investigations of subjects such as the following: Why is the divorce rate increasing and what could be done to help stabilize it? What does the average family do that contributes to inflation and what could they do to help minimize inflation? What wasteful energy habits do families in your town have and how can these practices be curtailed?

MAINSTREAMING 24

The concept of mainstreaming has come of age. Mainstreaming reverses the historical segregation of handicapped students in special classes or special schools. There is no common agreement on a definition of mainstreaming. However, the Education for All Handicapped Children Act, otherwise known as Public Law 94-142, does specify the conditions that must be met by educational institutions in order to receive federal funds. One of the key provisions of the law states that all disabled students up to the age of 21 have the right to a free public education in the least restrictive environment.

Concerns about mainstreaming often center on the inadequate training of educators, which limits their ability to work effectively with the handicapped; safety hazards; a lack of necessary equipment and materials; and the effect of mainstreaming on the progress of students who are not handicapped. But mainstreaming does not present insoluble problems. Current evidence points to increasing success under responsible administration.

HANDICAPPING CONDITIONS

There are a variety of handicapping conditions. Some of these are apparent at birth and others arise later in life as a result of an accident, a disease, or a latent hereditary disorder. Some individuals have only one handicapping condition and others have multiple handicaps.

Handicapping conditions can be classified in a number of ways. However, the categories cited in federal legislation focusing on the handicapped include the following: mentally retarded, hearing impaired, deaf, deaf-blind, speech-impaired, visually handicapped, seriously emotionally disturbed, orthopedically impaired, other health-impaired (cystic fibrosis, epilepsy), specific learning disability (brain injury, dyslexia, aphasia), and multihandicapped.

PLANNING FOR THE HANDICAPPED

The classroom teacher is not alone in working with handicapped persons. Public Law 94-142 specifies that on the basis of an individual assessment, an Individual Education Plan (IEP) must be designed for each handicapped student, and the plan must have parental approval. The child-evaluation team responsible for developing the plan includes a representative of the local education agency, a special education teacher/counselor, parents/guardians, and the student, if appropriate. The home economics teacher may serve as a member of the team or as a resource person.

Prior to the development of the IEP, an assessment is made of the student. The assessment is not a means of selection and classification of students. It serves to identify and to make provision for the needs of the student. An assessment might include:

- Having a personal interview with a student
- Obtaining background information from records and reports
- Testing psychometric and basic skills
- Obtaining samples of student work if needed and if available
- Making behavioral observations

State regulations regarding the specific content of the IEP differ. However, Public Law 94-142 states that the following must be included:

- Level of the present educational performance
- Annual goals and short-term instructional objectives
- List of services to be provided and statement of how much education students will receive in the regular classrooms
- Date when supportive services are due to begin and the expected length of services

In addition to the minimum requirements stated above, states may require some of the following information:

- Preferred learning styles
- Preferred learning situations
- Behavior strengths
- Talent and hobbies
- Special instructional media and materials needed

When working cooperatively as a member of a child-evaluation team or as a resource person, it is important that participants' roles be clearly defined in order to deliver services effectively and efficiently.

The special educator/counselor may be responsible for the following:

- Compiling educational, medical, and social information about the student
- Sharing information with the classroom teacher
- Arranging a meeting between the classroom teacher, the student, and the student's parents/guardians
- Assisting the classroom teacher in planning for the student's first experiences in class
- Following the student's progress and being available for consultation on matters such as assignments, means of evaluation, and handling other problems that may arise

The home economics teacher may have the following responsibilities:

- Assessing capabilities and limitations of the handicapped student
- Evaluating the architectural accessibility of the classroom and how problem situations can be modified
- Assisting in the development of the IEP on the basis of the assessment
- Cooperating with the special education teacher/counselor in working with the handicapped student

WORKING WITH THE HANDICAPPED

Home economics has the potential of providing many worthwhile experiences and opportunities for handicapped people. The previous experiences of the handicapped in their home and educational environments vary widely. Many have lived in a rather narrow world without the opportunity to participate fully in all the activities of life. Home economics can provide many opportunities to learn everyday living skills, socialization skills, and employability skills.

It is natural to have some concerns about working with handicapped persons, especially if you have had limited previous experience with the handicapped or if you have had no specific training in this area. It is understandable that you would be concerned about how effectively you could communicate with a person having a hearing or speech impairment, or about how much assistance to offer a sightless person or someone orthopedically disabled. New experiences are often awkward.

Identify your personal feelings about people with handicaps. How comfortable or uncomfortable are you? Your discomfort or sense of embarrassment is obvious to handicapped persons. People who are uncomfortable often become too helpful or solicitious. People who feel comfortable around handicapped persons recognize that the handicapped want to be as self-sufficient as possible. They will tell you when they need assistance, or you can simply say, "Let me know when and how I can help you."

There is a certain amount of risk in communicating openly and freely with handicapped persons—the risk of saying the wrong thing or being turned down curtly if you offer help. When you say to a person in a wheelchair, "Let's walk across the hall," or to a sightless person, "Have you seen Kim?" there can be a moment of embarrassment. It's natural to use the words *walk* and *see*. Blind persons know the meaning of *see*, and it would be even more awkward to say to a person in a wheelchair, "Let's roll across the hall." Learn to feel comfortable with commonly used expressions even when they are not always literally accurate.

If your offer of assistance is rejected in a very unseemly manner by a disabled person, don't take it personally or be embarrassed. You have little to lose when you receive a "no" response, and you have something to gain when someone says "yes."

You need not feel guilty if you encounter disabled persons you do not like. The important discrimination to make is that you dislike them for any one of the reasons that would lead you to dislike any other person and not because of their disability.

CONSIDERATIONS FOR SPECIFIC HANDICAPS

A number of adjustments and adaptations can be made in existing programs and facilities that provide more effective accommodations for handicapped people. Many of these accommodations would benefit nonhandicapped students as well. When you are considering making adjustments in the learning environment, remember to ask handicapped persons themselves what would be most helpful. Use brainstorming to gather additional ideas from all students.

Physical Limitations

- Provide access to the building and rooms for people using wheelchairs and crutches by having ramps installed.
- Facilitate the use of wheelchairs and crutches by requesting nonskid floor surfaces.
- Arrange furniture and equipment so there is ample space for wheelchairs to pass.
- Apply simple handles rather than knobs on cabinet doors and drawers for amputees with artificial limbs or devices, and for persons with limited use of their hands.
- Have some working surfaces lowered or recessed to accommodate wheelchairs.
- Purchase some one-handle rolling pins and mixing bowls with suction cups on the bottom. Remember that lightweight hand tools or tools with extra large handles are helpful to students with weak hands.
- Enlarge the handle or grasping edge of equipment when possible.
- Find alternative means of manipulating machines—by arm, knee, foot, or chin, for example. Make a bib with a pouch or pocket for holding the sewing machine foot control. The control can be operated with the chin, so that both hands can be used in guiding fabric, removing pins, and performing other similar tasks.

- Use a mobile demonstration table that can be moved from student to student.
- Request book holders, mechanical page turners, and other types of special equipment that might be helpful to particular students.
- Tape papers to the table to prevent students from dropping them on the floor. Laminate papers before giving them to students. The papers will be easier to handle, and can be wiped clean, written on, dried without damage, and used again. Place magnetized pieces on a metal board when using games.

Visual Limitations

- Seat students with partial or limited vision at the front of the room and use large print on visuals.
- Put frequently used material on cassette tapes or records.
- Let students examine equipment and tools, as a verbal description is given, to help students develop a "mental blueprint."
- Use tactile rather than visual marking on controls. Braille tape or raised marks can be used.

Hearing Limitations

- Arrange for students to work in small numbers whenever possible.
- Use visually oriented media instead of auditory media. Captioned films, charts, and overhead transparencies should be used whenever possible.
- Look directly at students who lip-read as much as possible during lectures or conversation.
- Try a total communication approach that includes speech, careful listening, sign language, finger spelling, gesture, and mime.

Learning Disabilities

- Plan your program with an eye to students' successes. Use an approach that leads students to the right answers. Reword the question or simplify the problem. Narrow response choices. Provide clues when necessary.
- Provide immediate feedback so that students know when responses are correct.
- Move in an organized, step-by-step procedure so that material drawing on basic knowledge and habits precedes more difficult material.
- Provide enough repetition over a period of time so that students overlearn.
- Use a minimum of change from one step to another.
- Plan carefully for the transfer of knowledge from one situation to another. Present the same concept in a variety of settings so students can transfer the common elements.
- Limit the number of ideas presented at any one time. Introduce new material only after old material is familiar.
- Keep written information at an appropriate reading level.
- Keep written and spoken material brief and simple.

- Use visuals and audiovisuals frequently.
- Accept verbal or illustrative responses to questions and tasks.

The question often arises as to whether all handicapped students can be integrated into regular classrooms. Children with severe impairments may need special considerations. For these children, there are a variety of options. Some can attend regular classes with supplementary aid; others attend a special class part-time; still others need to be in a special class full-time. For the most part, however, students with mild or moderate handicaps can be successfully integrated into the regular classrooms.

Some additional references on mainstreaming that you may want to pursue include:

- Agard, J. *Mainstreaming: Learners and Their Environments*. Baltimore, Maryland: University Park Press, 1978.
- Dahl, Peter R., Judith A. Appleby, and Dewey Lipe. *Mainstreaming Guidebook for Vocational Educators*. Salt Lake City, Utah: Olympus Publishing Company, 1978.
- Fairchild, Thomas N. and Ferris O. Henson. *Mainstreaming Children with Learning Disabilities*. Austin, Texas: Learning Concepts, 1977.
- Gearheart, Bill R. and Mel Weishahn. *The Handicapped Child in the Regular Classroom*. St. Louis, Missouri: C. V. Mosby Company, 1976.
- Glover, John A. and Albert L. Gary. *Mainstreaming Exceptional Children*. Pacific Grove, California: Boxwood Press, 1976.
- Henson, Ferris O. and Thomas N. Fairchild. *Mainstreaming Exceptional Children*. Austin, Texas: Learning Concepts, 1976.
- Lowenbraun, Sheila and Jame Affleck. *Teaching Mildly Handicapped Children in Regular Classes*. Columbus, Ohio: Charles E. Merrill Publishing Company, 1976.
- Paul, James L. et al. *Mainstreaming: A Practical Guide*. Syracuse, New York: Syracuse University Press, 1977.
- Phelps, L. Allen and Ronald J. Lutz. *Career Exploration and Preparation for the Special Needs Learner*. Boston, Massachusetts: Allyn and Bacon, Inc. 1977.
- Schleifer, Maxwell J. (editor). *Mainstreaming and the Federal Mandate (PL 94-142): Practical Guidance for Implementation*. Boston, Massachusetts: Exceptional Parent Press, 1978.
- Turnvull, Ann P. and Jane B. Schulz. *Mainstreaming Handicapped Students: A Guide for the Classroom Teacher*. Rockleigh, New Jersey: Allyn and Bacon, Inc., 1978.

CAREER EDUCATION 25

Career education may take two basic forms: 1) training for gainful employment in a specific occupation or cluster of occupations, such as is acquired in a vocationally oriented wage-earning program; or 2) a general orientation to the world of work, which can be integrated into every course, and which helps students learn about many career choices related to the field of study. Whatever approach is taken, career education programs must be adapted to meet the needs of particular students, particular schools, and particular communities.

Since many states have developed materials for teaching in cooperative and vocational preemployment programs, emphasis upon career education in this chapter will be for those teachers who work primarily in regular home economics classes. The type of career education in these programs does not focus upon a limited number of career goals, but instead covers a wide range of occupational opportunities at all levels and helps students develop positive attitudes toward work as a very important domain of life. Some teachers in the regular home economics program include career education as a separate unit while others integrate career education into the various subject-matter areas, such as food and nutrition, child development, and consumer education.

THE NEED FOR CAREER EDUCATION

Since home and family living cannot be separated from the realities and demands of working, the home economics teacher has a unique contribution to make to the total growth and development of the individual. Certainly, personal and family living patterns affect and are affected by the work people do. Working wives and mothers are a large and permanent part of society, and more men are assuming the roles of homemakers. Therefore, both boys and girls and men and women need help in preparing for multiple roles as breadwinners, homemakers, and family members.

The world of work is changing rapidly and constantly. Job requirements are being altered; careers that never existed before are now becoming realities; more women are employed in fields that were held by men in the past and vice versa; and there is a greater need for retraining because of changes in employment patterns. Therefore, students need to be aware of and to examine many alternatives in light of their own strengths, weaknesses, interests, goals, and values.

There are several reasons for young people to become acquainted with possibilities for work before the last two years of high school. For one thing, interest in a career often begins during early adolescence. It is during the middle-childhood and teen years that students learn to cooperate and compete with peers, to build positive or negative attitudes toward achievement, to build patterns of response to authority, and to establish a set of values concerning work. Finally, students who do not yet have career goals or even ideas will have time to explore, think, and plan before they graduate.

The ability to work well with others cannot be promoted by the development of appropriate work skills alone. Qualities of an effective worker also include a positive attitude and self-concept and a measure of self-understanding. In other words, the ability to adapt to working involves being able to make many personal adjustments successfully.

Home economists, with their concern for the total development of the individual and for the well-being of families, are in a unique position to accept a large part of the responsibility for helping young people develop desirable "work personalities." The home economics teacher can help students become more employable regardless of their chosen work.

Career Education as a Separate Unit

The separate-unit approach to career education could be used at the beginning of the school term to give students a different perspective of the concepts included in home economics or it could be used at the end of the term to show how all areas of subject matter relate to employment. When career education is covered separately, a general orientation to the world of work is usually given. Under the separate-unit approach, concepts related to selecting a career, getting and holding a job, and viewing the overall employment picture are more likely to be included than when career education is mentioned throughout the term as each content area is covered.

The learning experiences that follow could be integrated into a variety of subject areas or incorporated into a cooperative wage-earning program, but are particularly suitable for a separate unit because of the general and broad approach to career education.

- Divide into seven groups to investigate occupational opportunities in these areas of home economics: child development, food and nutrition, housing and interior design, family relations, management, clothing and textiles, and consumer education. Ask the class as a whole to suggest additional opportunities in each of the fields. After interviewing people engaged in the occupations suggested, develop a list of qualifications desirable for each position.

- Develop a slide presentation and script featuring people in the local community at work in a variety of home economics-related occupations.
- Make a bulletin board entitled, "Graze in the Fields of Home Economics." Around a picture, cutout, or silhouette of a giraffe or other appropriate animal, list occupations suggested by the class. Change these periodically.
- Make a bulletin board entitled, "Star-studded Careers in Home Economics." On large stars cut from construction paper, write the name of an occupation in the field of home economics. Change these as additional careers are suggested and studied by the class.
- Plan a career day in which people employed in home economics-related occupations discuss job qualifications and opportunities.
- Tell of one new idea gained or a skill developed in a home economics class that could lead eventually to a career or would help make a person more employable.
- Interview women to find out what was done and what was studied in home economics when they were in school. Discuss reasons for the changes in the curriculum today.
- Take a survey to discover how many mothers work outside the home. Compile a list of the types of work they do. Interview working mothers to find out the reasons they give for working. Compile a list to discover what reasons are given most frequently.
- List occupations in which women are more likely to be engaged than men. List occupations in which men are more frequently employed than women. Cite some of the reasons for these differences. Discuss which of these reasons are most valid and why. Suggest reasons that might cause an employer to prefer having a man, or a woman, in a particular job.
- Relate an experience of seeing a women who is employed in a "man's job." Tell about a man who works in a position that is usually held by a woman. Discuss the following: What were your reactions to finding these employees in these situations? How did you react and why did you react this way? What special problems may these employees face? Offer solutions that may be helpful to these employees in solving their problems.
- Collect articles about experiments involving a longer workday and shorter workweek. Discuss the types of plans being tried or proposed and the advantages and disadvantages of each. Discuss the effects of current employment trends on the use of leisure time and on family life.
- Investigate and read about job sharing as a new approach to employment. Point out how job sharing is different from an arrangement whereby two persons have two part-time jobs.
- Define "moonlighting" and give examples to illustrate an understanding of the term. Discuss the reasons that lead some people to moonlight and what the possible effects might be on family relationships, standard of living, health, and personal satisfaction.

- Investigate school and community resources that are available for both personal and vocational guidance and counseling. Prepare a report on the services offered through various offices and agencies. Discuss how school and community organizations provide opportunities and experiences that could influence one's choice of an occupation or career.
- Invite someone from the local branch of the state employment commission to talk to the group about the community employment situation and about local employment problems. Discuss the effects of the situation on teenagers and their families.
- List skills that may be acquired and trades that may be learned in the armed forces, both of which could later open up occupational opportunities for the individual. Tell about a person who was able to capitalize on skills learned in the armed service by using these in a vocation or hobby after being discharged.
- Define "fringe benefits" and give examples that illustrate an understanding of the term. Analyze the actual cost to the employee and to the employer of some of the fringe benefits suggested. Give examples of fringe benefits that would appeal to some individuals more than they would to others. Discuss the reasons for such a difference in preferences.
- Discuss opportunities in the local community for teenagers to make money. List possible part-time jobs associated with the seasons of the year, special holidays, harvest time, sports, tourist attractions, and local celebrations or special events.
- Discuss occupations that exist today that were unheard of ten, twenty, or thirty years ago. List occupations for which there was a demand in the past and for which there is little need today. Discuss the factors that brought about these changes.
- Research and discuss current demographic trends and technological developments that will influence the job market ten to fifteen years from now. Identify fields that should be strong then. What fields might have declining opportunities?
- Analyze your own personality traits, aptitudes, and interests. According to this analysis, select several occupations for which you might be suited. For each of these occupations, investigate the amount of education or training required, the advantages and disadvantages of each, the chances for advancement, and beginning and potential salaries. If possible, interview people engaged in one of these occupations to find out what they like and dislike about the work. Present these findings to the class in the form of an oral report.
- Collect and display a variety of job-application forms. Discuss the importance of completing these accurately and neatly. Discuss how the application can create either a favorable or an unfavorable first impression. Practice filling out some typical job-application forms.
- Bring to class photographs that are appropriate and inappropriate for use with job-application forms. Analyze the reasons that make each picture suitable or unsuitable. Compile a list of do's and don'ts for having pictures made for such a purpose.
- Write letters of application. One student may apply for a college scholarship. Another student may apply for a student assistantship at a college. Still another may apply for a part-time job while enrolled in college, or during the Christmas

vacation, or during the summer. Other students may apply for full-time jobs following graduation or answer want ads found in the local newspaper. Prepare a résumé to enclose with letters of application or to use in interviews.

- Identify the mistakes purposely planted in a skit about a person who is applying for a job through a personal interview. Have an "instant replay" that corrects the mistakes made in the first performance. Discuss the appearance, manners, and attitudes of the person being interviewed. Discuss why you would or would not employ this person. See page 108 for the skit titled *How to Lose a Job Before Getting One.*

DEVELOPING ATTITUDES TOWARD WORK

In any course in home economics, it is possible to incorporate a wide variety of learning experiences to help students prepare for employment of any type. A sense of responsibility, the ability to follow directions, a willingness to cooperate with others, punctuality, and the ability to accept constructive criticism are just a few traits that are assets in all endeavors. The learning experiences suggested here are designed to help students develop a broad understanding of factors contributing to success in all occupations.

- List personal characteristics that would be assets in all types of employment situations. List traits that would be liabilities in all occupations.
- Invite a school counselor to discuss the questions that employers most frequently ask about students and former students who are being considered for employment.
- Ask employers to participate in a panel to discuss qualities desired in employees, or interview employers to determine qualities they look for in prospective employees. Use the employers' ideas to develop a checklist and evaluate your own employability.
- List suggestions for good employee relationships with one's employer, customers, and other employees. Discuss reasons for similarities in the lists.
- Role play situations in which personality conflicts affect job performance. Suggest ways of improving the relationships depicted.
- Fold a piece of paper in half. On one side list the traits and qualities desired in a friend. On the other side list the traits and qualities you would look for in an employee if you were in the position of hiring a person for a job. Unfold the paper and compare the lists.
- Explain the meaning of the expression "Let George do it." How is the attitude reflected in this statement a handicap to success at home, in school, and on the job?
- List a dozen ways to lose a job. For each way listed suggest a means for improving the situation.
- Describe people who are considered responsible. Choose one way in which to become a more responsible individual. Develop a plan of action and keep a diary for a week, showing progress toward that goal.

- Discuss your responsibility as an employee in situations such as these:

  1. You break a piece of equipment.
  2. You are sick and cannot go to work.
  3. Your car will not start when it is time to leave for work.
  4. You see one of your friends taking something from the establishment.
  5. You are offered a similar job for more money.
  6. The employer goes away for a few days.

- Develop a checklist or rating scale that could be used by any employer in any field to decide which employees should get merit raises.
- Ask guest speakers—perhaps people who have risen from disadvantaged backgrounds to become successful and respected members of the community—to talk about the factors that aided them in succeeding.
- Make a bulletin board entitled "Are You on the Beam?" On one side of the display, use a silhouette of a flashlight, lantern, or pole lamp. List qualities desired in all employees, and label light beams with these characteristics.

INTEGRATING CAREER EDUCATION INTO SUBJECT-MATTER UNITS

In both comprehensive and specialized courses, the teacher has an opportunity to help students compare and contrast various home economics careers. Students need to look at clusters of jobs and employment opportunities in order to increase their alternatives. For example, there is a cluster of occupations in the area of services to children, and a family of careers related to food and nutrition, of which many students are unaware. When career education is incorporated into each subject-matter unit, it is often placed last so that the relationships among subconcepts can be viewed and linked in a different context. Career education is an effective closure for a unit because it substantiates the importance of that content area. Following are examples of learning experiences that can be used when incorporating career education into two subject areas, child development and food and nutrition.

Child Development

- Role-play situations in which parents are interviewing people to care for their children. Discuss the following in relation to the scenes:

  1. Which of the applicants would you employ? Why?
  2. What other questions might the prospective employers have asked?
  3. Why is each of these considerations important?
  4. What would prospective employees want to know about the family?
  5. Why would employees want to know these things?

- Divide a piece of paper or the chalkboard into two columns. Label one "parents" and the other "child-care employees." List competencies and attitudes desirable for each. Discuss the reasons for the similarities and differences in the lists.

- Observe a person working with children or a film showing a child-care situation. Point out the importance of a knowledge of child development and a positive attitude toward children in the situations viewed. Discuss which actions of the child-care employees reflect a concern for children and other qualities that should contribute to success in working with them.

Food and Nutrition

- List types of jobs in food services for which there is on-the-job training in the local community. Discuss the skills that people in these occupations need to develop.
- Take a field trip to a food-service establishment to observe the types of work performed at all levels from unskilled to highly skilled. Note the levels with the greatest variety of tasks. Discuss possible reasons for these findings.
- Suggest ways an individual could use competencies related to food preparation in part-time self-employment at home, such as in catering special parties, making and decorating wedding cakes, or preparing canapés and hors d'oeuvres for selected clients.

Additional content-related activities in career education are available in many state curriculum guides. A career education program should be adapted to the needs of the students and their community.

INDEX

1 2 3 4 5 6 7 8 9 10 KPKP 89 88 87 86 85 84 83 82 81 80